Nikoletta Kanavou
The Names of Homeric Heroes

Sozomena

Studies in the Recovery of Ancient Texts

Edited
on behalf of the Herculaneum Society

by

Alessandro Barchiesi, Robert Fowler, Dirk Obbink
and Nigel Wilson

Volume 15

Nikoletta Kanavou

The Names of Homeric Heroes

Problems and Interpretations

DE GRUYTER

ISBN 978-3-11-057820-1
e-ISBN (PDF) 978-3-11-042197-2
e-ISBN (EPUB) 978-3-11-042202-3
ISSN 1869-6368

Library of Congress Cataloging-in-Publication Data
A CIP catalogue record for this book has been applied for at the Library of Congress.

Bibliographic information published by the Deutsche Nationalbibliothek
The Deutsche Nationalbibliothek lists this publication in the Deutsche Nationalbibliografie; detailed bibliographic data are available on the Internet at http://dnb.dnb.de.

© 2015 Walter de Gruyter GmbH, Berlin/Boston
This volume is text- and page-identical with the hardback published in 2015.
Printing and binding: CPI books GmbH, Leck

♾ Printing on acid free paper
Printed in Germany

www.degruyter.com

οὐ μὲν γάρ τις πάμπαν ἀνώνυμός ἐστ᾽ ἀνθρώπων,
οὐ κακὸς οὐδὲ μὲν ἐσθλός, ἐπὴν τὰ πρῶτα γένηται,
ἀλλ᾽ ἐπὶ πᾶσι τίθενται, ἐπεί κε τέκωσι, τοκῆες.

(*Od.* 8.552–4)

Preface

The purpose of this book is to contribute to the appreciation of the linguistic, literary and contextual value of Homeric personal names. This is an old topic, which famously interested Plato, and an object of constant scholarly attention from the time of ancient commentators to the present day. Aside from numerous articles, there are a few books dedicated to particular aspects of the subject, notably von Kamptz (an etymological study), Peradotto (on names and narrative in the *Odyssey*) and Higbie (on name and identity). The present discussion considers both epics and is structured around the character and action of selected heroes in their Homeric contexts (in the case of the *Iliad*, a heroic war; the *Odyssey* chapter encompasses more than one planes of action). It offers a survey of modern etymologies, set against ancient views on names and naming in order to reconstruct (as far as possible) the reception of significant names by ancient audiences and further to shed light on the parameters surrounding the choice and use of personal names in Homer. The introductory chapter presents the particularly complex set of factors that affect all efforts to interpret Homeric names. Two chapters follow, one on each epic, which discuss main heroes and other memorable figures. A third chapter treats selected word-plays and potential puns and links among 'minor' names from both epics. Finally, an Appendix touches on the underexplored career of Homeric personal names as historical names, offering data and a preliminary analysis. The vastness of the material involved imposes a selection, with a view to discussing names of main characters (particularly the obscure names) at length, and to offering a taste of the rest; it is hoped that this work will provide impetus for further research.

The book is based on the first part of a DPhil thesis, which was completed in Oxford under the supervision of Dr S.R. West and has been thoroughly revised, extended and updated (a monograph based on the second part, on significant Aristophanic names, was published by De Gruyter in 2011). Special thanks go to the Foundation for Education and European Culture (IPEP) for financial support during the final stages of this book's preparation. Martin and Stephanie West read the whole manuscript, made valuable suggestions and saved me from a number of errors; I was extremely fortunate to receive their comments and advice. I am also grateful to Athanassios Vergados, who offered useful insights on the introductory chapter as well as on numerous Homeric names, and to Peter Thonemann who read and commented on the Appendix. Finally, I should like to thank the editors of the Sozomena series, especially Dirk Obbink, for accepting my book for publication in the series.   *Athens, October 2014*

Contents

Abbreviations — XI

1 Introductory notes — 1
1.1 Major and minor heroes (and heroines) — 1
1.2 Names and history — 5
1.3 Etymology and philosophy — 8
1.3.1 Etymology — 8
1.3.2 Philosophy of names — 14
1.4 Names, society, orality and literacy — 17
1.5 How to tell a 'speaking' name in Homer — 23
1.5.1 Notes to the reader — 28

2 Names from the *Iliad* — 29
2.1 The Warrior Heroes — 29
2.1.1 Achilles — 29
2.1.2 Aias — 36
2.1.3 Agamemnon, Menelaos — 44
2.1.4 Diomedes — 48
2.1.5 Idomeneus and Meriones — 50
2.1.6 Patroklos — 55
2.2 Heroic Old Men — 63
2.2.1 Nestor — 63
2.2.2 Phoinix — 67
2.3 Helen — 71
2.4 The 'Greek' Trojans — 76
2.4.1 Priam, Hekabe — 77
2.4.2 Hektor, Astyanax, Andromache — 80
2.4.3 Paris-Alexandros — 83
2.4.4 Aineias — 87

3 Names from the *Odyssey* — 89
3.1 Odysseus — 90
3.2 Odysseus' Family — 106
3.2.1 Laertes, Antikleia — 106
3.2.2 Telemachos — 107
3.2.3 Penelope — 110

3.3   Odysseus' Travels —— 113
3.3.1 Kalypso and Kirke —— 113
3.3.2 Polyphemos —— 118
3.3.3 Some Phaeacian names —— 120
3.3.4 Odysseus' companions —— 127
3.4   'Secondary' Names on Ithaca —— 128
3.4.1 The servants —— 128
3.4.2 The suitors —— 132

4   'Minor' speaking names —— 134

5   Afterword —— 151

6   Appendix. Homeric Personal Names as Historical Names: Preliminary Remarks —— 156

7   Bibliography —— 169

Name Index —— 185

Abbreviations

Names of ancient authors and works are abbreviated as in LSJ.

CEG	P.A. Hansen (ed.), 1983. *Carmina Epigraphica Graeca saeculorum VIII–V a. Chr. n.* (vol. 1). Berlin.
Comm. on Od.	A. Heubeck et al., *A Commentary on Homer's Odyssey*. Oxford.
— v.1,	1988. books 1–4 (S. West), 5–8 (J.B. Hainsworth).
— v.2,	1989. books 9–12 (A. Heubeck), 13–16 (A. Hoekstra).
— v.3,	1992. books 17–20 (J. Russo), 21–22 (M. Fernández-Galiano), 23–24 (A. Heubeck).
DGE	F.R. Adrados et al. (eds.), 1980–. *Diccionario Griego-Español* (7 vols). Madrid.
D–K	H. Diels – W. Kranz (eds.), 1974. *Die Fragmente der Vorsokratiker* (3 vols). Berlin.
FGrH	F. Jacoby (ed.), 1926–58. *Die Fragmente der griechischen Historiker*. Berlin / Leiden.
HE	M. Finkelberg (ed.), 2011. *Homeric Encyclopedia* (3 vols). Malden, MA / Oxford / Chichester.
IG	*Inscriptiones Graecae* (various eds.), 1877–. Berlin.
— II^2	*Inscriptiones Atticae Euclidis anno posteriores*. J. Kirchner (ed.), 1913–40 (3 parts). Berlin.
— IV	*Inscriptiones Argolidis*. M. Fraenkel (ed.), 1902. Berlin.
— XII(5)	*Inscriptiones Cycladum*. F. Hiller von Gaertringen (ed.), 1903–9 (2 vols). Berlin.
K–A	R. Kassel – C. Austin (eds.), 1983–. *Poetae Comici Graeci* (8 Vols). Berlin.
LfgrE	*Lexikon des frügriechischen Epos* (various eds.), 1995–. Goettingen.
LGPN	*Lexicon of Greek Personal Names.*
— I	P.M. Fraser – E. Matthews (eds.), 1987. Vol.I, *The Aegean Islands; Cyprus; Cyrenaica*. Oxford.
— IIA	revised version (April 2007) of: M.J. Osborne – S.G. Byrne (eds.), 1994. Vol.II, *Attica*. Oxford.
— IIIA	P.M. Fraser – E. Matthews (eds.), 1997. Vol.III.A, *The Peloponnese; Western Greece; Sicily and Magna Graecia*. Oxford.
— IIIB	P.M. Fraser – E. Matthews (eds.), 2000. Vol.III.B, *Central Greece: from the Megarid to Thessaly*. Oxford.
— IV	P.M. Fraser – E. Matthews (eds.), 2005. Vol.IV, *Macedonia,Thrace, Northern Regions of the Black Sea*. Oxford.
— VA	T. Corsten (ed.), 2010. Vol.V.A, *Coastal Asia Minor: Pontos to Ionia*. Oxford.
— VB	J.-S. Balzat et al. (eds.), 2013. Vol. V.B, *Coastal Asia Minor: Caria to Cilicia*. Oxford.
LIMC	*Lexicon Iconographicum Mythologiae Classicae* (various eds.), 1981–. Zurich.
LSJ	H.G. Liddell – R. Scott – H.S. Jones (eds.), 1940. *A Greek-English Lexicon* (9th ed.); Supplements 1968, 1996. Oxford.
M–W	R. Merkelbach – M.L. West (eds.), 1967. *Fragmenta Hesiodea*. Oxford.
N. Pauly	*Der Neue Pauly: Enzyklopädie der Antike* (various eds.), 1996–. Stuttgart.
OCD	S. Hornblower – A. Spawforth – E. Eidinow (eds.), 2012 (4th ed.). *The Oxford Classical Dictionary*. Oxford.
PMGF	M. Davies (ed.), 1991. *Poetarum Melicorum Graecorum Fragmenta I: Alcman, Stesichorus, Ibycus*. Oxford.

RE   A.F. Pauly, G. Wissowa, W. Kroll et al. (eds.), 1894–1980. *Real-Encyclopädie der classischen Altertumswissenschaft.* Stuttgart.
SEG   *Supplementum Epigraphicum Graecum* (various eds.). 1923–. Leiden, Alphen aan den Rijn, Germantown, Md., and Amsterdam.
TGrF   *Tragicorum Graecorum Fragmenta.*
    R. Kannicht (ed.), 2004. Vol.5.1: *Euripides.* Goettingen.
    S.L. Radt (ed.), 1977. Vol.3: *Aeschylus.* Goettingen.
    — (ed.), 1999². Vol.4: *Sophocles.* Goettingen.
    B. Snell (ed.), 1986². Vol.1: *Didascaliae Tragicae, Catalogi Tragicorum et Tragoediarum, Testimonia et Fragmenta Tragicorum Minorum.* Göttingen.
W   M.L. West (ed.), 1989, 1992 (2nd ed.). *Iambi et elegi graeci ante Alexandrum cantati* (2 Vols). Oxford.

1 Introductory notes

'...nowhere does Homeric and Hesiodic poetry, but especially the *Odyssey*, seem to be more self-conscious about language and its relation to things than when it comes to proper names.'

(Peradotto 1990: 94–5).

'...the personal name... is by nature partially or fully "opaque".'

(Paschalis 1997: 4).

1.1 Major and minor heroes (and heroines)

Personal names are present in both the *Iliad* and the *Odyssey* in great numbers. Almost every person mentioned in the epics is referred to by name, whether they are main heroes or minor (but active) characters. Names are important in view of the fact that the poet mostly recounts the action of heroic *individuals*,[1] not impersonal masses of warriors. Often uniquely mentioned figures with no function other than a single appearance in a collective list of persons (e.g. of fighting or slaughtered soldiers in the *Iliad*, cf. 5.9 ff., 144 ff., 533 ff., and of Phaeacians in the *Odyssey*) receive names too.[2] There are occasions when no names are given, e.g. for the slaughtered Thracians in *Il.* 10.485 ff., but on the whole there is a clear preference for naming the subjects in both poems. Naming is an essential part of character introduction, itself an aspect of a 'good and well-motivated plot', as observed already in antiquity.[3] Naming amounts to more than the identification of active characters; the personal name in Homer is a wholly fundamental referential means.

---

[1] The 'Homeric hero' is 'a man characterised by heightened courage and sense of duty, or specifically a male warrior in the vague universal category of heroic literature' (Clarke 2004: 78–9 goes on to define the notion of hero as superior to that of later man, drawing also on Hesiod's famous designation of the heroic generation). Note the different use of the term in e.g. 'main heroes' (in English semantics) as the central figures in the poems.
[2] Lateiner (2004: 12) counts 240 named battle dead (and many anonymous others). See Beye (1964) for a detailed discussion of the names of fighting and dying soldiers.
[3] See Nünlist 2009: 51–7, who draws attention to Sch. b *Il.* 2.494–877 *ex.*: τὸ γὰρ μὴ γνωρίζεσθαι τοὺς ἥρωας ζήτησιν ἐποίει ('not to know the heroes would cause confusion') and to Sch. b *Il.* 1.69b *ex.*: ὅρα πῶς ἐν ἀρχῇ διασαφεῖ τὰ ὀνόματα ('look at how clearly [the poet] names his heroes'); the Scholium implies the use of patronymics, which make the identification of named heroes secure.

In addition to their role as reference, most Homeric names have a recognisable sense (Greek names are generally meant to be significant constructions).⁴ This introductory chapter will explore the particular nature of this 'sense', and the external and internal factors that define it. More specifically, what follows will sketch a background to the potential of Homeric personal names to function as 'speaking' names (that is, names that are suited to their bearers and / or contexts),⁵ taking into account language, genre and poetics; also historical setting, and social and theoretical approaches to naming.

The crucial question, relevant to every Homeric study, just what is meant by 'Homer',⁶ will not be addressed here at length; but clearly the issue of Homeric onomastics is further complicated by assumptions on authorship and on the manner of epic composition. I accept M.L. West's propositions regarding these difficult topics, namely that the two epics were composed with the aid of writing (West is inclined to date both to the 7th c. BC)⁷ and that they belong to different authors.⁸ Separate authorship does not invalidate the connection between the two epics, as one poet may have known and used (to an extent imitated) the work of the other; it is in particular the *Odyssey* poet who seems to have drawn on the *Iliad*.⁹ The often observed continuities between the two epics in

---

4 See further Kanavou 2011: 2. This is true also for some Homeric place-names, which will not be discussed here, but see below p. 104 for an example; also M.L. West 2014: 56 n.11.
5 For a more detailed discussion of the meaning of this term see now Kanavou 2011: 2–3.
6 See Fowler 2004: 231, with bibliography.
7 See M.L. West 2011a: 15–9 and 1995: 213–9, where he argues that the creation of our *Iliad* should be dated after 688 BC and that Hesiod's wisdom literature antedates it; he dates the *Odyssey* to the last third of the same century (2014: 1). But the *Iliad* is still commonly dated to the last decades of the 8th c.; see Bennet 2014: 189. Ruijgh (2011: 260) placed both epics in the second half of the 9th c. On an evolutionary model of Homeric poetry, which presumably did not acquire its definitive form until the 6th c., see Nagy (1992: 52; 1996a: 13 ff.), followed by Seaford 1994: 144 ff. (also Nagy 2010 for a study of how the epics may have evolved during their oral phase, when different versions surely existed). Seaford (ibid: 144 ff.) has argued for a late date for the ending of the *Iliad*. On the tangled issue of how the texts came to be written down, see further Saïd 1998: 31–5 (with bibliography) and more recently Jensen 2011.
8 M.L. West 2011a: 7–8, 2014: 1; this is now a common belief, but same authorship is not altogether excluded, see e.g. Janko 1982: 83–4, 191.
9 Thus M.L. West 2011a: 70–2; 2014: 2, 25–7. Cf. Usener 1990; Rutherford 2001, who discusses Iliadic allusions in the *Odyssey* despite oralist objections (ibid.: 125–6 – this is not to lose sight of the fact that other poetry, which did not survive in writing, also circulated at the time). Note also M.L. West's (2014: 25) objection to 'Monro's law' (1901: 325; the *Odyssey* 'never repeats or refers to any incident related in the *Iliad*'). The view that the *Iliad* was not known to the poet of the *Odyssey* at all (thus Page 1955: esp. 149–59) is a very eccentric one, and has been adequately refuted (Rutherford ibid.: 120–1, n. 5). See also Saïd 1998: 302–4, with bibliography.

plot and characterisation, though not unbroken, allow us to regard them as a unity: the explanation of a name that appears in both epics will be uniform, but different nuances of meaning will be noted. I also accept the proposition that the *Iliad*, drawing on older oral poetry, emerged through a process of authorial expansions of an original shorter poem on the Trojan war, and that a number of untraditional figures were inserted in the poem during this process;[10] similarly that our *Odyssey* is descended from a proto-*Odyssey*, which centered on the basic story of an absent man's homecoming, and was gradually expanded with further wanderings.[11] We shall see the implications of these propositions for the interpretation of individual names.

While many names are derived from the tradition of heroic epic, some are certainly the product of the poet's free choice (but still reflect the demands of the epic genre[12]). Names of main heroes must be of the former type;[13] some have fairly straightforward etymologies (even if exact meanings are hard to grasp, e.g. Agamemnon and Menelaos). Others (e.g. Achilles, Odysseus, Aias, Nestor) are etymologically obscure, and the discussion of their meanings is entangled with difficult problems. The difficulties entailed in the discussion of main heroes' names (but certainly also of several 'minor' names) may have to do with their age, which reaches to the Mycenaean era. Indeed the justification of meanings of names is relevant to the varied strands (Indo-European inheritance,[14] Mycenaean civilisation, archaic Greece, as well as oriental influence) that influenced the composition of the epics. As a rule, main characters' names have a longer and more established presence in traditional stories and are more ancient than the names of minor characters, which could easily be added or taken out, forgotten or created to suit their bearers.[15] As regards the *Iliad* in particular, several main characters (e.g. Nestor) appear to have been at-

---

10 M.L. West 2011a: 42 ff.
11 M.L. West 2014: 2–3; 21–3; 93.
12 A heterogeneous genre which encompasses a variety of traditions across time and from all over the world (cf. Martin 2005; see also below pp. 19–21). For generic features associated with the Homeric epics see Foley 2004: 181–7; among these, the national character of the epics 'as a charter of group identity', with 'myth in the service of indigenous social history', finds expression in 'heroic actions, with a central focus on martial achievement' – this is admittedly where the inspiration for many Iliadic names comes from (the *Odyssey* is different in scope).
13 Cf. the doubts expressed by Burgess (2001: 63 ff., in relation to artistic representations) about the necessity of the claims that any major characters were the product of Homeric invention.
14 For a brief outline of this inheritance see Dowden 2004: 189–90; cf. M.L. West's programmatic notes (2007a: 15, 24–5). See also Nagy 1990.
15 Cf. Stanford (1939: 100; cf. 1965: xxi).

tracted into the story of the Trojan war from other bodies of legend,[16] and it is therefore not surprising if their names are not exactly transparent;[17] such names further appear to accentuate the remoteness of the major heroes from ordinary humans.[18] The figure of Odysseus is clearly much older than our *Odyssey*, 'a figure of ancient legend, at first probably not a warrior hero but a man celebrated for ingenuity and guile.'[19] Older scholarship has often sought the heroes' origins in the divine and religious sphere – but we shall see that this process entails much speculation and few solid results. An important aspect of the naming of main heroes is the frequent mention of patronymics, whose metrical utility is well-known, but which also underline the high social status of the heroes and complement their characterisation.[20] Names of fathers are often bound with their sons' in terms of significance (see below on the names of Atreas, Laertes, and of Odysseus' grandfather Autolykos).[21]

The problematic character of some of the well-known heroes' names is contrasted with the transparency of very many other names, which draw on regular linguistic patterns (as known from historically attested names). Not all of these names need to have been invented, though some may have been, while others may have belonged to a common stock.[22] Most of these may be linguistically analysed and categorised according to principles used for attested historical names,[23] and their significance is mostly easy to discern.

Important characters in the epics include some women, even though their presence and function in the plot is more limited than the men's; that said, the *Odyssey* contains some female characters of key importance. Regarding the explanation of their names, the premises described above stand true for female names too – clarity of significance varies considerably, from the 'dark' name Helen to the more transparent Nausikaa.

---

16 Cf. M.L. West 2011a: 29 ff.
17 Names of heroes who emerge from other mythical circles and only have a marginal presence in Homer (e.g. Meleagros, Eteokles, Bellerophontes) may also have a claim to great antiquity; see von Kamptz 1982 (1958): 26 ff. and below, on Meleagros' name.
18 This impression is confirmed by the scant use of many heroic names in historical times (see Appendix).
19 Thus M.L. West 2014: 2.
20 See Higbie 1995: 6–7 (and 43–68 on the utility of patronymics in metrical patterns).
21 On heroes' sons in general see M.L. West 2007a: 440–3, and on their names Germain 1954: 485.
22 As Scodel points out (2002: 29–30), 'invention' does not necessarily mean that such names (and their bearers) were created from scratch, but it may in fact equal recycling or recombination of traditional material from one context to another.
23 Von Kamptz 1982 (1958): 3.

Among parameters of name interpretation familiar to every onomastic study, to be discussed in the remainder of this introduction in relation to Homer, the historical parameter appears to be of rather limited use in the study of Homeric personal names.[24] The following section will show why; discussion will then move to the subject of etymology both as practice and as philosophical framework: the age and character of the Homeric material dictates more attention to this topic than to potential historicity.

1.2 Names and history

The archaic character of the epics means that we have limited access to the kind of information, which aside from etymology, is basic in any discussion of names, that is information about historicity. In literature of the classical period, we more or less know what is related to history and what is not: thanks to the considerable amount of epigraphic evidence that relates to personal names, made accessible now by the *LGPN*, we can often distinguish between real and fictitious names, real and fictitious characters.[25] The study of names in the two monumental epics may include historical sources, which date from their time or earlier, but the use of these sources is subject to such limitations as to allow only speculation and some doubtful conclusions on the historical nature of the names.

The earliest historical attestations of Homeric names are possibly found in the Hittite texts, which were made much more familiar to the non-specialist than they had previously been thanks to the work of Page.[26] Previously Forrer had 'identified' a number of Homeric references in the Hittite documents, such as a city of Troy, the name Achaea (*Ahhiyawa*), and the personal names Atreus, Alexander and Eteokles.[27] A few years later, Sommer demolished most of these identifications.[28] Recent research favours the possibility that Mycenaeans were mentioned in the Hittite texts, that the Hittite *Wilusa* is directly related to (or even is) Troy itself,[29] and that there is enough evidence in these texts to point to a tradition of a Greek-Anatolian conflict which may have been the his-

---

24 For a useful overview of modern research and bibliography on Greek historical names, with special relevance to Homeric names, see Neumann 1991: 311–4.
25 Cf., as an example, my study of names in Aristophanes (2011).
26 1959.
27 Forrer 1926.
28 Sommer 1932.
29 See Latacz 2004: 75–91, cf. M.L. West 2011a: 38–9.

torical core of the Trojan war.[30] However, personal identifications are treated with extreme caution, and they hardly are an object of agreement among Hittitologists.[31] Still, the relationship between Hittite (as well as other Anatolian languages of the Bronze Age) and the linguistic substratum often termed as pre-Greek[32] affects the understanding of 'difficult' Homeric names, as will become apparent later in the discussion.

The decipherement of the Mycenaean script has offered more solid ground for belief in the historicity of some Homeric names (the Homeric poems present, as often noted, an amalgam of bronze and iron age civilisation, and certainly preserve memories of Mycenaean Greece[33]). The Linear B tablets, the only Greek written source that is earlier than the Homeric epics, contain several Homeric names,[34] but due to the ambiguous character of this script the exact form of the names can often only be guessed at[35] (but some names, e.g. Achilles, are undoubtedly attested).[36] It is safe to infer that some Homeric names were in common use in the Mycenaean age, but this does not tell us much about their use in Homeric poetry. There are in fact many different possibilities. Some scholars have speculated that some of the persons named in the *Iliad* and the *Odyssey* originate in a lost Mycenaean poetry. Such poetry (with the same or different themes) must have existed, but Linear B preserves no literature.[37] Still, the assumption that the main lines of Greek mythology were laid down in the Myce-

---

30 Bryce 1998: 392 ff. (though there is no clear reference to the sack of Troy, see M.L. West 2011a: 39).
31 See Güterbock 1986: 33 ff. For a discussion of the *Alakšanduš* -Ἀλέξανδρος connection, which is thought to have particular force, see below, on 'Paris-Alexandros'.
32 See Finkelberg 2005: 42–54.
33 See Snodgrass 1974: 114–25 and Finkelberg 2005: 2–3. On the relevance particularly of later elements to the dating of the epics see Seaford 1994: 146–7; on their panhellenic character ibid.: 152–3.
34 58 according to Ventris-Chadwick (1973: 103–5; see also Gray 1958). This number has since not significantly risen. Notably *LGPN* excludes Mycenaean names. On the current state of research in Linear B texts see the Companion series edited by Duhoux and Morpurgo Davies (three volumes). See also Wachter's (2000) 'Homerisch-Mykenisch' word index.
35 Work on the decipherment of Mycenaean proper names continues (cf. Bartoněk 1995). For an account of the relevant problems see Morpurgo Davies 1995: 389. See recently also García Ramón (2011). The etymology of Mycenaean names, as far as it is possible to reconstruct, is discussed by Neumann (1991: 318–20) in comparison with the etymology of Homeric names.
36 See Jorro – Adrados (1985) s.v. *a-ki-re-u*.
37 Note, however, that Mycenaean texts have been thought to contain some metrical lines (Watkins 1995: 59). Cf. also Ruijgh (1995; 2011: 257–8, 281–5, 289–90) on the Mycenaean origin of the dactylic hexameter and on Homeric formulae that seem to go back to Mycenaean times (e.g. Διὶ μῆτιν ἀτάλαντος, λιπὼν ἀνδροτῆτα καὶ ἥβην).

naean age³⁸ may encourage connections between Homeric names that are attested in Linear B texts and myths as old as the Mycenaean era; but Linear B names apparently belonged to everyday people, and it is possible that they were only given to heroes at a later age. Gray³⁹ has summed up some possibilities: '…they [Homeric names] could have existed as a stock of "names suitable for heroes" on which the poets drew at will; or they could have come down attached to stories or incidents or professions, with the probability that some of them are historical'.⁴⁰

The possibility that the epics reflect historical people and events is attractive, and it has been sustained by scholars such as Denys Page, who argued in favour of the historical character of central heroes (Agamemnon, Achilles), as well as of the Trojan war.⁴¹ Heroes' names have further been connected with historical tribes.⁴² It goes without saying that if the *Iliad* could be read as history, the interpretation of names would become a totally different issue; notwithstanding antiquity's trust in the historical value of the Homeric epics,⁴³ external evidence is scarce, and the *Iliad* has admittedly emerged from centuries of oral tradition, probably merging persons and events of different times and places⁴⁴ and mixing history with myth.⁴⁵ This is not to disregard the value of oral tradi-

---

38 Thus Nilsson 1932: 12–3; more recently Dowden 1992: 44–6 and 2004: 190–1.
39 1958: 43.
40 Cf. Fick – Bechtel 1894: 363, who believe that real, historical names were given to heroes.
41 1959: 253 ff. Nilsson (1932: 251) recognised the capitals of heroic Greek kingdoms mentioned by Homer as Mycenaean sites and thought that Agamemnon was the name of a historical Mycenaean king, one who was not necessarily linked with the Trojan war. Dowden (1992: 65–8) does not exclude the possibility of 'an Agamemnon of distant, southerly, Mycenae' who took over Troy, but insists on our version of the Trojan war as a mythic construct of Indo-European origin. For a brief history of scholarship on this issue see Finkelberg 2005: 1–3.
42 Fick – Bechtel 1894: 363 (e.g. on Agamemnon, name of a king of Kyme [from the tribe of the Atreidai of Mycenae?] whose daughter married Midas according to Pollux *Onomasticon* 9.83); cf. Bowra (1930: 77 ff.) and see also Appendix. Names of heroes-founders of tribes (e.g. Dardanos, Tros) must have been invented on the basis of the respective tribes.
43 Even Thucydides thought Homer to provide evidence about the past (Graziosi 2002: 120–3, Hunter 2004: 240–1).
44 Despite such views as Webster's (1958 *passim*), who saw in the epics the potential to reconstruct the Mycenaean world, and Finley's (1957: 159; 1970: 82–4; 1977: 44–5, 150–2), who recognised a number of Mycenaean allusions, but believed the epics to reflect mainly the Dark Ages. Cf. also Kirk (1964a, esp. 32–3; 1964b: xi; Grethlein 2010: 129) on the difficulty of extracting historical information from Homer. Still, it cannot be denied that the *Iliad* reflects 'an idea of history', to be discerned in the heroes' engagement with their own past, e.g. in the stories of Nestor (Grethlein 2010: 131–4; 2006: 42–153).
45 The deeds of some Iliadic heroes may have been sung earlier than the alleged time of the Trojan war; and historical characters can of course be displaced and attracted into alien cycles

tion for our knowledge of Greek prehistory,⁴⁶ but the limits of this value are worth stressing: it cannot be decided whether any of the characters in the poem existed as such (or at least as reflections of historical models) or whether they were mythical or the products of poetic imagination; the identification of details such as personal names is impossible.⁴⁷ Even if derived from historical models, these names and characters become of course fictionalised once they enter a poetic setting.⁴⁸

1.3 Etymology and philosophy

The obscure historical roots of Homeric names hinder scholarly research into their etymology, especially in the case of main heroes' names, and hence into the possibility that they may carry appropriate meanings. The elucidation of names is further complicated by the artificial / poetic character of the Homeric language, which is based on archaic East Ionic, but blends elements from various dialects and chronological periods,⁴⁹ and contains many words (including names) that do not appear elsewhere in Greek literature, as well as personal names that occur in variant forms.⁵⁰ Despite these difficulties, research into the meaning of Homeric names, and indeed in many cases their interpretation as 'speaking' names, is encouraged by ancient etymological practice and by antiquity's view of names.

1.3.1 Etymology

The main way to establish meanings of words is, of course, etymology; a brief reminder of the meaning of this term (a frequent topic in classical scholarship)

---

of legend, which means that their historical nature can have been permanently blurred. See Vermeule (1986: 85–6). Cf. M.L. West (2011b: 97–112): 'The Trojan war ... remains in the end a mythical war'.

46 Cf. Finkelberg 2005: 9–12 (the Homeric poems are based on 'historical myth' which allows some insights into its Mycenaean backdrop, but also reflects the time when the poems where circulated). On the historical periods that affected the composition of the Homeric epics see Dickinson 1994, 2006, and Snodgrass 2000.
47 See Latacz 2004: 204–5. Cf. also Bell – O'Cleirigh – Barrell 2000: 206–10 and M.L. West 2011a: 40.
48 See Kanavou 2011: 11, n. 42.
49 See for a brief description Ruijgh 2011: 255 and further *HE* s.v. Language, Homeric (A. Willi).
50 See e.g. Reece 2009: 7 and *HE* s.v. *hapax legomena*.

is in order. Etymology certainly did not mean the same to ancient authors as to modern linguists. Ancient etymology – as practised by poets and prose writers, not just scholiasts and grammarians – is not bound by solid linguistic rules (hence it is also labelled as paretymology or folk-etymology), it is intuitive and flexible and leads to variable proposals. This sort of etymology is contrasted with modern scientific etymology, which is an established branch of linguistics, based on the foundations of historical and comparative linguistic science. The proposals of scientific and folk-etymology may at times overlap, but the scientific approach poses limitations which are not shared by popular etymology.[51] Ancient etymology and modern scientific etymology indeed differ in both principles and purpose: while ancient etymology can have a 'scientific' and a didactic purpose, especially in the hands of the scholiasts and grammarians,[52] its most essential role (that interests us here) is as a multi-purpose literary device: in poetry (particularly oral poetry), it is a source of mnemonic aids and functions as a narrative factor, unifying characters and themes.[53]

In the view of modern scientific etymology, the significance of the names of many major Homeric heroes is often hard to discern, because they were probably conceived at a time (or derived from a time) that was still pre-history, and for this reason they cannot be explained by means of linguistic rules for name-giving that were established in historical times. Such names, which often consist of components that are not found in historical times,[54] have often been regarded as originally non-Greek. Page[55] believed that names such as Achilles, Odysseus, Aias, Nestor, contain a foreign stem (though there can be no doubt about the

---

51 Lyons 1981: 55. On this distinction cf. also Higbie (1995: 4–5), who rightly notes that both types of etymology are useful to the Homeric scholar. See further the essays collected in Schmitt (1977) on etymological theory and method; Del Bello (2007: ch.1) on the place of etymology in modern linguistic science; Baxter (1992: 57 ff.) for a comparison between ancient and modern etymology; Willer (2003) on the intersection between the literary (playful and speculative) and the scientific face of etymology (he writes mainly on European romantic literature but provides an overview of ancient practice, ibid.: 28 ff.); and Olschansky (1996) on folk-etymology (note in particular the subtle distinction between 'folk-etymology' as a general term and 'gelehrte Etymologie', i.e. the learned, but not scientific by modern standards, etymology practised by ancient scholars, ibid.: 150–2).
52 Cf. Peraki-Kyriakidou 2002: 490–2.
53 It 'aims primarily at integrating words, myths, persons and things in a meaningful manner, and provides an internal justification for their presence and function in the poetic canvas' (Tsitsibakou-Vasalos 2007: 5–6). Greek poets clearly did not rely on accurate etymologies, but were keen on evocative names, as Aristole also remarks (*Rhet.* 1400b18 ff.).
54 Von Kamptz 1982 (1958): 7–8. Examples of obsolete or rare components include Βελλερο-, Ἠνι-, Ποντο-, Πρωτεσι-, -ερτης, -μεμνων.
55 1959: 215, n. 91.

Greek character of the suffixes). Earlier Ventris-Chadwick, discussing Mycenaean names, had expressed the suspicion that some names may have a non-Greek aspect.[56] Mycenaean evidence for a name does not guarantee 'Greekness',[57] as some names may originate from a 'substrate' language or belong to members of a non-Greek population.[58] Palmer was an enthusiastic and overall convincing defender of the Greek character of 'difficult' names,[59] and since then several attempts at a Greek explanation of various names have been made (as we shall see in the following chapters), even if a definite etymology often seems impossible.

Etymological analysis was the mainstay of scholarship on Homeric onomastics in the 19th century; further studies appeared in the 20th,[60] and scholarly interest in it has not ceased.[61] Notable contributions to the subject include the work of Sulzberger (1926) and Rank (1951), while a systematic linguistic study of Homeric personal names was the subject of a thesis by von Kamptz (1958). Von Kamptz's work includes a brief chapter on 'speaking names',[62] but a strict linguistic interpretation fails to identify clear selection criteria of names in this group, as the majority of names in other chapters are also said to be significant. The 1958 thesis (which was published without alterations in 1982) did not consider the implications of the decipherment of Linear B for Greek onomastics, which makes the discussion often seem outdated.[63]

Etymologies would arguably become clearer (and could be better trusted) if the names were placed in a system of classification, and if their significance could be shown to follow clearly defined linguistic patterns. A widely used categorisation of names was devised by Fick and Bechtel and was followed by von Kamptz and Masson.[64] This recognises three 'main' categories: 1) compound

---

56 But Achilles and Aias are categorised as Greek (1953: 93 ff.). Cf. Ventris-Chadwick 1973: 93, where it is stated that it is hard to define whether certain names are of Greek origin or not.
57 On the problematic use of this term for such an early period see Finkelberg 2005: 16–23. Homer's Greeks are Achaeans, Danaans and Argives, while 'Hellas' referred to specific Thessalian territory and the ethnic 'Greek' is an invention of the Roman period.
58 Cf. Varias 1998/9: 350–1.
59 1956: 7 ff. and 1963: 79.
60 Cf. e.g. the work of G. Curtius (1858) and Goebel, whose *Lexilogus* (1878–80) included entries for personal names; also the articles of McCartney (1918/9) and Linde (1924), who explored linguistic puns and plays. E.R. Curtius cited numerous examples of 'speaking names' from the Homeric epics in his *magnum opus* (1948). Cunliffe's *Homeric names* (1931) stays out of 'the very uncertain field of etymology' (ibid.: v).
61 See e.g. recently Liović (2012).
62 1982 (1958): 25–39.
63 See further the reviews by Meier-Brügger 1983: 341–2 and Janko 1984: 305–6.
64 Dobias – Dubois (in Masson 1990–2001 vol.1: VII ff.). Meier-Brügger (1992: 42) also distinguishes between 'Komposita' and 'Kurznamen'.

names, 2) short forms of these, 3) 'surnoms ou sobriquets', or 'die übrigen Namen' (*simplicia* that have not emerged from compounds). Compound names have the greatest potential for significance: they are believed to be inherited from Indo-European and therefore to be governed by very archaic composition laws; their components are usually linked by a syntagmatic relationship (there are infinite possibilities of combination between two parts)[65] and they usually (but not always) make good sense. In real life they are expected to express a moral / warlike / social / religious quality wished by the father, or appropriate relative, in a son (i.e. they can be 'motivated' names).[66] Sobriquets are clear cases of intended significance.[67] Challenging the old view[68] that compound names are older and *simplicia* originated from them, Szemerényi argued that the oldest names were monothematic (*simplicia*), while dithematic names (compounds) were originally meant as combinations of names with epithets; the use of the latter in name-giving would have emerged from later heroic songs which made them popular. Perhaps such names had some social stratification (they were somewhat higher onomastic designations and therefore were more appropriate for heroes). Thus compound names may have been 'an offshoot of an Indo-European type of poetic expression',[69] and their poetic origin would be felt in the use made of them in epic poetry. Some Homeric phrases seem to correspond to meanings of names (e.g. ὄρνυθι λαούς 'urge on the men', *Il.* 15.475, which corresponds to the name Laertes);[70] such phrases are also found in Vedic.[71]

---

[65] For an account of these possibilities, and the resulting difficulty in determining exact meanings, see Bouvier 2002: 358.
[66] Cf. Kanavou 2011: 2. In classical Athens it was also common for members of the same family (especially grandfathers and grandsons) to share the same name, but this hardly happens in Homer – one notable exception is Ortilochos, presumably named after his grandfather (*Il.* 5.542–49); it seems unlikely that the name should be spelt differently for grandfather and grandson (thus Kirk [1990: 114–5]: Ortilochos and Orsilochos respectively, following D.B. Monro and T.W. Allen [OCT 1920]). Glaukos mentions a great-grandfather called Glaukos (6.154 f.). Note also a Λαμπετίδης, son of Λάμπος (*Il.* 15.526).
[67] Cf. Dobias – Dubois (in Masson 1990–2001 vol.1: VII-XII).
[68] In Fick – Bechtel 1894: 2–3, followed by von Kamptz 1982 (1958): 3 ff. Cf. Dobias – Dubois (ibid.: VII-XII).
[69] Szemerényi 1996: 163–4 (with bibliography); cf. Schmitt 1967: 122–3. On personal names in Indo-European see also Meier-Brügger 2010: 431–4, with bibliography.
[70] Cf. the historical names Orselaos and Orsilaos, the reverse form of Laertes. But Dobias – Dubois (in Masson 1990–2001 vol.1: IX) somewhat exaggerate when saying that 'sans un syntagme vivant en grec ou dans une langue apparentée, la traduction d'un anthroponyme reste une chimère'.

A problem in the above classifications is the lack of precise criteria in the treatment of *simplicia*. The existence of parallel names (e.g. a charioteer's name appears both as Ἀλκιμέδων and Ἄλκιμος; *Il.* 16.197, cf. 19.392)[72] may indicate an evolution of form, but it is not clear whether the names' significance is affected, and whether some Homeric *simplicia* might derive their meanings from compounds: 'the diachronic development of personal names differs from that of other lexical items.'[73] A more descriptive (synchronic rather than diachronic) categorisation[74] in monothematic and dithematic names, without regard to the 'original' form of the name, avoids the pitfalls of the traditional groupings and shows more respect for the individuality of names: although patterns of name formation existed, there was plenty of room for creativity and originality (which means that no categorisation can encompass all names). The relation of Greek names to language (and secondarily to linguistics) is safely expressed only in the observation that all roots can produce personal names, and conversely names are explained by being attributed to roots.

This last premise is common to modern and ancient etymology. It is in any case the latter which should weigh more in our approach to Homeric names. As Del Bello notes,[75] 'the stress twentieth century linguists lay on morphology and phonology fails to account for the extralinguistic claims of ancient etymologizing.' Manifestations of ancient etymology include passages from Homer, which explain proper names (but also common nouns), Hesiod, and later Plato; the Homeric Scholia also contain numerous explanations of names.[76] Homeric names should be analysed against the relative definition of etymology, which the ancient evidence suggests; the most rewarding etymological approach is the one that takes into account the spirit of the ancient efforts.[77] This approach will prove particularly rewarding in the study of the 'difficult' names of Greek heroes,

---

[71] See Dobias – Dubois (ibid.: VIII) for an example. Vedic literature, recorded in writing in the 6th c. BC, but originating as early as 1200 BC, can be paralleled with Homeric poetry (see Puhvel 1987: 42 and below, pp. 56, 67, 74, 86).
[72] See further below, under 'Minor' speaking names.
[73] Morpurgo Davies 2000: 22–3. See also Dobias – Dubois (in Masson 1990–2001 vol.1: VII-XII).
[74] Hartmann 2002: 60–1; cf. Neumann 1991: 314–6. See further *HE* s.v. Names, Personal (R. Hitchman) on current linguistic approaches to the structures of Homeric names.
[75] 2007: 47.
[76] Erbse's Index (vol. 7: 92–105) of etymologies in the Iliadic Scholia contains several proper names. Note that the corpus of the Homeric Scholia (accessible in the editions of Erbse, Dindorf and now Pontani for *Odyssey* books 1–2) is too varied to allow us to infer how the epics were read and understood in any particular context; on the nature of the Scholia see further Nagy 2004: 18 ff.
[77] Cf. Sedley 2003: 29.

as well as of a number of Trojan names of suspected foreign origin (whose discussion is affected by the difficult problems of interpreting Bronze Age Anatolian linguistic stock, especially Luvian).[78] The evidence for ancient etymological practices confirms that it is legitimate to use etymology as an interpretative tool.

Linguistic analysis is still an obvious starting point for the study of meaning of Homeric names, and the scholar of today has a wealth of resources at his or her disposal.[79] But etymology is rarely seen as an end in itself, but rather as a springboard to diverse interpretations relating to one or more aspects of the use of Homeric names[80] – in fact, etymological analysis is now understood to work together with other interpretative aspects that arguably assist the understanding of names: the last few decades have seen more sophisticated approaches to characterisation,[81] and brought to the foreground issues like contextuality and intertextuality, and the point of view of the audience;[82] the perspectives of onomastic studies were multiplied and the understanding of names was deepened.[83]

---

[78] Perhaps such names were adapted by the Greek poets to form proper Greek-sounding names. The name Ἀλέξανδρος (from the Hittite *Alakšanduš*) is a possible example (to be discussed later).

[79] Etymologies of Homeric personal names are found in the entries of *LfGrE*, in Wathelet's dictionary of Homer's Trojans and in etymological dictionaries (Beekes, Chantraine, Frisk); also in the online (currently under preparation) *Dizionario Etimologico della Mitologia Greca* (*DEMGOL*, http://demgol.units.it), conceived as a replacement for Carnoy's now largely outdated mythological dictionary (1957) – see also Pellizer 2006.

[80] As the work of scholars such as Mühlestein (who used etymology to make attractive, if not always convincing assumptions on the history of text and characters) has shown. His numerous articles on Homeric personal names are collected in Mühlestein 1987.

[81] See Griffin 1980: 50 ff. In the old-fashioned analyst and oralist view, the nature of the poems poses limitations to the depiction of Homeric characters and hinders consistency and psychological depth; Taplin (1990: 82) was certainly right that 'characterization in Homer is not a self-sufficient element which can be extracted by itself. It is indivisible from critical interpretation in all its aspects.'

[82] See the bibliography gathered by Lateiner (2004: 29–30) as a starting point generally on these issues in Homer. Intertextuality is indeed a problematic concept to apply to orally conceived poems, but the texts of the Homeric epics should be considered sufficiently fixed to allow allusion (see Currie 2012: 574–80). Perhaps oral poetry too can be sophisticated enough to permit allusion; thus Pucci, whose book on intertextual readings in the two epics suggests that they influenced one another during their 'formative period', before they were fixed (1987: 18, 27).

[83] Modern book-length studies in the use of ancient literary names include Peradotto (1990, on the use of names as an element of Odyssean narrative technique), Higbie (1995, on heroic names and naming techniques in the framework of traditional oral poetry), Paschalis (1997, on names in Virgil's *Aeneid*) and Kanavou (2011, on Aristophanic names).

1.3.2 Philosophy of names

Ancient etymological practice is suggestive of an underlying theoretical approach to names and naming, which serves as further encouragement to the search for the meanings of Homeric names. Admittedly, there is no clearly expressed theory of names before Plato, but such a philosophy is implicit in Homeric contexts, which justify the choice of certain names.[84] The ancient Greeks – perhaps as early as Homer, but certainly by the classical period – did not only have a set of 'rules' governing the use of names in society, but had also compiled a philosophical framework for the nature and use of names (one might say a 'philosophy of names'). A theory of names is implicit in presocratic philosophy, most famously in the philosophy of Heraclitus, who believed that names (especially divine names) had 'true' meanings, hidden in their etymology.[85] Etymology of proper names was reportedly also practised by sophists, who saw it as part of their arsenal of rhetorical weapons; Protagoras' etymology of the name of Hera (from ἀήρ)[86] is a frequently cited example.

An elaborate theory of names was developed by Plato, especially in the *Cratylus*; this work discusses the arguments in favour of both linguistic 'naturalism' and 'conventionalism' and significantly aligns itself with naturalism. Much like in presocratic philosophy, the argument in favour of the 'correctness' of names in the *Cratylus* is not purely linguistic: although the etymologies used in the dialogue are likely to be meant seriously,[87] it is implied that linguistic 'naturalism' cannot be fully defended by etymologies (as we have seen, etymology was a fluid concept). The existence of 'true' meanings is better suggested by philosophical theories such as the flux-doctrine (which goes back to Heraclitus), ancient opinions about the history of language (which lie in the field of what we nowadays

---

[84] Cf. e.g. the name of Meleagros' wife Kleopatre – Alkyone (*Il.* 9.561–4; the name Alkyone was chosen by her parents to remind of the cry of the seabird ἀλκυών as a metaphor for her mother's grief).

[85] Cf. the suggested (though not altogether clear) association between Ζηνός (gen. of Ζεύς) and ζῆν 'to live' in fr. 32 D – K; 23 D – K on the name of *Dike* 'Justice'. See Kahn 1979: 201; Kraus 1987: 120–33; Kirk-Raven 1957: 71 (on Pherecydes; but note that his Ζάς, gen. Ζαντός, is less suggestive of a connection with ζῆν than is Ζηνός).

[86] Plato, *Protagoras* 404c2–4.

[87] Thus Sedley 2003: 4–5, but see also Barney (2001: 19–20), who suggests that Plato's ambivalence 'between serious engagement with etymology and making fun of it' is a difficult one to resolve. For a recent, exhaustive discussion of the etymologies section of the dialogue see Ademollo (2011, esp. ch. 6 and 7), who holds that Sokrates' character in the dialogue is convinced of the correctness of the etymologies, and suggests that his humorous tone should be seen as a literary and philosophical device rather than as a sign of lack of seriousness.

call anthropology) and the theory of an original 'divine language' (which was believed to reflect the true nature of things).[88] Furthermore, a clear distinction is made between common nouns and personal names (of humans); Sokrates concludes that the latter are not a safe guide to the correctness of all onomastic labels – the reason for this is not linguistic (all personal names are originally given for a reason, but this rational link does not necessarily last[89]) and needs to be sought in the motives that lie behind naming (expression of wishful thinking [not of a person's essence], element of chance etc.).[90]

However, Plato's etymologies seem to imply that a recognisable meaning was often part of what the ancient Greeks saw in a name.[91] Plato also provides essential clues about perceptions of meanings of Homeric names. He notes that Homer μέγα τι καὶ θαυμάσιον λέγειν... περὶ ὀνομάτων ὀρθότητος 'he gives ... great and wonderful information about the correctness of names' (*Cra.* 391d; transl. Fowler), where ὀρθὰ ὀνόματα (*correct* names) are names that suit their bearers and context. He treats examples from Homer in a manner that seems unaffected by the concept of the 'artificiality' of literature. It is suggested that the wisdom of the poet imitates 'natural' naming (and of course Homeric names were thought to belong to real people). The scale of 'correctness' of names ranges from the language of gods, to Homer, to every-day names, used by ordinary Athenians, which lack poetic wisdom. It can be inferred that the Greeks of Plato's time would see many names (in real life and in literature) as appropriate names; but they would not think that of *every* name.[92] Aristotle famously took steps towards a more 'conventional' view of names, though he too notices the significant use of some names in literature (*Rhet.* 1400b) and the occasional use of names in real life in fun, anger or foreboding. Concerning the use of names in real life, the debate presented in Plato's *Cratylus* is still current.[93] There is of course no disagreement about the 'naturalistic' use of personal names in literature.[94]

---

88 Sedley 2003: 20 ff. Cf. Barnes (1982: 368–71) on the influence of Democritus' thought on the origins of language.
89 Cf. Debus 2002: 21.
90 See Sedley 2003: 86–9.
91 If it is allowed that Plato's *Cratylus* reflected, to an extent, a common feeling about names.
92 Ancient interest in the etymology of names continued with the Stoics, who used it on divine and mythological names to uncover allegorical meanings (brief overview in Del Bello 2007: 49–50). The term ἐτυμολογία was probably invented by them; see further Allen 2005. On etymologising with names, in the broader frame of ancient philosophical views on language, see also Gambarara 1984: 23 ff.
93 This is not the place for a proper treatment of this subject, but see Peradotto (1990: 95 ff.) for a brief history of the debate. Conventionalism's most famous proponent, J.S. Mill, argued that names were 'meaningless marks' (Mill 1973–4 (1843): 24 ff.); others (like O. Jespersen) defend

Even if the choice of names in real life is mostly conventional (and their etymological meanings are not relevant to the bearers), naturalistic aspects of their function are worth pointing out. First, names are informative in themselves (they provide more information than just themselves); e.g. they may express the geographical origin of the bearer or his / her social status.[95] An argument used in the *Cratylus* (384d) to support the conventionality of names seems in that sense to backfire: slaves were re-named by their owners (as frequently seen in Delphic manumissions). The later philosopher Diodorus Cronus named his slave Ἀλλαμήν ('But-then'), probably in order to make a point about conventionalism[96] – but the name expresses his point and is therefore 'speaking'; no doubt it also attracts speculation about its motives and implications. On the other hand, it is easy to see the repeated use of a common (hence not noteworthy) name for different persons as purely conventional; but a name may acquire special content and associations for each person, and represents this individual wholly and totally. Even in real life, names become connected with their bearers in special (if not always conscious) ways, and they are never 'empty' forms.[97] To return to Greek names, we are now inclined to believe that a strictly conventionalist view of names, 'that (their) primary function in real life was not connotative or descriptive, but only to identify the bearer, to mark his / her place in a community',[98] cannot have an absolute force.

The belief that the use of names in literature cannot be seen as entirely separate from real-life practice is expressed already in ancient scholarship. As already mentioned, the Homeric Scholia include comments on significant names

---

'naturalism': 'proper names (as actually used) "connote" the greatest number of attributes' (Jespersen 1924: 66).

94 See further Debus 2002: 57–73.

95 A striking modern example is found in M. Arnold's essay on 'The Function of Criticism at the Present Time' (1865, referred to by Stray 1998: 77), where the author hinted at the inferior alienness of the working class by his sneers at such plebeian names as Higginbotham and Wragg. (He notably went on to contrast these ugly names with beautiful Attic names).

96 Ammonius (*In Int.* 38, 17 ff.); see Gera 2003: 208 and n. 87.

97 See Debus 2002: 23–6. Note also the following remark by Lévi-Strauss (1966: 172): that names lack in signification is not a fact that may easily fit the observations of ethnologists on name-giving in primitive societies (e.g. Indians). These construct proper names from clan appellations, thus names have the value of codes (this would hardly be possible if logicians / linguists like Mill are right in thinking that names are 'meaningless').

98 Morpurgo Davies 2000: 21 and n.14: denotation and connotation are terms used by J.S. Mill; for him names 'connote nothing, have no signification'. The problematic character of these terms is seen in that they are understood differently by Eco (1976: 88), who believes that a name's reference to an unknown individual does not constitute denotation, but an imprecise connotation (the name refers generically to a person).

(which will be brought into the discussion of individual names), as well as a theoretical description of this kind of naming, which shows awareness of both the practical / historical and the literary dimension of naming (Sch. *Od.* 7.54, which explains the Homeric term ἐπώνυμον, reads: ἐπώνυμόν ἐστι τὸ ἀπὸ γενέσεως μὲν αὐτομάτως τεθὲν, ὕστερον δὲ κατὰ τύχην δοκοῦν τεθεῖσθαι.)[99] This definition was elaborated in Byzantine times by Eustathius (776, on *Il.* 9.563, cf. on *Od.* 7.63 ff.), who also attempts a basic categorisation of significant names (in two groups: names that proved 'right' in later life, e.g. Αἴας, and names which were considered significant from the start and were assigned to heroes at birth, e.g. Ὀδυσσεύς). Such notions may underscore the use of personal names in the epics, and certainly affect our understanding of them.

1.4 Names, society, orality and literacy

Homeric names may appear to lack a firm historical basis, but the use of significant names has clear social and literary precedents. The use of 'correct' names is known to be a primitive habit, traces of which seem to survive in the archaic age. Significant names in Homer reflect, to some extent, the archaic concept of descriptive meaning, according to which 'a name was often relevant to a person's own condition or (more often) to that of some close relative of his at the time of his naming'.[100] This concept is reflected in the explanation of Odysseus' name (*Od.* 19.401–9), which implies that Autolykos' wish to include a hint at his own personality in the naming of his grandson leads to the absorption of this personality trait in the character and future development of Odysseus. In another famous passage from the *Odyssey* (8.550–4), Alkinoos' plea to Odysseus to reveal his name, naming is associated with the beginning of a person's life.[101] Nobody is nameless; even the deceitful appellation *Outis* functions in fact as a name (as we shall see in the *Odyssey* chapter). The personal name is the landmark of a person's place and role in society, and a basic piece of identification

---

99 Cf. Sch. A *Il.* 5.60: ὀνοματοθετικὸς ὁ ποιητής (on the term *eponymon* see also below, p. 124).
100 Stanford 1939: 99.
101 'Tell me the name by which they called you at home, your mother and your father and other folk besides, your townsmen and the dwellers roundabout. For there is no one of all mankind who is nameless, be he base man or noble, when once he has been born, but parents bestow names on all when they give them birth.' This suggests that a name is *personal* even if shared by more individuals.

(though not the only one: the mention of family and ethnic origin is also required).¹⁰²

The above remarks seem to be in keeping with the finds of anthropological research, especially the work of Claude Lévi-Strauss¹⁰³ on the power of personal names in primitive societies, which preserve traits of very early social structures. Lévi-Strauss' study of the Nambikwara Indians of South America has significantly enhanced our knowledge on name-tabooing. Arbitrary appellations, such as Portuguese names, had to be used by the anthropologists to identify individuals because the Nambikwara would not reveal their Indian names, and instances of revelation of these names by children were clearly considered illicit acts. This suggests that in 'primitive' or 'mythical' thinking there is an internal unity between name and bearer; the name is not a label for the person, the name *is* the person. Ancient Greek name-giving and the use of names in Greek society had, among other origins, visible roots in myth and cult.¹⁰⁴ Names were expected to have special power (more so than in modern societies with rationalistic thinking), such as 'programmatic' power. Wish-names (or names of good will) reflect faith in a name's positive force; conversely, the tabooing of names (the non-mentioning of a name to protect a person's welfare) – which finds an example in the epics in the treatment of the name Odysseus¹⁰⁵ – suggests a belief in the negative power of names.¹⁰⁶ Ethnography, in its essence a type of anthropological re-

---

102 See Debus 2002: 9 ff., Higbie 1995: 5 ff. and Gera 2003: 7.
103 1976: 364–5; 1966: 172 ff. Cf. Frazer 1922: 244 ff.
104 'The Greeks ... kept something of the primitive feeling that the connexion between a person and his name is significant, not accidental, φύσει not νόμῳ' (Dodds 1960: 116–7); cf. Peradotto 1969: 4–5. Evidence of magical and religious usages in the Greek (and Roman) world with regard to names has been collected by Jones (1996: 3–28). Religious assumptions must have played a part in the creation of 'theophoric' names (a very large category); a name 'Kephisodotos' in an inscription at an altar dedicated to Kephisos (*IG* II² 4546) suggests the belief that Kephisodotos was granted in response to prayers to the river-god Kephisos. Notably, names did not often allude to powers of the Underworld. See further Parker (2000: 53 ff.), who however notes that the use of 'theophoric' names was in many other cases conventional.
105 See further below, under 'Odysseus'.
106 Abusive Aristophanic names might be related to the use of vulgar names in every-day life, which must have had a superstitious, possible 'apotropaic' function (there are many such examples from primitive societies). See Dobias – Dubois (in Masson 1990–2001 vol.1: XIII). Herodotus (4.184) may be giving an example of name-tabooing when stating that the Atarantes did not use proper names. Cf. Gera 2003: 193 ff.

search, also finds interest in personal names as expressions of cultural identities.[107]

However, it is beyond doubt that the motivation behind the choice and use of names in the epics was mainly literary; this is made clear by the very nature of the poems, which offer a purely poetic treatment of their subject.[108] The origins of at least some Homeric names could dwell in poetic pre-history; tradition of the poetic treatment of the Trojan war is reflected in the poems of the epic cycle (they are only fragmentary, and most are probably later than Homer, but can still contribute to the appreciation of the history of Homeric heroes and their names).[109] Some names have been shown to express poetic ideas that may be as old as Indo-European poetry.[110]

By the time of the *Iliad* the use of 'speaking' names seems to have been an established literary habit. 'Speaking' names are found as early as the Mesopotamian epic of Gilgamesh, which has arguably donated poetic motifs and techniques to the *Iliad*.[111] There are remains of several versions of the epic, dating from various periods, which preserve different forms of the heroes' names. The examples used here are names as they appear in the standard Babylonian epic: the name Gilgamesh is thought to mean 'heroic ancestor',[112] presumably a reflection of how the hero was perceived. The name of the hero's companion, Enkidu, is understood in its older spelling as 'Lord of the pleasant place', perhaps a generic name; but a later spelling (the one used in the Standard Babylonian epic) delivers the meaning 'creature of Ea' (the Mother Goddess was responsible for his birth). The name of Gilgamesh's mother, Ninsun, can be translated

---

107 Cf. the rise in recent years of the subfield of linguistic anthropology (including the 'ethnography of communication'), which involves the study of proper names; see e.g. Blount 2009. See also below, on Phaeacian names.
108 Cf. Gomme 1954: 4–5.
109 As demonstrated by neoanalysis, see below p. 25. On the epic cycle and the tradition of the Trojan war see Burgess 2001.
110 See M.L. West (1988) and Watkins (1995: 507) on the name Πρωτεσίλαος. Cf. Watkins (1995: 27) on the name Ἕκτωρ. See also above (p. 11) on the Indo-European origins of Homeric poetry.
111 See Burkert 2004: 21–45 and Currie (2012: 553, 568–9) who stresses the proven historical influence of Mesopotamia on Greece in the archaic period; I assume that the transmission of *Gilgamesh* would have been made possible by billingual poets, but see M.L. West 2014: 31–2 for a different view.
112 Because spelling in languages written in cuneiform script (such as Sumerian) includes a complex of signs (significant elements), and the name Gilgamesh has a long history (and a variant form, the Sumerian Bilgames), it is not easy to pin down its significance; scholars have put forward different possibilities (within more or less the same semantic range), see George 2003: 71 ff. (mainly 74–5).

as 'lady of the wild cows': she was conceptualised in the epic as a cow. The name of the prostitute Šamhat appropriately denotes superlative beauty of the flesh. The name of the divine ale-wife Šiduri has different possibilities of meaning in Akkadian ('she is my wall', i.e. protection; indeed she supports the hero with solid advice) and Hurrian (the generic meaning 'young woman'). Finally, the name of the Flood hero Ūta-napišti is seen as significant; in spite of the confusion regarding its form, it is agreed that it was appropriately associated with the meaning 'life' ('Life of distant days'? 'He found life?' – notably he was awarded eternal life after having survived the Flood).[113] Etymology in its broad sense seems to have been a factor in the understanding of the names of the Mesopotamian epic,[114] as is the case with quite a few Homeric names.

The use of 'speaking' names is further associated with the oral aspect of epic composition; our study of them can only be a study of how they behave in the epics as written texts,[115] but certainly heroic names originate in oral poetry on which Homer draws. The Homeric poems, relying on oral tradition, resemble oral poetry in the treatment of names. To mention one example, personal names have a great stylistic and symbolic importance in African oral literature, especially in narrative tales, where actors are given 'descriptive' names, which are either generic terms (to suit prototypical characters) or specially created for the tales.[116] Homeric patterns of naming, the scenes in which names are requested and given, also display features of an oral technique (where repetition of certain elements of narrative pattern coexists with variation).[117] Naming and denomination also hold an important place in narrative texts in general,[118] while significant naming is a persistent feature of epic poetry in particular. Another

---

[113] George 2003: 138–40, 147–9, 152–3. Cf. Maul 2014: 155.
[114] See e.g. George 2003: 140, 149.
[115] M.L. West (2011a: 13) has pointed out the dangers of imposing a one-sidedly oralist approach on the Homeric poems. Indeed 'the search for a scientific and precise measure of oral as against written composition may turn out to be a fruitless one', Finnegan 1977: 72, cf. Foley 1997: 162–3 and Fowler 2004 (with bibliogaphy).
[116] Biebuyck 1987: 47–71, esp. 61. Some examples from Nyanga tales (eastern Zaire): 'Busene' = Poverty and 'Butumba' = Wealth (generic names); names suggesting physical or moral attributes and set the mood of the tale: 'Iyange' (refers to the girl's beauty), 'Karumbirumbi' (= 'always asking for beer'). Cf. Finnegan 1970: 470–9. Names are known to have a social, ritual and psychological significance also in the real life of African societies.
[117] See Higbie's analysis of naming 'type-scenes' in Homer (1995: 69 ff.). But note also the possibility that some of the repetitions are of the poet's own work and not of phrases and motifs learned from others (M.L. West 2011a: 50–1). On repetition as a building block of Homeric poetry ('strukturierendes Prinzip zum Kalkül des Dichters'), see Bannert 1988.
[118] Cf. de Jong 1993: 289.

epic poem, set in a completely different place and time, but whose origins are also oral,[119] is known to make significant use of meaningful naming: the medieval epic *Beowulf*. The examples may be divided from Homer by centuries, but are telling.[120]

The above examples, that suggest significant naming as a generic practice in Homer's type of poetry (oral and epic), reach far in time and space. We should not lose sight of the fact that etymological play with names is equally at home in other early Greek hexameter poetry:[121] the poetry of Hesiod contains some examples, such as *Th.* 195–8 on the name of Aphrodite: ... τὴν δ' Ἀφροδί-την .../κικλήσκουσι θεοί τε καὶ ἀνέρες, οὕνεκ᾽ ἐν ἀφρῷ /θρέφθη; 'Gods and men call her Aphrodite, the foam-born goddess' (transl. Most); *Op.* 80–2 on the name of the mythical Pandora: ... ὅτι πάντες Ὀλύμπια δώματ᾽ ἔχοντες / δῶρον ἐδώρησαν '[Hermes named her Pandora ('All-Gift')], since all those who have their mansions on Olympos had given her a gift' (transl. Most);[122] so do the Homeric hymns, such as *h.Ven.* 198–9 on the name of Aineias, from αἰνὸν ... ἄχος 'terrible sorrow';[123] *h.Pan.* 47 on the name of Pan: Πᾶνα δέ μιν καλέεσκον, ὅτι φρένα πᾶσιν ἔτερψεν 'and they took to calling him Pan, because he delighted them all (*pantes*)' (transl. West). I shall avoid the question whether one poet's technique functioned as a model for the others: the relative chronology of Hesiod, Homer and the *Hymns* is a vexed issue.[124]

---

119 Cf. Foley 1990: 17. Our knowledge of the poem's manuscript history is meagre, but research has shown that we are dealing with 'at least an oral-derived text.' Currie (2012: 574) asserts that the epics of medieval Europe were composed in an environment that mixed orality with literacy, much like the Homeric epics.
120 There is, for example, *Hyge-lāc*, explained as 'instability of thought', the name of a hero who goes on a misjudged raid; it is contrasted with his wife's name, *Hygd* 'thought', 'mind', which reflects her better judgment in not following her husband on the expedition and, after his death, in offering the kingdom to Beowulf. The hero's name was traditional, but the wife's name must have been purposely invented by the poet of *Beowulf*. Other examples include 'Wolf' and 'Boar', the names of two especially thuggish young warriors; see Chickering 1977: 6–7 (and for further comparison between the *Iliad* and the *Beowulf* tradition Griffin 1980: 14 n. 34, 39 n. 98, 93 n. 35, 98; between the *Odyssey* and *Beowulf*, Foley 1990 [who recognises common core ideas but emphasises the divergence of traditions]). By contrast, the Yugoslav epic poems (also oral-derived) predominantly use historical characters.
121 For further examples (including some from Homer), see Salvadore 1987: 13–52.
122 On Hesiod as an etymologist see further Koning 2010: 227–30 (and 220 n. 127 on Pandora's name).
123 See further below, the discussion of Aineias' name.
124 See e.g. Janko 2012: 20 ff., with bibliography. He argues that Hesiod's poetry postdates the Homeric epics (this is the commonest view; opposite view in M.L. West [1995 and 2011a: 17] who

Lyric poetry, especially the poems of Archilochus of Paros, is another early context of the practice of significant naming. There are demonstrable points of contact between the iambic and epic traditions,[125] and Archilochus' work is now often thought to be more or less contemporary with the Homeric epics.[126] His fragments contain names such as Λεώφιλος (fr.115W) 'people's friend', an appropriate name for a leader of the people, perhaps a demagogue,[127] and Κηρυκίδης (fr.185W) 'herald's son', with a play on ἀχνυμένηι σκυτάληι, suggesting a 'grievous messenger'.[128] Another famous seventh century poet to use significant names is Alcman; his Partheneion (fr. 1 *PMGF*) names one Ἁγησιχόρα, a very appropriate name for a chorus-leader; in fr. 3 *PMGF*, Ἀστυμέλοισα ... μέλημα δάμωι 'a concern to the people' (ll. 73–4) is an obvious word-play; and in another fragment we find the more ambiguous Πολλαλέγων and Πασιχάρεια (fr. 96 *PMGF*).[129] The practice continues in the early classical period with Pindar[130] and Aeschylus (his etymologies are relevant to the explanation of the names of Homeric heroes,

---

thinks Hesiod to be earlier than the *Iliad*), and that the *Hymns* are later still, with the exception of the *Hymn to Aphrodite* which can be as early as the *Iliad*.
125 See now Rotstein 2010: 20, with bibliography. The figure of Thersites and his significant name (on which see further below, pp. 154–5) is an often cited example. Cf. M.L. West 2014: 34–5.
126 'There is no good reason to believe that the *Iliad* is earlier ... than the generation of Archilochus.' (M.L. West 2012: 235).
127 Cf. Rankin 1977: 82.
128 Cf. Gallavotti 1949: 139 and Kirkwood 1974: 46–7; further Bonanno (1980) on fictitious names used by Archilochus. There are also the more 'difficult' and much-discussed names Λυκάμβης (a wolf-name to imply a treacherous nature, with a pun on ἴαμβος?) and Νεοβούλη ('who changed her mind' – about marrying Archilochs?); see M.L.West 1974: 26 and Rankin 1978: 7–27.
129 Proposed meanings range from the early interpretation by Aristeides (*Orationes* 45.32): man 'who says much' and wife 'who takes pleasure in all (that she hears', to 'woman who gives pleasure to all men' and 'man who collects much (thanks to the gains of his promiscuous wife). See Henderson 1975: 23, McKay 1974: 413–4, and Maas 1973: 191. Πασιχάρεια has one, much later attestation (Epidauros, imperial period, *LGPN* IIIA).
130 His word-plays with names include: Ἐπιμαθέος ... ὀψινόου 'late-thinking Afterthought' (*P.* 5.27–8; transl. Arnson Svarlien); ἴων ξανθαῖσι καὶ παμπορφύροις ἀ-/ κτῖσι βεβρεγμένος ἁβρὸν / σῶμα· τὸ καὶ κατεφάμι-/ξεν καλεῖσθαί νιν χρόνῳ σύμπαντι μάτηρ / τοῦτ' ὄνυμ' ἀθάνατον '... his tender body washed in the golden and purple light of violets (ἴων). Therefore his mother declared that he should be called for all time by this immortal name, 'Iamus.' (*O.* 6.55–7; transl. Arnson Svarlien. Note the pun on Ἴαμος, mentioned earlier in 1.43). Both examples are very 'Homeric.' See further Braswell 1988: 104, 254.

as we shall see).¹³¹ It thus cannot be doubted that audiences of Homeric poetry in the archaic and classical periods were attuned to the use of 'speaking' names.

1.5 How to tell a 'speaking' name in Homer

It emerges from the above that the use of 'speaking' names in the Homeric epics is placed within an established literary tradition, and that the search for such names within the epics is well justified. But not every name in literature is a 'speaking' name; how do we decide whether a Homeric name is appropriately significant? This is not an easy question, as the answer should need to take account a variety of factors relevant to language, text, performance and audience. These factors are not fully predictable, and some cases are clearer than others; discussion nevertheless depends on a specific set of considerations, laid out below.

A 'minor' name may be attributed to more than one character, and it need not be assumed that its significance was equally noticed at all times: some contexts activate puns, others do not. The use of significant names in Homer is often signposted by means of a *calembour* or word-play (a playful 'explanation' of a name by semantical or etymological cognates which lie in close proximity, or even by words of similar sound that are chosen for euphony and are eventually thought to be etymologically connected). Word-plays with personal names form part of a general Homeric practice that encompasses all types of words, not just proper names; word-plays constitute rhetorical figures¹³² and contribute to the formulaic system and to memory-friendly verses. Word-play is occasionally developed in the form of a short narrative or description that may connect a name with basic feature of the bearer's character or appearance (cf. the explanation of the name Odysseus in *Od.* 19.399 ff. and of the name Κύκλωπες in Hesi-

---

131 It is worth noting here *Sept.* 658: ἐπωνύμῳ δὲ κάρτα, Πολυνείκη λέγω 'As for him, whose name is so very fitting...' (transl. Smyth). Polyneikes is deservedly called 'rich in contention' (577 ff., 830), and his name, 'insulting but not jocular', has been thought to have been coined (clearly before Aeschylus, cf. *Il.* 4.376 ff.) for this story; thus Hutchinson 1985: 186. See also Finglass' note (2011: 265, on S. *Aj.* 430–1) for bibliography on tragic etymologies.
132 On these see further Edwards (1991: 55–60). Word-plays can be categorised on the basis of various figures of speech, e.g. 'equivox' in the famous Οὖτις, 'paronomasia' in many cases, e.g. in Πρόθοος θοός *Il.* 2.758, which is also a 'parechesis' (assonance); see McCartney 1918/9: 343 ff. and more recently the categorisation proposed by O'Hara (1996: 59–60; see also his detailed definition of word-play, ibid.: 2–3). For examples of Homeric word-play (especially involving assonance) not concerning proper names, see e.g. Macleod 1982: 50–3. See also Peraki-Kyriakidou (2002: 482–9) on etymologising 'through synonyms or synonymic phrases' in Homer.

od, *Th.* 139 ff.). In its rare uses, the term (ὄνομα) ἐπώνυμον[133] is another way of attracting attention to a name's significance; it expresses the poet's own comments on proper names, which offer valuable insights in the literary intentions surrounding their use.

However, explicit references to names' meanings are not particularly common in Homer. It has been noted that while in Hesiod the meaning of names is often explained, the *Iliad* and the *Odyssey* hardly ever make the appropriateness of names explicit.[134] Allusions to main heroes' meanings do not seem to have entered the formulaic system, even for names that frequently appear in formulas, such as Achilles.[135] Hence the discussion of the meanings of 'difficult' names in both epics clearly entails a degree of speculation. However, relevant allusions may be found in a broader context of semantic relations: a name may be explained by the semantic environment in which it occurs, as well as by related semantic environments elsewhere in the narrative.[136] It may also be explained by the generic or individual characteristics of the bearer: we shall see that names mostly express features which are rather of the former type, apparently reflecting the emphasis given by the poems to the social status of the heroes (good warriors and leaders),[137] as opposed to strictly individual elements. Indication of suitability of personal names will occasionally be found in the depiction of respective characters in art.[138] Sometimes a proposed connection between a name and its semantic context will appear too subtle; but we should not underestimate the semantic power hidden in the names themselves as lin-

---

133 E.g. for the name Arete (*Od.* 7.54; see more in 'Names from the *Odyssey*', under 'Some Phaeacian Names'). This sequence demonstrates the poet's consciousness of the appropriateness of a name, see Hahn (1969: 94–101). For a different explanation of the term see Sulzberger (1926: 421–2), who takes it to refer to a name suggestive of a paternal characteristic.
134 Risch 1947: 79. In their different naming concepts, Risch (ibid.: 89–90) sees the poets' different relationship with the world, Hesiod's more solemn spirit and troubled thought in contrast with the lightness, poetic confidence and elegance of the Homeric epics. Hesiod's tendency to *Namensdeutungen* may also reflect his linguistic distance from the Ionic forms, or, more likely, the didactic spirit of his poetry.
135 On the use of names in the formulaic system see Higbie 1995: 43 ff. The formulaic repetition of words and phrases is reflected in the concordances to the epics (by Prendergast and Dunbar).
136 See Paschalis 1997: 1–4. The function of meaningful names within broader narrative or semantic patterns has become the object of some important modern studies; cf., e.g., Nagy (1979), Peradotto (1990), de Jong (2001).
137 Cf. Clarke 2004: 77. Also S.R. West (2012: 532) points out that oral narrative emphasises the function of its characters and shows little concern for subtle psychology.
138 Note that the distinction of specifically Homeric images (especially in early art) is hard (see Burgess 2001: 54 ff.), but early epic images from other mythological (non-Homeric) tradition can also be useful for the appreciation of a character's history and name.

guistic formations. To perceive this power, one must sometimes only rely on feeling and not on poetic rules and tricks.¹³⁹ A name may be understood as significant without the intervention of a word-play; puns certainly assist *our* understanding of 'speaking' names, but *ancient audiences*¹⁴⁰ may not have needed them in order to understand a name as significant. The early Greek interest in etymologies, as well as the choice and use of names in real life, further suggest that audiences of the archaic period were ready to notice meanings in personal names – and probably did not need much help to do so.¹⁴¹

The discussion of individual names will mostly rely on a unitarian working hypothesis, but will further show that exploitation of their meaning is often inherent in particular episodes (or sub-plots) of the epic story (which may at times reflect a broader epic background). This approach profits from neoanalysis, and is also associated with episodic performance, which is a feature of oral epic poetry;¹⁴² although the Homeric epics as we have them are clearly meant to form coherent wholes, their length should hinder continuous performance, and certain episodes could (and would) be singled out by rhapsodes.¹⁴³ A name can

---

139 Note Quintilian's poor view of word-play, 'quod etiam in iocis frigidum' (*Inst. Or.* 9.3.69).
140 The term, used here collectively, represents in fact a variety of audiences and settings (Thalmann 1984: 119), spread geographically and in time (from the archaic period onwards), who probably as late as the hellenistic period heard and read different versions of the text than ours (see Lamberton 1997: 33–4; the question of who exactly were the Homeric audience is a very difficult one to answer, and different perceptions exist, see also Graziosi 2002, esp. 86–9). On the *polis* as audience and on the potential of the epics to inspire 'politically significant emotion' (Athenian interventions in the text served this purpose), see Seaford 1994: 152, 182–3 (a panhellenic audience, on the other hand, was envisaged at the Panionian celebrations). It is worth remembering that bards could modify the text in performance to suit the interests of their audiences.
141 On the knowledgeability of ancient audiences, which might extend to the ability to detect intertextual allusions, see Currie 2012: 574, with bibliography.
142 On neoanalysis see generally Willcock 1997. For instances of the importance of neoanalytic claims for the interpretation of Homeric names see below pp. 57–8. For a survey of 20th century approaches to the Homeric text (analytic, neoanalytic, unitarian, oral poetics) see Heubeck 1974 (but note Willcock's remark [1997: 175] that neoanalysis and oral poetry theory are not mutually exclusive; cf. Currie 2012).
143 Cf. Scodel 2002: 48–9. The epics were traditionally divided in episodes (cf. Hdt. 2.116, Th.1.10, Pl. *Ion* 539b; these were arranged into coherent wholes at the time of Peisistratos according to ancient tradition, see Seaford 1994: 151–4). In an episodic performance, parts may stand for the implied whole (an observation that applies broadly to epic traditions, cf. Foley 2004: 177). On the exceptional length of the Homeric epics and on the possibility of continuous performance at great festivals (the *Panathenaia*) see Seaford ibid: 149–54, 182–3, 189 (who guesses that Homeric material also existed in the form of episodes performed on a variety of occasions;

also be appropriately significant in the sense that it may reflect a hero's basic feature and his characterisation throughout the epic story.[144] The notion of a significant name is clearly broader than the sense of a pun.

The involvement of personal names in the plot has given rise to the question whether names should be seen as merely reflecting the narrative or as being the motivating sources of the stories. Paschalis rightly hints at the impossibility of such a question.[145] It is more sensible to interpret names as elements of the plots and patterns of a story, rather than to try to extract the narrative from them. Old heroic names were probably not created with the purpose of evoking any specific narrative, but were exploited (and etymologised) for the sake of (or in accordance with) narratives within which they were used. In that sense they obtained the power 'to condense concepts, descriptions, and short narratives.'[146] Because of this power, they are not (and should never been seen as) marginal elements; they are central to the interpretation of plots and characters. They are further empowered by their fluidity of meaning: when more etymological meanings are possible, even of unequal degree of explicitness, the poems may appear to hint at one meaning in one context, and to a different one in another context. They can also function as allegories, when audiences are encouraged to look for meanings and levels of significance hidden beneath the obvious etymological sense[147] (the significant polyonymy of Odysseus, to be discussed in the *Odyssey* chapter, is a good example of this). It is no surprise that the study of personal names and denomination has found a place in virtually every reading of the epics (e.g. the already mentioned ethnographical readings), including modern ideological approaches.[148]

---

the oral nature of the narrative certainly also resulted in a variety of versions, influenced by the demands of different audiences).

144 Cf. the definition of the significant name in von Kamptz (1982 (1958): 25): it is the name which 'auf die Vorstellung Bezug nimmt, die von ihnen (= den mythischen Figuren) besteht oder *erweckt werden soll*' (emphasis is mine).

145 1997: 4; 'the issue whether the meaning of names generates the meaning of the narrative or whether names encapsulate the meaning of the narrative, cannot be resolved'. Risch (1947: 76) implies a similar question, whether names owe their existence to the stories that inspired them (which presupposes that stories pre-existed) or names pre-existed, and stories only reflected an effort to justify the names.

146 Paschalis 1997: 3.

147 On the intersection between etymology and allegory see Del Bello 2007: ch. 2.

148 See e.g. Clayton's (2004: 35) analysis of Penelope's name in connection with a feminist evaluation of her function in the *Odyssey*. The power of Odyssean female characters has inspired a fair amount of feminist scholarship on this epic, see Doherty 2009: 12 (with bibliography).

Among modern approaches, special mention must be made of intertextual and of narratological readings. Given the narrative nature of the epics, the association between etymology and narratology has proved particularly fruitful.[149] However, the traditional character of epic heroes and names imposes limits to narrative exploitation: for example, familiarity with a character's name and the story may work against the potential of its etymology to 'foreshadow' events (which the audience already knows about and expects). The assumption that etymologies may work within a narrative nexus spanning more than one book is plausible in terms of poetic composition,[150] but it should be kept in mind that circumstances of performance did not guarantee that two books would be recited in a row.[151]

The above notes will serve as a framework to the attempt that follows to reconstruct meanings of selected Homeric names. While linguistic derivations will serve as a starting point, emphasis will be given to the connection between names, plot and characterisation, and to the point of view of the audience. The use of the term 'Iliadic, Odyssean (or Homeric) audience' will mostly refer to ancient audiences (especially of the archaic period),[152] and does not of course envisage a uniform body; where more than one interpretation seems possible, some listeners would no doubt immediately think of one, others of another (and with very familiar names which were not immediately transparent, awareness of any significance may not have been very widespread). It is clear that a study of Homeric personal names involves the various views and suggestions found in the rich reserves of Homeric scholarship. The aim here is a fresh

---

149 Narratological readings are interested in the proper name as a type of *anaphora*, while uses of, suppression of, and substitution of personal names are all relevant to the characters' focalisation (cf. de Jong 2001: 18, 168; see also Skempis-Ziogas 2009).
150 Specific allusion is not impossible in oral poetry; see the arguments in Currie 2012.
151 E.g. it is therefore hard to maintain (with Skempis-Ziogas 2009: 217) that the use of the verb ἀράομαι at *Od.* 6.323 anticipates the etymological meaning of Arete's name – heard for the first time at 7.54. On Homer as an oral performer see also Ong 1982 *passim*.
152 Modern audience-oriented theory (on which see *HE* s.v. Contemporary Theory [J. Peradotto]) has brought forward varied perceptions of 'audience'. The focus here will be placed on actual audiences, of specific chronological periods (the evolution of the names' meanings will be considered, and of course listeners from different geographical places would perceive names differently – the term 'Homeric audience' is highly conventional, see also above n. 140). Archaic audiences may be assumed to have a more immediate grasp of the language of the epics than later ones (there is evidence for the increasing obscurity of Homer's language already in the classical period, see e.g. Aristophanes fr. 233 K–A). That being said, learned listeners (and readers) of later times would be able to discern instances of more subtle and implicit etymologising.

and, as far as possible, conclusive analysis of the names in question, without losing sight of the great diversity of views and interpretative frameworks, which demonstrate the 'openness' that characterises the study of Homeric onomastics. We will look mostly at names of prominent figures (and often of persons in their genealogies, when these are mentioned in the poems), but also selectively at names of secondary characters, from both the *Iliad*[153] and the *Odyssey*. Some names will be noted to have an etymology that becomes 'obvious' through proper word-plays, not all equally strong; other names, i.e. names whose meaning cannot be teased out through the examination of the verses where they occur, will be treated as meaningful too, but their meanings will be teased by association with epic language in general (and hence are open to doubt and argument). Regarding the latter names, the discussion will explore two possibilities: that some seemingly 'dark' names are significant in their contexts, and that their significance can emerge from their reading as Greek words.

1.5.1 Notes to the reader

References to the Iliadic text follow the latest Teubner edition by M.L. West (1998–2000), and to the *Odyssey* P. Von der Mühll's Teubner edition (1984). Translations of lines and passages usually follow the most recent Loeb (*Iliad:* transl. A.T. Murray, revised by W.F. Wyatt, 1999; *Odyssey:* transl. A.T. Murray, revised by G.E. Dimock, 1995). Translations of other ancient Greek texts also mostly follow Loeb (translators' names are given in brackets).

Decisions on the transliteration of Greek names are not easy to make, and absolute consistency is hard to achieve. I have favoured direct transliteration of all proper names discussed as significant, to facilitate etymological understanding by reflecting the original Greek more accurately. However, names of ancient authors and works adhere to the familiar latinised spelling. I also retain commonly used English forms (e.g. Homer, Aristotle).

---

[153] For a categorisation of characters based on their importance for the Iliadic plot, see Stoevesandt 2000: 135–43. Discussion of the name of Odysseus, one of the leading figures in the *Iliad*, is reserved for the *Odyssey* chapter.

2 Names from the *Iliad*

2.1 The Warrior Heroes

2.1.1 Achilles

Achilles has attracted and continues to attract the largest amount of attention among the Iliadic figures. His origins are extremely ancient, as demonstrated by the presence of similar figures in other Indo-European poetic traditions.[1] He is the hero who motivates the poem's action; his importance suggests his name as a particularly worthy object of exploration.

The Scholia explain the name as significant: οὕτως ἀναγνωστέον δι'ἑνὸς λ ... διὰ τὸ ἄχος (ὅ ἐστι λύπην) ἐπενεγκεῖν τοῖς Ἰλιεῦσιν. Οἱ δὲ παρὰ τὸ μὴ θιγεῖν χείλεσι †τροφῆς†· ὅλως γὰρ οὔ μετέσχε γάλακτος (Sch. AT *Il*. 1.1) '[the name] must be spelled with one λ ... because of the *achos* (which means 'grief') that he brought upon the people of Ilion (=Troy). But according to others, because he did not touch food(?) with his lips (χείλεσι); indeed he never had any milk.'[2] But despite antiquity's effort, etymology has failed to yield any straightforward results, and Achilles' name (Ἀχιλ(λ)εύς – with single or double λ according to metrical needs) emerges as one of the most difficult problems in Greek onomastics. There are various ancient etymologies,[3] and there is no lack of variety in modern efforts: the name was thought to be pre-Greek[4] with various explanations, or Greek from ἄχος 'grief', either as ἀχ-ίλος[5] or as Ἀχί-λαϝος.[6] The discovery of the name on the Mycenaean tablets[7] encouraged its explanation in Greek terms, and for a short while gave life to the attractive possibility of

---

[1] The ancient Sanskrit epic *Mahābhārata* features a warrior hero named Arjuna, who like Achilles on Skyros, disguised himself for a time among girls (the daughters of the court) (Puhvel 1987: 84). The staging of action and basic creation of the Sanskrit epic 'antedate the middle of the first millennium BCE' and thus may be concurrent with the composition of Homer's epics, Puhvel ibid.: 68–9.

[2] Cf. the alternative, equally incredulous derivation from ἀ-χεῖλος by the imperial author Ptolemaeus Chennos ('the Quail'), allegedly because one of Achilles' lips was burnt while Thetis was making him immortal (as reported by Photius; on Ptolemaeus see Kim 2010: 18–20).

[3] For an overview of these see Roscher 1884–90 : 64.

[4] See Bosshardt 1942: 139. Risch (1974: 158) accepted that the ending –ευς is often present in Greek names, but still regarded the name as 'offenbar vorgriechisch'. Cf. von Kamptz 1982 (1958): 348.

[5] Kretschmer 1913: 305–8, and earlier Roscher 1884–90: 64.

[6] Palmer 1963: 78–9.

[7] Pylos tablet Fn 79 and Knossos tablet Vc 106.

Achilles being a real, historical warrior's name[8] – but even if this were true, it would throw little light on the meaning of the name; this should be sought in its poetic function.[9]

The difficulty in establishing an etymology for the name was clearly reflected in the dispute between Holland and Nagy on the issue of the name's significance.[10] Nagy has rightly argued that this should not necessarily rely on 'right' etymology; popular etymology is equally worth considering.[11] The old linguistic debate has characteristically never been brought to an end,[12] but it is worth considering that the name acquires significance in specific contexts. A large portion of modern scholarship[13] concentrates on the ancient connection between the hero's name and the notion of ἄχος: this is found in the Scholia (see previous page) and Callimachus (Ἀχιλεὺς γὰρ ἀπὸ τοῦ εἶναι ἄχος τοῖς Ἰλιεῦσιν, ἤγουν τοῖς Τρωσί, κατὰ φερωνυμίαν· ὑπὸ γὰρ θείας προνοίας, ὡς ἔφη Καλλίμαχος, ἐκλήθη οὕτως, fr. 624 Pfeiffer. 'Achilles is named after the *achos* he caused the people of Ilion, i.e. the Trojans; indeed he got his name under divine providence, as Callimachus says'). Nagy[14] argued that this notion is intrinsic to the hero's function in myth and epic. This is a hazardous assumption, given that Achilles is apparently a later insertion in the Trojan saga, and he has a separate tradition as a free-roamer warrior which is independent from it.[15] Still, he is clearly essential to the conception of the *Iliad*, and it is worth considering that the poet took advantage of the name's sound in ways that suited the contents of his poem.

---

8 See Page 1959: 25 ff.
9 Palmer (1979; 1980: 37–8) assumed that the wrath of Achilles was already a poetic theme in Pylos at that time (as early as the 14th c. BC), which is very uncertain (cf. Grossardt 2009: 57–8: 'Ein hohes Alter der Sage vom Zorn des Achilleus ließe sich dann aus dem Namen des Helden nicht scließen'). While real-life names may reflect a capacity of the father or a positive characteristic, Palmer argued that Achilles' name fulfills neither function, and that a literary motive for its choice should be sought instead; the name is 'evidently a speaking name invented for the purpose of the story and inseparable from it'.
10 Holland (1993) and Nagy (1994).
11 See also 'Introductory notes'.
12 See Latacz 2000b: 15: 'Seine Etym. ist trotz vieler Spekulationen (e.g. ἄχος) bis heute nicht geklärt; der Name ist vielleicht vorgr.' (cf. *N.Pauly* s.v. Achilleus [D. Sigel]) and recently Beekes (2010 s.v. Ἀχιλλεύς) who concludes that 'the meaning of the name remains unknown' (though I cannot agree that 'this is unimportant').
13 See most recently *HE* s.v. Achilles (S. Schein).
14 1979. But Nagy is right to look for implicit ideas in the epic, an underlying system of meanings, which takes flesh in a specific tradition of heroes and plots, and which is also duly expressed in names.
15 I fully endorse M.L. West's arguments here (2011a: 42–7).

Indeed the numerous textual references (events, facts and verbal elements that deploy what can be seen as the ἄχος of a λαός 'people' or 'army') make a relevant explanation of the name a likely one;[16] synonymous expressions[17] would also be noticed by the audience and felt to confirm the theme. The connection between ἄχος and the plot is evident, as the grief that the hero causes by staying away from the war is very central in the epos, and is connected with the prominent theme of μῆνις, the reason for the hero's withdrawal;[18] when the hero stops grieving for his compatriots by eventually returning to fight, he obviously starts causing grief to the Trojan side.[19] The connection of Achilles with grief amounts to more than the pain he causes or prevents: he experiences personal grief for the death of Patroklos, a grief which is appropriately denoted as ἄχος (18.22).[20] Achilles himself is doomed to a sad fate which makes grief an inseparable part of the way he is generally perceived as a hero; this idea is strongly felt in the *Iliad*, especially in his mother's lament over his sad fortune (18.52–64), where she refers to the son's grievings with the appropriate verb ἄχνυται 'he has sorrow' (18.62).[21] Towards the end of the poem, the hero's grief obtains a philosophical note, as he and Priam are briefly brought together in sorrow (24.525–6). As a 'Man of pain', in both an active and a passive sense, Achilles arguably fits a recognised heroic profile (we shall see in the next chapter that Odysseus too both inflicts and receives pain).[22]

The verbal puns on *achos* gain further strength from the realisation that they suggest the name as suitable to the hero's broader psychological profile. This profile consists not just of grief, but of other emotions too, which are all akin to grief. The very beginning of the epic surrounds the name of Achilles with emo-

---

16 There are about a hundred occurrences of vocabulary from that root in the *Iliad*. In addition to these, the name Achilles itself is mentioned about 400 times! (Agamemnon's name is mentioned about half as often).
17 Gathered by Nagy 1979: 7 ff.
18 Generally understood as 'anger'; Muellner (1996), in his study of the particular function of the term in its cultural and poetic context, interprets *mēnis* as cosmic anger against morally transgressive behaviour – a description that may seem to account for the magnitude of the consequences of Achilles' anger in our poem.
19 Note that the Scholium to *Il*.1.1 reads as second part of the name Ἰλιεῦσιν (as another name for the Trojans; cf. the Callimachus fragment). See also Holland (1993: 26) who proposed, among other possible interpretations of the name, 'he who frightens the λαός'.
20 Cf. *DGE* s.v. ἄχος (1) on the various triggers of this emotion in the epic.
21 Nagy (1979: 7 ff., esp. 7 ff.) may be right in thinking that the name incorporates an underlying, archetypal theme of the poem; note that the word ἄχος is often used in formulaic expressions (e.g. αἰνὸν ἄχος in *Il.* 8.124, 17.83).
22 See Cook 2009: 11 ff. (who also mentions the example of Herakles).

tional vocabulary (μῆνιν 'wrath', ἄλγεα 'sorrows'). The name of the victim of grief, the λαός as Ἀχαιοῖς, is an ethnic name that, like Achilles, seems to start with the root for ἄχος.²³ Achilles' *mēnis* is balanced by pity: he feels anger against Agamemnon, then against him who caused the death of Patroklos, but also pities himself (for being the victim of Agamemnon's egotism, for his fate to die young) and Priam, as the last book of the *Iliad* shows;²⁴ both of these emotions are part of the hero's *achos*. *Ochthein*, which is also used for Achilles, depicts a similar psychological state (agitation / indignation, e.g. 20.343).²⁵ Another related emotion frequently associated with Achilles in the *Iliad*, *cholos*,²⁶ may be felt as a weak pun on his name; a Myrmidon claims that Achilles nursed on *cholos* 'bile' (*Il.* 16.203), and this may account for the formation of an angry temperament.²⁷ Finally, Achilles experiences 'angry grief'²⁸ (a combination of *achos* and *mēnis*) at the death of his friend Patroklos, which finds expression in prolonged, excessive lamentation and in his particularly aggressive form of revenge. Grief and anger constitute the main elements of a raw emotionality that led Plato to treat Achilles in the *Republic* (books 2 and 3) as the archetype of uncontrolled *thymos*.²⁹

A name that expresses emotion would defy the predominant tendency of the poet of the *Iliad* to name his heroes for generic heroic features (such as martial valour). Of course a view of war not merely as a field of heroic activity, but also as a source of emotional turmoil and suffering, is not absent from the *Iliad* (cf. e.g. 4.8 ff., and in Achilles' words, 9.31 ff.). More importantly, though, the name would be in keeping with the depth of Achilles' characterisation, which is unique in the poem. Achilles' name, with the nuances described above, follows the character's development³⁰ as he responds to experience. Some of the senses of *achos* are linked to action that contributes to heroic ideology – other senses are suited to the hero as he challenges or even subverts it (as at the peak of his individu-

---

23 Cf. Nagy 1979: 8 ff.
24 See further Most (2003: 50–75) on the structural importance of anger and pity ('sides of the same coin') in the *Iliad*.
25 Cairns 2003: 22 n. 42.
26 See the instances gathered in Cairns 2003: 22 n. 39, 25 n. 57, 26 n. 64, 27 n. 70.
27 Hanson 2003: 185–6.
28 Cf. Seaford 1994: 165, and ibid.: 166 on the extreme closeness between the two as an expression of the fact that they are almost identified in fate.
29 See further Hobbs 2000: 19 ff.
30 Treated at length by Zanker (1994), who argues that the evolution of the hero's character culminates in 'magnanimity' or altruism (expressing his pity for Priam).

alism, when he causes grief to his fellow Greeks).³¹ The significant echo of his name clearly has more implications for his characterisation than the content of the frequent formulas that accompany it.³²

The assumption that the hero's essence should be older and wider than his epic image is associated with another interpretation of the ἄχος etymology. In a recent attempt to etymologise the name against an Indo-European background, *achos* is taken to be closely connected with the notion of death, and the name is explained as 'the one who overcomes death'.³³ This significance may allude to the story of Thetis' attempt to make her son immortal by anointing him with ambrosia;³⁴ this story is not in the *Iliad* but was obviously well known in antiquity (cf. Sch. D on *Il.* 16.36). Of course, Achilles has a career as a warrior who defeats death in a variety of war settings before he meets his fate – and his poetic fame ensures that his *kleos* never dies.

The association between the etymology of Achilles' name and the idea of death is an old one. Kretschmer³⁵ had connected the name with Ἀχέρων, the stream of the Underworld, and argued that Achilles is one of the young figures in mythology who were predestined to suffer an early death (like Adonis and Hyakinthos) and for whom cults (*Trauerfeiern*) were founded. Although this view does not include a poetic justification of the name, more recent attempts at a 'religious' explanation have brought the Iliadic context to the foreground. Hommel,³⁶ like Kretschmer, noticed the name's similarity to Ἀχέρων (and further to Ἀχελῷος, Ἀχερουσία λίμνη) and argued that Achilles was no less than a divine figure (probably a water-god, the ruler of the Kingdom of the Dead, settled in re-

---

31 Seaford (1994: 184–5) assumed that the development of Achilles' characterisation was influenced by historical factors, in particular the increasing importance of hero-cult; the relevant aetiological myths possess a narrative structure of dishonourment, wrath and restoration of honour, found also in the story of Achilles (but one needs to accept a late date for the elaboration of these themes into the long epos).
32 E.g. 'swift-foot' (πόδας ὠκύς) – of no particular interest for characterisation.
33 Nikolaev 2007; he proposed a new scientific etymology of *achos*, which brings it close to the Indo-European formulaic theme 'hero slays death'. This etymology further suggests a new, grammatical explanation to the alternation of λ and λλ in the name's form (ibid.: 168–9). The etymology of ἄχος is controversial. Chantraine 1999 and Beekes 2010 (s.v. ἄχνυμαι) suggested derivation from an Indo-European root with the meaning 'fear'; a connection with ἄγχω 'strangle' has also been proposed (Stefanelli 2008).
34 Nikolaev ibid.: 170–1.
35 1913: 305–8. A connection of the name with a supposed pre-Hellenic root *αχ- meaning 'water' was assumed by several linguists of the late 19th c. See further Van Windekens 1949/50: 19 ff.
36 1980: 38–9.

mote waters). He then drew attention to *Il.* 21, where Achilles is fighting like a demon against the Trojan river-gods and their sons, having his own death in front of his eyes, and where Ἀχελῷος also finds a mention (1.194). He accordingly perceived Achilles' figure in the *Iliad* as one which, to the informed, is intrinsically connected with the concept of death, 'gleich als ob er damit dem Wissenden seinen Ursprung als Gott der Toten verriete'.[37] Finally, he thought that the origin of the hero as a 'Lord of the dead' is further implied by the presence of a cult of Achilles in the Pontic region, in particular at Λευκὴ νῆσος,[38] which is connected with the hero in the *Aithiopis* and which Hommel identified with the Island of the Blessed on the basis of two Pindaric passages (*O.* 2.78–80 and *Nem.* 4.49–50).[39] It is further noteworthy that Achilles in his new armour is compared to Sirius, a star described as the brightest of all, yet a deadly omen, 'a sign of evil [that] brings much fever on wretched mortals' (*Il.* 22.25–32).

As far as the *Iliad* is concerned, however, the theme of death is linked with the notion of grief; there is no compelling suggestion of a god of the Underworld. In *Il.* 21 the hero features much more as the enemy of river-gods than a water deity himself, and takes pains to differentiate himself from these by claiming that he is a descendant of Zeus (187). It might appear somewhat significant that a direct association between Achilles and the realm of the Dead is made in the *Odyssey* (11.485, Odysseus to Achilles: νῦν αὖτε μέγα κρατέεις νεκύεσσιν 'now you rule mightily among the dead'), but the diction there does not point to Hommel's preferred etymology, while, interestingly, it includes a word-play on the notion of grief as ἄχος (μή τι θανὼν ἀκαχίζευ, Ἀχιλλεῦ 'grieve not at all that you are dead, Achilles', 486). Also the identification of Λευκὴ νῆσος is far from certain, and even if thought to be, Achilles' presence there does not imply a 'Lord of the Dead',[40] nor is there a strong indication that he was later worshipped as a god on Leuke and not just as a hero. It is not impossible, however, that the whole scene of fighting around the waters (with Achilles' confrontation of the water-gods and his final jump into the river, 233–4) may echo the remains of an older mythology about him, which may have been vaguely heard in the name.

---

[37] Hommel 1980: 43 (with bibliography).
[38] On this cult see e.g. Parker 2011: 244–6.
[39] The earlier mentioned dialogue between Thetis and Hera from *Argonautica* (4.811) includes a reference to the hero's future residence on the Elysian plain. The fact that in the same passage naiads are presented to help raise the young hero may reflect his mother's maritime nature, in which he too may participate.
[40] See Hooker 1988: 4–5.

Achilles may have divine origins (though not necessarily as a god of Hades or the water),⁴¹ and then entered the mythic circle as a hero; the use of the name in myth and poetry would have then led to new etymological associations and assumptions of meanings. Notably the Achilles – ἄχος connection does not exhaust the potential of the name for significance. After all, ancient attempts at explaining the name do not offer a uniform etymology but diverge into different views, offering glimpses of a variety of traditional stories associated with the hero. A derivation from χιλός, which is mentioned in a Scholium and in a fragment of the poet Euphorion,⁴² is connected with an important aspect of Achillean mythology: the hero's time with the centaur, who kept him on a diet of animal entrails and bone marrow.⁴³ The story has a serious claim to a primitive date, as its portrayals in art date from the archaic period. The evidence from art, in combination with the later literary references, may suggest an old epic about the childhood and the youth of the hero, in which allusions to the relevant meaning of the name may have been present.⁴⁴

Homeric poetry does not suggest a clear significance for the name of the hero's father, Peleus, but engages it in a memorable sound-play that spans three lines (*Il.* 16.142–4); notably Peleus' name is not mentioned, but is artfully suggested by

---

41 Such an etymologically unclear name can hardly be used to support a solid argument about the nature of his bearer, see Hooker 1988.
42 Ἐς Φθίην χιλοῖο κατήϊε πάμπαν ἄπαστος / τούνεκα Μυρμιδόνες μιν Ἀχιλέα φημίξαντο (fr. 81 Lightfoot, cf. Sch. *Il.* 1.1, *Et. Gen.* and Tzetzes, *Ex.* 61.3. 'When he came to Phthia he had never tasted proper food, which is why the Myrmidons called him Achilles' [privative a+χιλός]). Euphorion was apparently quite fond of appropriate naming (if we accept, with Meineke, the inclusion of fr. 184 Lightfoot, with the explanation of the name Περσεύς, in his work). Van Groningen (1977: 130) notes in respect to fr. 81: 'C'est une remarque de poète savant, peut-être même originale.'
43 Apollod. 3.172. Χιλός (a word not found in Homer) is normally used for animal fodder; its use in Euphorion's passage may be inspired by the centaur's nature, which was half equine. Note that conversely Phoinix later fed Achilles with meat and wine (*Il.* 9.488–9).
44 See *LIMC* I s.v. Achilleus, esp. 53 (A. Kossatz-Deissmann). Admittedly, it cannot be excluded that Euphorion's etymology was a hellenistic invention, as we cannot be sure that the details of Achilles' diet were part of the early myth. The unlikely etymology privative a + χεῖλος 'without a lip' (Sch., Tzetzes *ad Lyc.* 178) may have emerged from that same myth. Cf. Apollod. (3.172) where the centaur is said to have given Achilles his name for not drinking his mother's milk (ὠνόμασεν Ἀχιλλέα ... ὅτι τὰ χείλη μαστοῖς οὐ προσήνεγκε) and A.R. (4.812, Hera addressing Thetis: ὃν δὴ νῦν Χείρωνος ἐν ἤθεσι Κενταύροιο / νηιάδες κομέουσι τεοῦ λίπτοντα γάλακτος 'he whom now in the home of Cheiron the Centaur water-nymphs are tending, though he still craves your mother milk'). Apollodorus apparently assumes that Achilles' name was chosen to reflect a feature of the hero's upbringing and was not given to him at birth; hence his birth name was a different one (Ligyron). Cf. the Callimachus passage which attributes Achilles' naming to divine planning.

πατρὶ φίλῳ (143) and by the surrounding vocabulary that is similar in sound to the name (πάλλειν / πῆλαι / Πηλιάδα / Πηλίου). Peleus gave his son a spear, that 'Achilles alone was skilled to wield' (... ἀλλά μιν οἶος ἐπίστατο πῆλαι Ἀχιλλεύς, Il. 16.142). The spear was given to Peleus by Cheiron from the peak of mount Pelion (16.143–4), where Peleus' wedding to Thetis also took place according to the *Cypria*. An allusion to mount Pelion was perhaps also heard in Patroklos' complaint that the harsh and stubborn Achilles was born not of Peleus, but of 'the sheer cliffs' (16.33–5).[45]

2.1.2 Aias

Obvious literary exploitations of the heroic name Aias are found outside Homer and concern the greater Aias (never the lesser); this is not surprising, given the greater mythical importance of the Telamonian. Relevant texts and contexts contain the following:

1) Pindar (*I.* 6.4 ff.) narrates that Aias would be named after the eagle, αἰετός, that appeared to his father Telamon as a good omen following Herakles' prayer to Zeus that Telamon may beget an invulnerable son. The Scholia (Sch. P. *I.* 6.53) name the Hesiodic *Catalogue of Women* (fr. 250 M–W) as the source for this etymology.[46]
2) Euripides too may have implied a connection between Aias and αἰετός in his tragedy *Meleagros*; one fragment (*TGrF* 5.1 fr. 530 [Kannicht]) refers to Telamon and a shield adorned with an eagle.
3) For Sophocles the name echoes an exclamation of grief, αἰαῖ, caused by the misfortunes suffered by the hero (*Aj.* 430–2: Αἰαῖ· τίς ἄν ποτ' ᾤεθ' ὧδ' ἐπώνυμον /τοὐμὸν ξυνοίσειν ὄνομα τοῖς ἐμοῖς κακοῖς; / νῦν γὰρ πάρεστι καὶ δὶς αἰάζειν ἐμοί 'Aiai. Who could ever have thought that my name would thus correspond to my sorrows? For now I may say *ai* twice indeed.'[47]

Although there is no explicit etymology of the name Aias in Homer, some of the above mentioned etymological connections may be evoked at different moments. At *Il.* 13.821–5, Aias receives a good omen before battle in the form of an eagle (note a possible word-play: Ὣς ἄρα οἱ εἰπόντι ἐπέπτατο δεξιὸς ὄρνις / αἰετὸς

---

[45] On the word-plays see Edwards 1987: 122. Derivation from Pelion does not constitute 'scientific' etymology; see M.L. West 1988: 160 and cf. von Kamptz 1982 (1958): 300–1.
[46] A scholarly etymology of Αἴας (old form ΑἴϜας) as a diminutive of αἰϜετός was supported by Wilamowitz (1884: 245) and Kretschmer (1894: 48).
[47] Transl. Finglass 2011: 265.

ὑψιπέτης· ... ὃ δ' ἀμείβετο φαίδιμος Ἕκτωρ· <u>Αἶαν</u> ἁμαρτοεπὲς, βουγάϊε, ποῖον ἔειπες;); this is reminiscent of the omen that precedes his birth, mentioned in Pindar and the *Catalogue of Women*.[48] In the *Odyssey* (11.543–4), the dead Aias is said to resent still the loss of Achilles' arms to Odysseus: οἴη δ' Αἴαντος ψυχὴ / Τελαμωνιάδαο / νόσφιν ἀφεστήκει, κεχολωμένη εἵνεκα νίκης...; ('alone of them all the spirit of Aias, son of Telamon, still full of wrath for the victory [of Odysseus]); this expression of grief is reminiscent of the suffering evoked by the Sophoclean etymology.[49] However, none of these explanations of the name corresponds to the way Aias is presented in the Homeric poems: the hero's birth is of no concern to the poet of the *Iliad*, and Aias' famous association with grief comes later in his story than the end of the *Iliad*.[50] It is therefore worth exploring further ways in which the name Aias may have suited the Homeric character. The Iliadic Aias is the main focus (the Odyssean one being no more than a passing figure). Additionally, any effort to explain the name in its Iliadic context has to consider not one hero, but two: not just the Salaminian Aias, son of Telamon, but also the Locrian Aias, son of Oileus. Despite the greater importance of the Telamonian (he is ranked second after Achilles,[51] and he is mentioned in what is arguably the oldest part of the poem,[52] while the Locrian is not), the presence of two Aiantes in the poem as we have it cannot be ignored. One needs to ask the question whether the name would suit one or both its bearers, and if so whether it might have the same meaning for both.

One scholarly etymology of Αἴας, thought to be supported by evidence from the Linear B tablets from Knossos, assigns it to the same root as αἰόλος.[53] Whether Aias' name is a short form of Αἴολος[54] (there are some examples of Homeric

---

48 Note, though, that eagles are a standard type of omen; the fact that neither Hektor nor the poet hints at any connection with Aias' name makes it uncertain that the audience heard a pun.
49 Of course the use of χόλος forbids a specific pun. Note also that neither the tragic exclamation nor the verb αἰάζειν are used in Homer.
50 The *Little Iliad* gave an account of the hero's disappointment for the assignment of Achilles' arms to Odysseus, and of his violent reaction and final suicide. These events are dramatized by Sophocles in his *Ajax*.
51 See M.L. West (2011a: 121), with references.
52 Books 1–3.14 and 11.8 ff., identified by M.L. West (2011a: 63) as the 'primary layer'.
53 *āyu-* 'moving', see von Kamptz 1982 (1958): 368. The Mycenaean tablets have rendered the form *ai-wa* (Np 973), which has been identified with the name Aias, and also *ai-wo-ro* (read Αἴ-Fολος, Ch 896, 1029, 5754). See Ventris-Chadwick 1953: 94, 1973: 537 (name of an ox); cf. Mühlestein 1967: 42. The identification is doubted by Chantraine 1963b: 12–15 and Lejeune 1963: 1–9.
54 The name is of course prominent in book 10 of the *Odyssey*. Perhaps the right accentuation is Αἰόλος; see Chandler 1881: §391.

diminutives in –αντ),⁵⁵ or the two names are simply derived from the same root, a connection between the two implies that the name Aias may reflect the meanings of the adjective αἰόλος. Based on this etymology, Mühlestein seemed to kill two birds with one stone by showing that αἰόλος in its different uses is relevant to both of the name's bearers. The adjective at times accompanies the greater Aias' most important characteristic of appearance, the shield (σάκος; cf. 7.222 and 16.107). The use of αἰόλος in relation to armour seems to suggest the meaning 'flashing' (cf. τεύχε' ... / αἰόλα παμφανόωντα 'armour ... all bright and flashing', *Il.* 5.294–5), perhaps for a glittering metal surface (like a shield of bronze, e. g. 7.219–20 σάκος... χάλκεον), though there is also another possibility: the Mycenaean *ai-wa* and *ai-wo-ro* have been seen as names of oxen, and Aias' shield is known to have been covered with ox-hide (cf. 7.220 ἑπταβόειον).⁵⁶ The importance of the shield is probably also reflected in the names of persons that are closely related to the hero: his father's name Τελαμών (cf. the patronymic Τελαμώνιος), a word used in the *Iliad* as a noun meaning the belt for carrying or supporting the shield (from the root τελα- 'bear', e. g. 16.803 ἀσπὶς σὺν τελαμῶνι, 2.388–9, 5.796–8 etc.),⁵⁷ and his son's name Εὐρυσάκης ('with broad shield'; not mentioned in Homer, but in S. *Aj.* 575, cf. Plu. *Sol.* 10). It is therefore possible that the name Aias alluded to the hero's all-important shield, especially when the combination σάκος αἰόλον was heard in close proximity to the personal name (as at 7.219–22). But αἰόλος in the *Iliad* has a further meaning, unrelated to the shield: 'swift', as in πόδας αἰόλος ἵππος 'horse of swift-glancing feet' (19.404). This meaning would be appropriate for the lesser Aias, as rapidity is a recurrent characteristic of his, duly expressed in the standard (formulaic) epithet ταχύς 'fast'. The fast movement is moreover intrinsic to the type of warrior that he is (he fights with the javelin and therefore has to run around) and is also reflected in the character of his men, the Locrians, in 13.71 ff.⁵⁸

---

55 Gathered by Risch (1974: 2 f.): Φείδας (*Il.* 13.691) from Φείδιππος, Βίας (*Il.* 4.296 e.a.) from Βιήνωρ, Περίφας (*Il.* 5.842 e.a.) from Περιφήτης, etc.
56 Mühlestein (1965: 49) believed that the formulaic use of αἰόλος is older than the metal-surfaced shield, which was a later poetic version (cf. Page 1959: 23 ff.), and that the traditional meaning of the formula would have to relate to the old-style, leather shield. Drawing on a Hesychian gloss, Mühlestein suggests the meaning ποικίλος 'spotted', 'dappled' for αἰόλος, referring to the dappling of the hide.
57 For a detailed description of the function of the τελαμών see Greco 2002: 563.
58 Cf. the textual references gathered by Mühlestein 1965: 46–7. The potential tautology ταχύς Αἴας is not a serious problem, as it is not alien to the formulaic spirit and would be reminiscent of tautological word-plays such as Πρόθοος θοός (see also below, under 'Minor' speaking names).

The basic feature of the lesser Aias, rapidity, may have inspired one further word-play, with the verb ἀΐσσω 'to dart out'. The verb, possibly a cognate of αἰόλος,[59] denotes force of movement: ἀλλ' ὅτε δὴ τάχ' ἔμελλον ἐπαΐξεσθαι ἄεθλον,/ ἔνθ' Αἴας μὲν ὄλισθε θέων, βλάψεν γὰρ Ἀθήνη (a possible word-play, *Il.* 23.773–4). The greater Aias might in turn be associated with a more general sense of force and vitality (cf. αἰών in the sense of 'vital force',[60] e.g. *Il.* 16.453). The name would then suggest a meaning such as the one proposed by Carnoy: 'l' énergique, le débordant de force'.[61] Such a meaning is appropriate for a hero who is obviously very active and strongly present in the poem.

The objection can be raised that a homonymy is indeed more obviously interpreted as a way of establishing a link between two objects rather than as encouraging a separate reception. The closeness of the two heroes in action[62] reinforces this link. Though they are differentiated in the *Catalogue of Ships* (2.52 ff. and 55 ff.), the two are mostly mentioned together: the lesser Aias is clearly less often mentioned alone and more often in the company of the greater Aias, especially when he takes important part in the action (e.g. in the defence of the ships, 13.70 ff. and in the fight for the dead Patroklos, 17.70 ff.). Eustathius emphasises their closeness on several occasions (246.28, on *Il.* 2.404–8: ...ὁ μικρὸς Αἴας ὁ Λοκρός, ἀεὶ τῷ μεγάλῳ καὶ συμπαρομαρτῶν ἐξ ἀνάγκης, cf. 471.5 on 4.273 and 1124.48 on 17.724–9). But their significant differences are also brought up, often in the form of opposite characteristics (cf. Sch. T 13.66, 13.203): the lesser Aias is small in size and carries light equipment (2.529–30),[63] while the greater Aias is big and carries the huge and heavy shield; the lesser Aias is violent, coarse (23.47 ff.), the greater has πινυτή (7.288). In both character and action, the lesser Aias seems to supplement the functions of the greater. Their clearly differentiated roles in the *Iliad* allow a nominal dichotomy. Even the dual Αἴαντε, often seen as the landmark of the association between the two Aiantes, does not necessarily suggest unity. This very ancient dual, which occurs about 20 times in the *Iliad* (there are additionally five occurrences of the plural Αἴαντες), must have originally referred not to the two Aiantes, but to the greater Aias and his half-brother Teukros, who formed a pair of brother-heroes, possibly like the obscure Ἀκτορίωνε Μολίονε of the *Iliad* and, in later liter-

---

59 Cf. Chantraine 1999 s.v. αἰόλος (presupposing the root *āyu-*).
60 *DGE* s.v. αἰών (A.I.1).
61 1956: 117.
62 See *LfgrE* s.v. Αἴας ὁ Ἰλῆος (M. van der Valk).
63 The genuineness of these two lines has been doubted, though there can only be serious objections to 530 (see Kirk 1985: 202), and not to 529 that mainly contrasts the two Aiantes.

ature, the *Castores* or *Polluces* (Verg. G. 3.89).⁶⁴ Teukros is indeed, like the Locrian Aias, strongly connected with the Telamonian (cf. 8.26 ff., 13.169–82, 13.26 ff., 15.437–99), and traces of the old poetic tradition are still occasionally felt in the *Iliad*, not just in the dual, but also in plural forms of the name;⁶⁵ it is unclear whether the Homeric Αἴαντε always meant the two namesakes.

Notably, however, later poetry relating to the death of the two heroes and to the events preceding that end created further links between them: infamous deeds – not of equal seriousness – were committed by both (the rape of Kassandra by the Locrian,⁶⁶ the slaughter of the sheep by the Telamonian); they both faced the hostility of the gods – apparently of the same goddess, Athena (hostile to the lesser Aias during his journey home, *Od.* 4.502, and at the games of *Il.* 23.774,⁶⁷ and to the greater Aias in Sophocles, possibly an echo of an earlier story⁶⁸); the deaths of both were sad and unheroic (suicide for the Telamonian, drowning at sea for the Locrian). Perhaps significantly, the link between the two seems to have persisted in historical times: the two heroes had similar cults.⁶⁹ The homonymity, as well as the similarity of stories, have been thought to suggest one original hero, for whose death different versions existed, and who was subsequently duplicated.⁷⁰ This possibility is also felt in the Homeric represen-

---

64 See further Nappi 2002: 212–3.
65 This was first noticed by Wackernagel (1877: 302–10), but since then there has been disagreement as to which occurrences of the dual (and the plural) presuppose the old function, cf. Chantraine (1986: 29), Nappi (2002: 211–35) and recently M.L. West (2011a: 144). Kirk (1985: 158) limits the presence of the old traces to 4.273 and 13.197. See Greco 2002: 573, n.42 for more bibliography.
66 See Call. fr. 13 Pfeiffer. Locrian Aias' assault on Kassandra is far more serious, as he commits sacrilege by removing Athena's statue, where Kassandra had taken sanctuary.
67 Note that the hero gets an *ox* as a prize and is (ironically?) called φαίδιμος 'illustrious', an adjective usually applied to his more prominent namesake.
68 See Von der Mühll 1930: 2 ff.
69 Both were believed to be present and help at battles, the Locrian Aias by the side of the Italian Locrians, the Telamonian with the Athenians e.g. at the Salamis battle (cf. Hdt. 8.64, 83, 121). Their cults may have drawn on very ancient mythological material that linked the two namesakes together, as e.g. the story of the 'Dioskouroi', helpers of the Epizephyrians at the Sagra battle (Paus. 3.19.12; D.S. 8.32), who can originally have been the two Aiantes (Von der Mühll 1930: 28–9), given that the Locrians celebrated a pair of twin heroes in Amphissa (Paus. 10.38.7), while the Opountian Locrians had depictions of both Aiantes together (Eust. 275.44, on *Il.* 2.529). Von der Mühll (1930: 14) was perhaps right to assume that: 'Gerade deswegen, weil was vom Lokrer erzählt wird, den Telamonier zu verstehen hilft, ist die Identität der Gestalt der Beiden gesichert'.
70 Von der Mühll (1930: 3 ff.) assumed that both Teukros and the Locrian Aias were the products of duplications of the greater Aias, who were then developed into partners / helpers of the original, predominant hero; cf. Mühlestein 1967: 51–2. Greco (2002: 571–3) sees the presence of

tation of the two Aiantes, where the Telamonian Aias, probably old enough to be Mycenaean,[71] is the leader of the pair, while the Locrian Aias, being contrasted with the Telamonian in nearly everything, could be seen as the 'lesser' half of one original hero's personality.

One wonders what the name of the 'proto-hero' might have meant – and arguably the *Iliad* contains traces of such a 'proto-meaning', visible in the close phonetic association between the name Αἴας and αἶα 'earth' (a Homeric word, e.g. *Il.* 2.850, 8.1).[72] This seems to fit the character of the greater Aias: an 'earthly' name is suitable for a hero who is primarily a defender, who is not known to move much and attack in battle, but to stand still and keep the enemy away by the sheer size of his body and by his strength (note the popular designation of Aias as ἕρκος Ἀχαιῶν 'the bulwark of the Achaeans', e.g. 7.211). The hero may not be defending a home country,[73] but the Achaeans still defend a cause, and Aias in particular defends the Achaean military positions, especially their location by the port and the ships. Significantly, the greater Aias is further designat-

---

two closely connected heroes (emphasised in the dual) as a reflection of the necessary collaboration between two different types of warriors, the carrier of the shield and the archer; this view finds support in Eust. (471.6, on *Il.* 4.273), who acknowledges the need for fighting in pairs (ὁ μικρὸς ἐδέετο τοῦ μεγάλου... ὡς ἄρα εἷς ἀνὴρ οὐδεὶς ἀνήρ). In the case of the two Aiantes, it seems that one member of the pair was older, and the other underwent transformation: perhaps the original brother-figure was replaced by the lesser Aias at a time when the original meaning of Αἴαντε was no longer understood or remembered; the 'new' hero was then contrasted with the greater Aias in appearance and behaviour so that an individual character for him could be established. See *LIMC* I s.v. Aias II (O. Touchefeu); cf. Nappi 2002: 22 ff. Mühlestein (1967: 51–2) attributed the duplication of the original Aias to the double significant potential allowed to the name by the ambiguity of the adjective αἰόλος; similarly Nappi (2002: 232) argued that the two-sided significance of the name may explain the shaping of the new Aias' character.
71 See Greco 2002: 56 ff. and n.2 with bibliography. Aias' antiquity is implied by Mycenaean evidence for his name, his shield, the dual and his old patronymic (on which see Nappi 2002: 234–5); note, however, that the name of the father of the lesser Aias, Oileus (perhaps from Ϝιλεύς), also sounds very ancient (cf. Myc. *o-wi-ro*; see Chantraine 1999 s.v. Οἰλεύς). Friis Johansen's interpretation of an archaic Attic vase painting (mid. 8th c. BC) as the duel of Aias and Hektor (*Il.* 7), and thus as possible evidence for a pre-Homeric Aias, has been proven unjustified (Snodgrass 1998: 26).
72 The name Aias is not brought into the discussion of the meaning of Aia, land of the Golden Fleece, by M.L. West (2007b). West suggests an original meaning 'Dawnland' (see esp. 196–8), which presumably evolved to 'Land' through its use in particular formulaic contexts. Note that the *Iliad* contains examples of masculine names that derive from feminine nouns in –α; see von Kamptz 1982 (1958): 168: Φόρβας (9.665, 14.490), Βίας (4.296 e.a.), Φύλας (16.181, 191). However, according to the etymology of αἶα proposed by West (ibid.), it was never *aiwa, so it could not count as a scientific etymology of Aias' name.
73 Fick (1911: 7) proposed the meaning 'Landwehrmann'.

ed by the epithet πελώριος 'huge' (3.229, 7.208, 17.174, 360), which reflects one of the most important elements of his image, his greatness of size (often expressed formulaically in various ways, e.g. μέγας Τελαμώνιος Αἴας 5.610 etc.).[74] The use of πελώριος implies a connection with chthonic mythology: it is found in the formula γαῖα πελώρη 'huge Earth', which, though not used in Homer, is at least as old as the Hesiodic *Theogony* where it occurs five times (159, 173, 479, 821, 858).[75] The adjective is the basis of the name Πέλωρ(ος), borne by one of Kadmos' *spartoi*, the giants that sprung out of the earth, mentioned as early as Hellanicus (*FGrH* 4 F 1) and the logographer Pherecydes (*FGrH* 3 F 22). Peloros is finally an epithet of Zeus in a context relevant to the Earth: according to the hellenistic historian Baton of Sinope (*FGrH* 268 F 5), a Zeus Pelor(os) was celebrated at the Πελώρια, presumably in honour of a man called Peloros, who gave warning of a forthcoming movement of the earth (but it is uncertain how old this last usage of Peloros is). The epithet might have thus activated a chthonic meaning in the name, pointing perhaps to the origins of Aias' figure: a gigantic hero[76] with chthonic features,[77] traces of whom are the huge shield (big enough to be compared with a tower at 7.219, 11.485, 17.128), his supernatural voice (15.686), his invincibility by humans (13.32 ff.). All these peculiarities, combined with the superficiality and briefness of his description in 2.557–8 and by Helen in 3.229, imply that his connection with the *Iliad* was probably loose and late, and that he might have belonged to an older generation of heroes,[78] with a much stronger presence in unknown pre-Homeric poetry. The sense of Τελαμώνιος is not alien to the notion of the defender and gigantic hero, as ταλάσσαι may evoke more generally the notion of support. This seems to be allowed by other uses of the word: τελαμών means the base of a στήλη or στήλη (stone block) in epigraphical evi-

---

[74] These may refer not just to size but also to the terrifying effect produced by the hero's presence, cf. the references gathered by Von der Mühll (1930: 5).
[75] See Von der Mühll (1930: 7) for similar examples from later literature.
[76] Though other heroes in the *Iliad* are said to be great in size, there is no doubt that this is particularly emphasised and exploited in the case of Aias.
[77] The hero's possible connection with the earth has been thought to point to an original chthonic deity ('Erdgott' or 'Berggeist', cf. Solmsen 1909a: 78 n.2). This belongs together with equally unprovable speculations about the already discussed Achilles and Nestor.
[78] This is possibly also suggested by the failure image that the poem creates of him on important occasions, such as the duel with Hektor (a hero also thought to be a late addition to the Trojan epic) and the contest for Achilles' arms, reflecting a critical view of a hero who represents old-fashioned ideals and war techniques. See Kirk 1985: 208 and Greco 2002: 570–1 with bibliography.

dence,[79] it is used as the name of the Roman Atlantes (*Telamones*, Vitr. 6.7.6) and is a term in architecture for the colossal male figures that functioned as bearing-pillars.[80] Such connotations would suit Aias not just as the defender, but also as bearer of the shield, and as the gigantic character of an earlier mythical stage.[81] Conceived for the original hyper-hero, in the case of his duplicate the name would still suggest a 'hero of the earth' as a general concept with strong mythological relevance.[82]

It emerges that the 'proto-meaning' may not only reflect the origins of greater Aias, but also corresponds to several aspects of his Iliadic image. However, it appears that the poet at times played with the other possible etymological connections too; such puns, however vague, could mirror the development of distinctive characteristics for both the primary Aias and the secondary one. Moreover, it is not impossible that an audience would understand a name in different ways under the influence of varied contexts (this can happen with names of multiple etymological potential, such as Achilles, Nestor, Odysseus). The name Aias could thus at times evoke αἰόλος (in either of its two meanings) or ἀΐσσω or αἰετός. The eagle association in particular connects the greater Aias with his grandfather Aiakos (mentioned at *Il.* 21.189; Aiakides for Achilles and Peleus): according to the myth, Zeus went to Aiakos' mother, Aegina, in the form of eagle – a scholium says that this is why the child got the name Aiakos (Sch. T 21.189: ἐπειδὴ ἀετῷ εἰκασθεὶς ἐμίγη αὐτῇ, τὸν παῖδα Αἰακὸν ὠνόμασεν, cf. Ath. 13.566d, Nonn. *D.* 7.11 ff., 21 ff.). Aias and Aiakos were both connected with Thessaly: Aiakos as father of Peleus, Aias through the mount Aiantion in west

---

79 E.g. *IG* IV 517 (more in Richardson 1896: 47–8). This use of the word was apparently more frequent in the Euxine area, see *Bull.Épigr.* Index IV (1966–73): 182.
80 Chantraine (1999 s.v. τελαμών) assigned to the noun the general meaning 'ce qui sert à porter' and saw the name as possible cognate of Tantalos and Atlas, 'l' endurant'. Solmsen (1909a: 7 ff.) alleged that it belonged to the architectural vocabulary of South Italy already in archaic times.
81 Solmsen (1909a: 78) saw in the name Telamon the meaning 'bearer of the celestial globe'.
82 A connection between Aias and the identical sounding αἶα 'grandmother', cf. a lemma from the *EM* (Αἶα. Ὑπὸ Κυρηναίων τηθὶς καὶ μαῖα) is difficult. The Telamonian Aias was more privileged than his half-brother Teukros regarding his maternity, his mother being the lawful wife of Telamon, while Teukros was a bastard; cf. *Il.* 8.284 (νόθον) and 12.371 (ὄπατρος 'son of the same father', not ὁμογάστριος 'born of the same mother', see also Hainsworth 1993: 357). But if the name is to be seen as relevant to this story, αἶα should rather mean 'lawful wife'. A meaning 'bastard brother' is implied for Teukros by a later source (Hsch. τεῦχρος = ἀδελφὸς νόθος). Such a correlation between the names would suit nicely the assumption of Aias' and Teukros' initial unity as a pair of heroes. But τεῦχρος or τεῦκρος is not a Homeric word (and is only found in Hesychius), while the required semantic possibilities of αἶα receive no support from the Homeric context (see Chantraine 1999 s.v. αἶα).

Magnesia (cf. Ptol. *Geog.* 3.13.6). The similarity of their names perhaps reflects their mythical and genealogical ties.[83]

2.1.3 Agamemnon, Menelaos

Does the leader of the Achaeans bear a 'speaking' name? The centrality of his role in the *Iliad* compels us to address the question, and as far as etymology goes, his name is comparatively easier to analyse than either Achilles or Aias. Its first part, ἀγα-, expresses excess, and must intensify the meaning of the second component, -μέμνων, which may be etymologically relevant to μένω[84] and to the notion of endurance; if so, Agamemnon is the 'much enduring (in battle)'. Plato suggests a similar etymology in his *Cratylus* (395a-b): ἀγαστὸς κατὰ τὴν ἐπιμονὴν οὗτος ὁ ἀνὴρ ἐνσημαίνει τὸ ὄνομα ὁ Ἀγαμέμνων 'so the name Agamemnon denotes that this man is admirable for remaining' (transl. Fowler), referring to Agamemnon's endurance of the long war.[85] But -μέμνων can be explained in more than one ways, and other etymologies are not lacking. An allusion to μέδομαι 'rule' (Homer uses the term μέδοντες[86] for leaders, e.g. *Il.* 9.17, *Od.* 13.186) is an attractive possibility:[87] Agamemnon is of course a great leader, the first in power among the Greeks and head of the Trojan expedition. The capacity of ruler is the most frequently encountered element of Agamemnon's personality, as references to it are recurrent and most of the formulae used for him denote his kingship.[88] A line from the *Iliad*, where Achilles suggests to Agamemnon that the leaders of the Achaeans should remain present during

---

83 For Von der Mühll (1930: 22) Aiakos originally was Aias' father and Telamon a later addition to the myth. See Solmsen 1909a: 78, n.2 for the possibility that Aiakos, like Aias, was originally meant as a chthonic deity.

84 From an original *-μεν-μων; cf. Heubeck 1968: 360; 1987: 229, n.12. See also Anttila 2000: 30–2.

85 Cf. *EM* s.v. Ἀγαμέμνων; Choerob. *in Theod.* 109.2.

86 Chantraine 1999 s.v. μέδω 'organise in a thinking way.' See also below, under 'Minor' speaking names.

87 An etymology *-μέδμων > -μέσμων is possible; Ἀγαμέσμων is attested on an Attic vase (cf. the also attested Μέσμων). See von Kamptz 1982 (1958): 81, with bibliography. Eustathius (289.37) has Ἀγαμέδων as an alternative name for Agamemnon.

88 The formulae ἄναξ ἀνδρῶν and ποιμὴν λαῶν are most common. Cf. the epithet βασιλεύς (1.277, and βασιλεύτατος, 9.69). This does not signify that he possessed absolute authority, but that his role is comparatively wider than that of other Achaean rulers: he leads more ships (book 2), and he raised the expedition together with his brother, taking the lead as the most powerful of the two. Cf. Taplin 1990: 62–7 and Raaflaub 1997: 633–4.

the preparation of Patroklos' funeral (ἀγοὶ ... μενόντων, 23.160), with Agamemnon's name immediately following (1.161), may suggest a pun on the name.[89] Finally, the name of Μέμνων, the mythical king of Aithiopia who came to help the Trojans (*Od.* 11.522),[90] might be seen as relevant to kingship. However, the association between μέδομαι and -μέμνων / Μέμνων is somewhat discouraged by the phonetic difference.[91]

μεν- may alternatively allude to μένος, implying a meaning such as 'forceful, passionate (in battle)'.[92] Though of course nearly every front-line hero is a much-enduring and vigorous fighter, these features do not exhaust Agamemnon's characterisation; his action is not always consistent with the notion of endurance and persistance in the war: he loses courage and proposes to stop the war three times (2.110–41, 9.1 ff., cf. 14.82–103, where Agamemnon's ability to command is even put into question – his name would perhaps sound superior to his character in these contexts, if not a little ironic), but these disappointing moments are balanced by his ἀριστεία in book 11.[93] Agamemnon's forcefulness (μένος) is demonstrated in a number of ruthless killings (e.g. 11.101–21). Excessive violence borders on madness, as the similarity between μένος and the verb μαίνομαι may suggest (cf. a possible word-play at 6.100–1, of Diomedes).[94] Madness may further be regarded as a feature of Agamemnon's error of judgement and ill-timed anger. μένος signifies also anger: Achilles' anger is termed thus (1.207), and the verb μενεαίνειν is used in the context of anger (19.65–8: Achilles ceases his *cholos* – it is not right to persist in *meneainein*).[95] Agamemnon reacts with anger (*menos*) to Kalchas' revelation of the reason for Apollo's wrath against the Acheans, and at having to forfeit Chryseis (1.101–5). His behaviour is aggres-

---

89 Cf. Anttila 2000: 31.
90 The Odyssean reference is to Memnon's personal beauty, while at one other point (*Od.* 4.187–8) he is indirectly (without name) mentioned as the killer of Antilochos. The first explicit mention of him as king of the Aithiopians is in Hes. *Th.* 984–5, while his role in the Trojan war is known in more detail from Proclus' summaries.
91 Despite Beekes 2010 s.vv. Ἀγαμέμνων and μένω. Opposite view in Chantraine 1999 s.v. μέμνων (who rejects a derivation from μέδομαι for both Memnon and Agamemnon). Later uses of μέμνων as a bird-name and as a synonym of ὄνος 'donkey' (Chantraine ibid.) must be secondary to the personal name.
92 Cf. θρασυμέμνων, of Herakles (*Il.* 5.639), which can be explained either from μένος ('brave spirited', LSJ) or μένω ('firm in the fight', transl. Loeb).
93 Even if this is briefer and less distinguished that that enjoyed by other Achaean heroes, as Taplin notes (1990: 72).
94 ...ἀλλ' ὅδε λίην / μαίνεται, οὐδέ τίς οἱ δύναται μένος ἰσοφαρίζειν 'but this man rages beyond all measure, and no one can rival him in force'. See also Clarke 2004: 81, with bibliography.
95 See also Cairns 2003: 22, 41–2.

sive to Achilles, and he is also credited with *mēnis* (1.247). Incidentally, *mēnis* and *menos* are believed to be etymologically related.⁹⁶ Nestor urges him to cease this *menos* (1.282). Agamemnon's anger holds central place also in book 9 (e.g. 9.516, *chalepainein*). Even at the point when he yields in the need to make amends to Achilles so that he returns to battle, and after admitting his blindness (9.115–20), he shows remarkable arrogance; his anger is transformed into stubbornness (another aspect of μένω?) as he does not quite abandon his grudge against Achilles, even during the reconciliation attempt (esp. 9.158–61).⁹⁷ Excessive selfishness takes Agamemnon's behaviour to the level of *hybris* (in Athena's words, 1.214). Indeed, in whatever way an audience chose to interpret its second component, the name sounds appropriate for someone like Agamemnon, who is characterised by excess: extreme selfishness, as well as supreme power and great performance in battle.⁹⁸

The etymology of Agamemnon's name from the root *men-* (of μένω, not μένος) has the advantage of linking this name with Menelaos': the epics often assign cognate names to members of the same family.⁹⁹ If seen as semi-homonymic, the two names further encourage comparisons between the two heroes – and they may suggest common elements in their identities, perhaps even an exchange of identities. True, Menelaos does not have a particularly strong presence in the *Iliad*.¹⁰⁰ He is nevertheless a key-figure in the plot, as he is directly connected with the cause of the war. It is reasonable to assume that he is one of the oldest figures in the story – perhaps older than Agamemnon (whose increased importance may date to a later stage of the relevant tradition);¹⁰¹ his pre-Homeric function was almost certainly that of a fighter of the first rank. His role in the *Iliad* may be comparatively weaker, but his abuse as ἐλέγχιστος πολεμιστής 'contemptible warrior' (17.26) and μαλθακὸς αἰχμητής 'weakling warrior' (17.588) is not justified by the Homeric narrative; his appearance at 3.3 ff. fills Paris with terror. Menelaos' traditional warlike nature is expressed in the formulaic epithets which accompany his name: ἀρήϊος 'warlike' (e.g. *Il.* 3.339) and

---

96 See Watkins 1977: 198–9 and Muellner 1996: 186–7.
97 As Taplin notes (1990: 71).
98 Cf. *LfgrE* s.v. Ἀγαμέμνων (M. van der Valk). The view that Agamemnon's portraiture in the *Iliad* is based on a real Mycenaean king (Kalinka 1943, see also above, 'Introductory notes') with a nasty side to his character, is unfounded. On Agamemnon's characterisation in Homer see further *HE* s.v. Agamemnon (T. van Nortwick) and the bibliography gathered in Taplin 1990: 60–1 and n. 2.
99 See also below, under 'Minor' speaking names.
100 Cf. *LfgrE* s.v. Μενέλαος (B. Mader).
101 This may be true also for Paris in relation to Hektor, see under 'The "Greek" Trojans'.

ἀρηΐφιλος 'dear to Ares' (e.g. *Il.* 17.138).¹⁰² Indeed he has, like Agamemnon, a good warrior's name, apparently derived from μένω and λαός.¹⁰³ There are several possible meanings for an audience to choose from: Menelaos can be understood either as 'he who stands fast in the face of the enemy' or 'he who stands by his war-folk'¹⁰⁴ (depending on how λαός is interpreted, as in the case of the name Achilles); both possibilities reflect a heroic spirit. Another appropriate meaning might be 'he whose army holds strong';¹⁰⁵ it is rather discouraged by linguistic evidence for similar compounds,¹⁰⁶ but perhaps in this case too linguistic rules gave way to poetic etymology. The Iliadic Menelaos does credit to his name on numerous occasions. He shows great concern for public opinion, as well as responsibility for the Achaeans who got involved in the war for his sake,¹⁰⁷ thus justifying the allusion to λαός (in the sense of his compatriots) in the second part of his name. He also contributes to the fighting (cf. especially his ἀριστεία in book 17, even if judged inferior compared to the achievements of other major heroes); this allows the possibility of an allusion to λαός as 'the enemy'. On the whole, Menelaos' behaviour offers support to an active sense of the name.¹⁰⁸ We may conclude that the etymologies of both Menelaos and Agamemnon correspond to the heroes' actions in the epic in general, despite the fact that they do not seem to be activated through precise word-plays.

A discussion of the names Agamemnon and Menelaos should include a comment on their father's name, Ἀτρεύς. This name is granted further importance by the frequent use of the patronymic (Ἀτρείδης) as a way of referring to the two brothers. The name clearly lends itself to significant interpretations, as was noticed already in antiquity. A good example is Euripides' word-play (*IA*

---

102 Cf. Willcock 2002: 221–9. For the different war *ethos* of the two brothers in the *Iliad* (Menelaos – smoother, Agamemnon – more ferocious), cf. 6.62 with Most 2003: 55.
103 Cf. Beekes 2010 and Chantraine 1999 s.v. μένω.
104 Cf. von Kamptz 1982 (1958): 60, 62.
105 Sommer 1937: 192.
106 'Exocentric' compounds (as opposed to 'endocentric') are a less common type of compound which 'find their point of attachment outside themselves' (Palmer 1980: 258), and they do not seem to occur as names of epic heroes. Parallel names with -λαος (on which see section on Nestor) and epithets starting with μενε- (μενεδήϊος, μενεπτόλεμος, μενεχάρμης = 'he who endures battle'), support a transitive reading of the verbal element. A name that stands apart is Μενεσθεύς < -σθένης : 'with enduring force', cf. von Kamptz 1982 (1958): 62 or 'he who repulses the [enemy's] force'.
107 Cf. his initiative for the duel in book 3 and his reaction when wounded in 4.148–87, where he does not retreat from battle. On Menelaos' character see further Hohendahl-Zoetelief 1980.
108 Cf. also Barck 1971: 8–9.

321, Agamemnon speaking): μῶν τρέσας οὐκ ἀνακαλύψω βλέφαρον, Ἀτρέως γεγώς; 'Shall I, the son of Atreus (= the fearless), close my eyes from fear?' (transl. Coleridge). Plato (*Cra.* 395b-c) mentions various possibilities: that the name reflects his ruinous acts (ἀτηρὸν) in respect to Thyestes,[109] his stubbornness (ἀτειρὲς) and his fearlessness (ἄτρεστον). The last two etymologies are repeated in lexicography.[110] Among the different possibilities, it is the verb τρεῖν that has the greatest phonetic similarity to the name and is the most likely source for its significance – it may indeed constitute its true etymology.[111] τρέω 'to be struck by fear' and 'shrink from the fight' is a Homeric verb (cf. e.g. *Il.* 5.256, 21.288) and would produce an appropriate meaning: 'he who stands fast / does not panic in battle'. In accordance with the well-known habit of epic naming, the father's name appears to be semantically relevant to the names of his sons.[112]

2.1.4 Diomedes

Names with the second component -μήδης have a long history, as the Mycenaean *e-ke-me-de* (probably *Ἐχεμήδης[113]) suggests. Diomedes, son of Tydeus, may indeed be a hero of great antiquity: references to his background in book 4 (372–99) may imply an older epic tradition with special relevance to Thebes, of which he seems to have been part.[114] -μήδης (from μήδομαι) is not uncommon in heroic

---

109 Thyestes is mentioned briefly at *Il.* 2.106–7, but nothing is said of his feud with Atreus; perhaps the poet of the *Iliad* ignored this myth (thus Sch. A 2.106).
110 *EM* s.v. Ἀτρεύς: παρὰ τὸ τρεῖν, τὸ φοβεῖσθαι...· καὶ μετὰ τοῦ στερητικοῦ α, ἀτρεύς, ὁ ἄφοβος. Ἢ παρὰ τὸ τείρω, τὸ καταπονῶ, μετὰ τοῦ στερητικοῦ α, ἀτειρεύς· καὶ συγκοπῇ, ἀτρεύς, ὁ ἀκαταπόνητος.
111 Palmer 1980: 36, Szemerényi 1956/7: 17 ff., M.L. West (2001: 263; from *Ἀτρε(σ)-). The old effort to identify the name with the Hittite *Attar(is)siyas* (Forrer 1924: 21; cf. Schachermeyr 1986: 161–75) was given new force by West, who sees it as a Greek name (ibid.: 265–6). Von Kamptz 1982 (1958): 126, 336–7 assumed foreign origin, and a possible relevance to the Thessalian place name Atrax (which is however not mentioned before Strabo, 9.5.19); interestingly this region is known for the frequency of the historical use of heroic names (see also Appendix).
112 On the treatment of the names of Atreas and his sons in Greek poetic tradition see also Tsitsibakou-Vasalos 2007: 205–16. Notably Atreas belongs to a genealogy (*Il.* 2.104–6) in which all names are potentially significant: the name of his father Pelops (von Kamptz 1982 (1958): 331), brother Thyestes (ibid. 237–8) and grandfather Tantalos (*Od.* 11.582, von Kamptz ibid. 31). See further Tsitsibakou-Vasalos ibid.: 10 ff., 185–9, 207.
113 See Jorro – Adrados 1985 s.v. *e-ke-me-de*.
114 Cf. M.L. West 2011a: 146. Burgess (2001: 84–5 and n. 135) argues in favour of his long standing in the tradition of the Trojan war. This view is not universally shared: Diomedes has also

naming, and presumably alludes to the power of the mind, a quality which enjoyed much appreciation in the heroic world, mostly expressed in the form of 'good judgement' or 'excellence in counsel': a hero is expected to possess these features, along with prowess in battle (as the poem often suggests[115]). Some heroes (such as Nestor, Odysseus and the less prominent Polydamas from the Trojan side) even seem to rely more on their minds than on their warlike abilities.[116] In the *Iliad* there is also Θρασυμήδης (a son of Nestor, mentioned again in the *Odyssey*)[117] and the feminine names Ἑκαμήδη (*Il.* 11.624–6) and Διομήδη (*Il.* 9.665, the feminine form of Diomedes, name of a Lesbian girl captured by Achilles during one of his raids).[118] Diomedes and Diomede are not the only Homeric names with the first component Dio-: there is also Διοκλέης (son of Ortilochos of Pherai, mentioned in both epics) and Διώρης,[119] name of two Iliadic heroes. Διο- may allude to Zeus or to the Homeric adjective δῖος 'of/from Zeus' (there is also a personal name Δῖος, a son of Priam);[120] Diomedes may mean 'Jove-counselled' (LSJ); the second part of his name is heard in the expression ἄφθιτα μήδεα εἰδώς, which is used of Zeus at *Il.* 24.88.[121]

The sense of 'hero with divine mind' might be more than a generic designation: the *Iliad* presents Diomedes as a distinguished warrior of good lineage, but

---

been seen as an invented hero (thus Andersen 1978), who adds to the Achaean exploits during Achilles' absence, but fades when Achilles returns to battle. For a summary of the relevant views (including that Diomedes was imported into the Trojan cycle from Theban myth; cf. Kullmann 1960: 88) see Burgess ibid.
115 See the instances gathered in Schofield 2001: 225–7, with extension to other heroic poetry
116 See further Schofield 2001 (who argues convincingly in favour of the central place of sound and sophisticated thinking and debating in the heroic code, as opposed to earlier views on the subject which take a rather primitivist approach).
117 Note also Εὐμήδης (a name that suggests mental ruse), father of *Doloneia*'s Dolon 'Sneaky' (10.314 etc.): the two names may be a purposeful combination (cf. von Kamptz 1982 (1958): 26. *Doloneia* is certainly an addition to the *Iliad* by a different poet, see e.g. M.L. West 2011a: 233–5.
118 In female names this element may occasionally have been connected with 'dark' powers and sorcery (cf. Medea and perhaps also Hekamede, see more under 'Minor' speaking names).
119 A formation unknown to historical onomastics; on a possible etymology see von Kamptz 1982 (1958): 88. Note that Διώρης has long ι, while Diomedes and Diokles have short ι, so they are closer in sound to Ζεύς-Διός, not δῖος.
120 See von Kamptz ibid.: 189; 230.
121 On this expression, which also occurs in Hesiod, see Richardson's note (1993: 286). Rousseau (2012) supports the name's relevance to Zeus, arguing that it evokes the god's design to honour Achilles; despite the often noticed connection between Achilles and Diomedes (the latter has been thought to reflect the former in some instances; cf. Burgess 2011: 63), Rousseau's argument is difficult and certainly secondary to the name's connection with its proper bearer.

stresses also his good quality of mind.¹²² This is the content of Nestor's praise at 9.53–4: 'Son of Tydeus, above all men are you mighty in battle, / and in council are the best among all those of your own age'.¹²³ Diomedes has a striking presence in book 9, one of the most important books of the *Iliad*, where much depends on counseling (its main event is the embassy to Achilles). He is not selected as member of the embassy (presumably he is not senior enough), but he is the first to speak after Agamemnon at the beginning of *Il.* 9 (his instigation to continue fighting, against Agamemnon's suggestion that they should abandon their cause and return home, receives great applause), and the book closes with another short speech by him that sums up the situation of the Achaeans after Achilles' refusal to return to battle. His mental ability is further demonstrated at the beginning of book 14 (esp. 11 ff.), where (characteristically, together with Nestor and Odysseus) he advises Agamemnon (despite his young age, 14.112); in the awareness of his limits in battle (5.81 ff., 6.12 ff.); in the fact that he criticises Agamemnon (9.3 ff., Ἀτρείδη, σοὶ πρῶτα μαχήσομαι ἀφραδέοντι 'Son of Atreus, with you first will I contend in your folly'; ἀφραδέοντι, at the end of 32, provides a good contrast to Diomedes' name, significantly placed at the end of the next line). We may conclude that to Diomedes' name, too, the *Iliad* offers justification.¹²⁴

2.1.5 Idomeneus and Meriones

The name of the Cretan leader Ἰδομενεύς is of obscure etymology, and the lack of obvious puns on it in the epics or in later literature may imply that it was not understood as particularly significant. However, Idomeneus is clearly one of the epic's main heroes: he is named by Agamemnon as one of three βουληφόροι ἄνδρες (counselors) together with Aias and Odysseus (*Il.* 1.144–5), and he is identified by Helen as one of the premier Greek warriors (3.230–3). His impor-

---

122 See *LfgrE* s.v. Διομήδης (B. Mader). Cf. Schofield 2001: 257 ('Diomedes is after Odysseus the most perfect hero of the *Iliad*, and he is so because in him *euboulia* … and warrior prowess are better balanced than in anyone else but him.'). See also Higbie 1995: 87–101.
123 Note, however, the next line (56): 'you have not reached a final end (*telos*) of words'; on the meaning of *telos* ('goal'? 'conclusion'?) see now Elmer 2013: 118–9, and cf. Hainsworth 1993: 67 on Nestor's patronising tone: Diomedes has spoken well for his young age, but cannot compete with the old man's wisdom.
124 A very ancient cult of Diomedes (6th c. BC) in the Adriatic (noted by Farnell 1921: 289–93) has now been proved by archaeological evidence; see Kirigin-Čače 1998: 63–110; cf. Parker 2011: 245–6. Divine status could have endowed Diomedes' name (especially its 'theophoric' element) with a special kind of relevance.

tance in the *Iliad* and the sound of the name, which is reminiscent of Greek words, invite further consideration of its possible significance.

The old assumption that the name is of pre-Greek origin[125] largely rested upon the hero's great antiquity: he is part of the old Cretan world, generally thought to preserve a pre-Greek substratum. He is already old in the *Iliad* (13.361–2, 23.476; he is associated with Nestor, 11.497–520, 2.404–5 as among the oldest Greeks in Troy).[126] His antiquity is further indicated by the names in his genealogy: Idomeneus is a son of Deukalion (*Il.* 13.451–2) who is involved in very old stories about the creation of mankind (cf. [Hes.] *Cat.* fr. 234.3 M–W), and grandson of Minos himself (*Il.* 13.449–53, cf. 12.117, 17.608). Both ancestors' names are very ancient and of uncertain etymology: Μίνως is very likely non-Greek (Greek etymologies are short, and the name is of a linguistic type which is believed to be foreign[127]) but Δευκαλίων is attested in Mycenaean,[128] and possible Greek etymologies include an original *Λευκαλίων from Λευκαρίων (an alternative form of the name[129]), or a connection with the Homeric ἀ-δευκής 'harsh, untoward, unkind' (cf. *Od.* 4.489, 6.273, 10.245), ἐν-δυκέως 'kindly, with care' (*Il.* 23.90, 24.158, 187, 438, more common in the *Od.*), and the personal name Πολυδεύκης, mentioned in the *Iliad* at 3.237 (cf. also Hsch. δεύκει· φροντίζει).[130]

A couple of names that are similar to Idomeneus are attested in Mycenaean (*i-do-me-ne-ja* = *Ἰδομένεια, *i-do-me-ni-jo* = *Ἰδομένιος).[131] This encourages the possibility that the name – whatever its origins – acquired significance in Greek. The search for a meaning for Idomeneus' name may follow two possible

---

125 Von Kamptz 1982 (1958): 165–6, 350, assumed a pre-Greek *Ἰδαμνο- = Ἰδαῖος ('the man from Ida') of which Idomeneus may be a hellenised form. –μν- is thought to signpost pre-Hellenic names, as in the Cretan place-name Rithymna.
126 Cf. *LfgrE* s.v. Ἰδομενεύς (W. Beck).
127 Von Kamptz 1982 (1958): 127. The name has been thought relevant to the Pisidian place-name Minassos, like the personal name Κνῶς to Knossos (von Kamptz 1982 (1958): 373, following Kretschmer 1951: 17 and 1896: 397). More recent scholarship sees it as a title (rather than a personal name) of uncertain (pre-Greek) etymology (though it resembles a Mycenaean word, see Jorro-Adrados 1985 s.v. *me-nu-wa*); see *LfgrE* s.v. Μίνως (G. Steiner) with bibliography.
128 See Jorro-Adrados 1985 s.v. *de-u-ka-ri-jo*.
129 *EM* s.v. Λευκαρίων: Καθ' ὑπέρθεσιν Δευκαλίων καὶ Λευκάδιον, τροπῇ τοῦ δ εἰς ρ, Λευκάριον. Cf. *Et. Gen.* s.v. Λευκαρίων and Epich. fr. 116 K–A (Πύρραν γα μῶται Λευκαρίων). See also Schulze 1933: 115 A.3.
130 –αλ- may be explained as an independent element, also found in Homeric αἰθαλόεις, possibly also in the ethnic Θεσσαλός. Cf. von Kamptz 1982 (1958): 130. On the possibility of a non-Greek name see *LfgrE* s.v. Δευκαλίων* (B. Mader).
131 Jorro-Adrados 1985 s.v. *i-do-me-ne-ja, i-do-me-ni-jo*.

directions: one is to connect the first part of the name with the root (F)ἰδ- 'see'[132] (though admittedly this connection is made difficult if Idomeneus is related to the Mycenaean forms). A pun on 'see' may be present in [Hes.] *Cat.* fr. 204.56–63 M–W,[133] where it is apparently said that Idomeneus, as one of Helen's prospective suitors, was keen on *seeing* Helen for himself rather than on relying on hearsay about her. The word-play, however, depends on the restored form of an incomplete text (a form ἴδοιτο in l.61 is a mere conjecture); and l.61 is at a distance of five lines from the name. Additionally, the verb in question is far too common to attract particular attention.

The second direction is to connect the first part of the name with the Cretan place-name Ida, which must be the first component of the very similar name Ἰδαμενεύς.[134] An allusion to Ida initially seems suitable for a hero with Cretan connections. The second part of the name could in that case have emerged from the root μεν-, present in such names as Μίμνερμος, Μενέμαχος (possibly also in the names of Agamemnon and Menelaos).[135] However, the appropriateness of Ida as a Cretan allusion is not without problems. The Homeric Idomeneus is nowhere specifically connected with Ida. He originated from Lyktos according to the *Iliad* (17.611) or Knossos in later sources (D.S. 5.79). Ida might be perceived as a generic reference to Idomeneus' Cretan provenance,[136] but Homeric mentions of the place-name discourage this possibility. The Homeric Ἴδη (which occurs about 35 times, in 15 different books) refers to the mountain-range of Mysia (the first mention of a Cretan Ida is [Hes.] *Cat.* fr. 145, 1 M–W). The place-name appears as a component of personal names mostly of Trojans (rather than

---

132 For a relevant etymological attempt see Georgiev (1966: 116, 123), who assumed that the name was derived from the participle ἰδόμενος (but connected the Mycenaean *i-da-i-jo* = Idaios with Ida).
133 ἐκ Κρήτης δ' ἐμνᾶτο μέγα σθένος Ἰδομ[ενῆος] / Δευκαλίδης, Μίνωος ἀγακλειτοῖο γενέ[θλης·] / οὐδέ τινα μνηστῆρα μ[ε]τάγγελον ἄλλ[ον ἔπεμψεν], / ἀλλ' αὐτὸς [σ]ὺν νηΐ πολυκλήϊδι μελαίνη[ι] / βῆ ὑπὲρ Ὠγυλίου πόντου διὰ κῦμα κελαιν[ὸν] / Τυνδαρέου ποτὶ δῶμα δαΐφρονος, ὄφρ[α ἴδοιτο] / Ἀ]ρ[γείην] Ἑλένην, μηδ' ἄλλων οἷον ἀκ[ούοι] / [μῦθον, ὅς] ἤδη πᾶσαν ἐπὶ [χθ]όνα δῖαν ἵκαν[εν]. See Peradotto 1990: 109–10.
134 Kretschmer 1894: 238. Historical attestations of Idameneus (two from Rhodes, one from the early 6th c. BC, *LGPN* I) seem to be earlier than of Idomeneus (attested in Athens no earlier than 500 BC, see *LGPN* IIA and Appendix).
135 See above, on 'Agememnon, Menelaos'. Cf. Carnoy 1957 s.v. Idomeneus; Camera 1971: 135. Bosshardt (1942: 112) argued that the name is from Ἰδαμένης, with Ἰδο- (like Hom. ὑλο- [instead of ὑλη-] τόμος).
136 Mühlestein (1969: 74) detected such an allusion to Crete in the name of the Trojan Phaistos, killed by Idomeneus (*Il.* 5.43–7, see below, p. 136; this however does not really affect the interpretation of Idomeneus' name). Mühlestein further assumed a connection between Phaistos and φάος, which could make the association of Idomeneus' name with vision a little stronger.

Greeks). There are two Trojans named Ἰδαῖος, a herald (Il. 3.24 ff., 7 passim, 24.325, 470) and a son of the priest Dares (Il. 5.9–24). A Greek hero named Ἴδας was originally connected with Aitolia; he is mentioned in the epic as the husband of Marpessa (Il. 9.558) and later as one of the divine twins (with Lynkeus) of Messenia.[137] The personal names may allude to ἴδη 'forest'.[138]

An alternative etymology relates Idomeneus to the place-name Ἰδομεναί or Ἰδομένη,[139] the name of a town in Macedonia, attested as early as Thucydides (2.100), and of two hills in Epeiros (Th. 3.112). This could suggest a connection with northern Greece, which is relevant also for the explanation of the name of Μηριόνης, who is Idomeneus' younger companion and subordinate (Il. 2.650–1; Od. 3.191–2; his cousin according to the genealogy suggested in D.S. 5.79).[140] Meriones' name is reminiscent of the name of the Thracian mountain Μηρισός (Call. fr. 238, 29 Pfeiffer) and the Dardanian place-name Μηρίων.[141] But the relevant place-names are rather late.[142]

The key to the understanding of both heroic names (as well as of other old Cretan heroes' names, such as Minos and Rhadamanthys) must lie in their roots in an old Minoan poetry, which was probably influenced by West Asiatic traditions; this allows the possibility that they were of Eastern origin.[143] This has particular strength for the name Meriones, which is similar to the Hurrian word *maryannu* 'élite chariot warrior',[144] and forms part of what is thought to be a pre-Homeric formula (Μηριόνης ἀτάλαντος Ἐνυαλίῳ ἀνδρειφόντῃ· Il. 2.651, 7.166, 8.263; the formula is in tune with the hero's name in implying high social sta-

---

137 Cf. Pi. N. 10.6 ff., Theoc. 22.13 ff. See LfgrE s.v. Ἴδης (B. Mader).
138 Von Kamptz 1982 (1958): 307. Similarly Mühlestein (1969: 67–70) in his interpretation of the names Dares and Idaios. See further under 'Minor' speaking names.
139 See von Kamptz 1982 (1958): 154, 291. The place-name is notably similar to the Mycenaean names mentioned above.
140 They form a 'typical heroic duo', comparable to Achilles and Patroklos (HE s.v. Meriones [B. Louden]). They fight separately at first, representing two distinct parts of the Cretan contingent, but later they join forces. M.L. West (2011a: 63) notes that unlike Idomeneus, Meriones is absent from the poem's 'primary layer.'
141 Von Kamptz 1982 (1958): 292.
142 The effort to connect the two names geographically is further complicated by the fact that the name of Meriones' father, Molos, may be seen as suggestive of Aegean / Asia Minor origin. There are three early attestations of the very similar name Μόλης (in the Aegean islands, 6th-5th c. BC, LGPN I), and the name resurfaces in Asia Minor where it was apparently common in the imperial period (107 attestations, nearly all from Lycia, LGPN VB; there is also one from Ephesos, LGPN VA).
143 See M.L.West 1997: 612.
144 This interpretation of the name is favoured by M.L.West 1997: 612 and Makkay 2003: 29–33.

tus).¹⁴⁵ But as we have seen for Idomeneus, subtle Greek puns on the name Meriones are equally possible. Such a pun might allude to the hero's manner of fighting:¹⁴⁶ 'archer', 'bowman', if Μηριόνης is associated with μήρινθος 'cord', 'string'.¹⁴⁷ In the *Iliad* (23.854; its sole attestation in Homer) it denotes the string that binds the pigeon serving as target at the shooting contest, while a later occurrence (Ar. *Th.* 935) suggests the meaning 'fishing rod'; perhaps 'bowstring' was another possible sense. It would not be unsuitable for Meriones if he was a 'bowman' by name, as he occasionally appears as an archer (*Il.* 13.650–1; cf. 10.260 where he gives Odysseus a bow, and 23.850–83, where he joins Teukros in the archery context and wins the prize). However, this is not his only capacity – he is otherwise a spearman (e.g. 16.619: Μηριόνης δουρικλυτός 'famed for his δόρυ = spear').¹⁴⁸ It further seems a bit disconcerting that on the whole the *Iliad* takes a poor view of archery.¹⁴⁹ Other possible etymological associations are not lacking: the name is phonetically close to μηρία. As part of the vocabulary of ritual, the word referred to the thigh-bones of the sacrificial victim, but μηρός is also the place where a sword hangs (cf. *Il.* 1.190). The thighs are further praised in Homer as an element of a good body figure (*Il.* 4.146–7), while it is also a part of the body that is often wounded (e.g. *Il.* 11.583).¹⁵⁰ It is thus not impossible that an audience heard in the warrior's name the word for 'thigh'.¹⁵¹

---

145 On the formula see Ruijgh 2011: 287–9. Cf. Janko (1992: 78–9) on Meriones' probable career in pre-Homeric poetry. Notably his personal history involves elements of great antiquity: according to *Il.* 10.170–271 he inherited a six-generation old boars' tusk helmet from his father, an object which belonged to the early Mycenaean period, and whose origins are presumably pre-Mycenaean (Makkay 2003: 2 ff.; Dickinson 2006: 74, 157); but note that such objects may also belong to the later Mycenaean period, cf. Bennet 2014: 210; Gancarski (2002: 83–5) on collections of perforated boar's tusk platelets from graves of hunter warriors from central Europe.
146 Von Blumenthal 1930: 50.
147 Probably pre-Greek, see Beekes 2010 s.v. μήρινθος. The word might be related to μηρύομαι 'to lower –wrap?- (a sail)', cf. *Od.* 12.170 (von Kamptz 1982 (1958): 352). Cf. Chantraine 1999 s.v. μήρινθος. Another possible cognate, μέρμις, is used in the *Od.* (10.23) for the thong that binds the bag of Aiolos' winds.
148 See *LfgrE* s.v. Μηριόνης (W. Beck).
149 Cf. 11.385–90 (contempt for archers). See further Snodgrass 1967: 39–40 and Hijmans 1976: 343–52 (who points out however that skill in archery is respected). Generally (and briefly) on the (small but important) role of archers in Homeric battle see van Wees 2004: 154–5, 161.
150 See *LfgrE* s.v. μηρός (W. Beck).
151 Interestingly an epigram of *AP* (5.36) comically relates the name to the same word, μηρός, in that context alluding to the 'female genitalia'. Names inspired from parts of the body were not uncommon in historical times, see Bechtel 1917: 479–84; cf. in particular the name Κνῆμος (Th. 2.66.2) and Εὔκναμος (Plu. *Mor.* 761d) from κνήμη 'shank'.

2.1.6 Patroklos

Patroklos has a place among the prominent Iliadic figures for being closely connected with the principal Achaean hero, and – perhaps even more importantly – for being the key that unlocks the chain of events leading to Achilles' return to battle and the death of Hektor. The hero's importance increases interest in the meaning of his name, which is further encouraged by the name's etymological transparency.

The name, which occurs also (less often) as Πατροκλέης, is a compound of two easily recognisable parts: πατρο- and -κλέος (more clearly visible in the longer, full form of the name), which suggest a meaning connected with 'father' and 'glory'. Given that 'speaking' heroic names commonly reflect paternal characteristics (the famous example is Telemachos), the name is traditionally explained as: 'der durch seine Geburt (seinen Vater) glänzende oder berühmte',[152] or 'den Ruhm seines Vaters habend = weitertragend'. Might this significance be specifically appropriate for Patroklos? The fact that Patroklos' father Menoitios, though mentioned in the *Iliad* several times, is a rather colourless figure, makes this difficult. πατρο- could also evoke πάτρη 'family, clan'.[153] Menoitios appears as a brother of Peleus in a Hesiodic fragment (fr. 212 M – W), which would make Achilles and Patroklos cousins; Patroklos' name could then allude to his kinship with Achilles (and his heroic glory). However, a relationship between Peleus and Menoitios does not feature in Homer. Moreover, none of the (rare) occurrences of πάτρη in Homer has any other sense than 'homeland' (except for *Il.* 13.354 where it means 'ancestry'[154]), while πατρο- clearly has the meaning 'father' in several Homeric compounds (such as πατροκασίγνητος 'paternal uncle', πατροφονεύς / πατροφόνος 'murderer of one's father').[155]

Attempts at a suitable explanation of Patroklos' name include Mühlestein's, who argued in favour of a connection with (ἔ)κλυον (a Homeric word) 'listen', 'harken to',[156] suggesting the meaning: 'he who listens to his father', and

---

[152] Thus Pape-Benseler 1911 s.v. Πάτροκλος. Cf. Untermann (1987: 30): 'einer, dessen Ruhm sein Vater ist'. See also Bouvier (2002: 383) for a summary of suggestions.
[153] Cf. e.g. Pi. *P.* 8.38, *N.* 6.36. See von Kamptz 1982 (1958): 215, following Sommer 1948: 14 ff.
[154] Zeus and Poseidon are said to share ὁμὸν γένος ἠδ' ἴα πάτρη 'one stock and one parentage'; see further Janko 1992: 91.
[155] Cf. Chantraine 1999 s.v. πατήρ; ὀβριμοπάτρη as an epithet of Athena clearly gives a better sense if connected with πατήρ ('daughter of a mighty father') than if connected with πάτρη.
[156] Chantraine 1999 s.v. κλέος; cf. Hooker 1980b: 140 – 6. Note that ἔκλυον is used also with the meaning 'are ... glorious' (for the harmonious couple in the ideal marriage that Odysseus wishes for Nausikaa, *Od.* 6.181– 5); see also Schein 1995: 22 – 3.

obeys.[157] But the second component of Patroklos' name can hardly evoke any other sense than 'glory'. The ample attestation of such names in Mycenaean[158] suggests that they were used in everyday life, initially perhaps with the connotation of '(good) reputation', which would have been in most cases supplanted by the heroic usage.[159] Indeed κλέος in the sense of glory is one of the most powerful epic concepts – more important than obedience or mere good repute – and Homeric names with this element should as a rule allude to 'glory', especially when this meaning is encouraged by relevant epic diction.[160] The exact sense of the combination 'glory' and 'father' may elude us; but a line from the *Iliad* (6.446) sounds surprisingly close to Patroklos' name: Hektor says there that by fighting for Troy he glorifies his father as well as himself (ἀρνύμενος πατρός τε μέγα κλέος).[161] This may suggest the meaning: 'he who brings glory to his father' – a fundamental heroic obligation.[162]

The name of the Iliadic Patroklos is bound up with the problem of his origins, which Mühlestein sought in a different hero, Nestor's son Antilochos, and in another poem, the *Aithiopis*. Mühlestein partly relied on the unconvincing assumption that Patroklos' name (either invented or selected among known contemporary names) could express an action of Antilochos, who hears and responds to his father's call for help as the latter is attacked by the Aithiopian king Memnon and indeed saves his father's life, losing his own,[163] and on the similarity of roles: Antilochos too is presented as a friend of Achilles (*Il.* 23.556; Patroklos

---

157 Mühlestein 1969: 8 ff. (for the verb in the sense of yielding or obeying cf. *Il.* 7.379, 9.79, *Od.* 3.337, 3.477 etc.).
158 Even if not fully preserved; for examples see Risch 1987: 6 ff.; García Ramón 2011 *passim*.
159 Note that at *Od.* 1.282–3 (ἥ ὅσσαν ἀκούσῃς / ἐκ Διός, ἥ τε μάλιστα φέρει κλέος ἀνθρώποισι), κλέος is better understood as 'news, tidings'; κλέος in the sense of 'report, what is heard' is used only once in the *Iliad* (11.227) – 'glory' is clearly the main meaning of the word. Cf. Hooker (1980b: 146), who argued that either the root (-*kleu*-) embraced both meanings from the start, or the glory-related sense developed within the epic context.
160 For a list of these see von Kamptz 1982 (1958): 203. Some examples which suggest a connection with glory: Βαθυκλέης (*Il.* 16.594; κλέος βαθύ 'profound fame', see below, p. 139), Ἐπικλέης (*Il.* 12.379; 'glorious'), Ἐχεκλέης, -κλος ('he who has *kleos*': *Il.* 16.189; cf. 17.143 κλέος ἐσθλὸν ἔχει, *Od.* 1.95 κλέος ἐσθλὸν ... ἔχῃσιν), Φέρεκλος (*Il.* 5.59; cf. *Il.* 22.217 οἴσεσθαι μέγα κῦδος Ἀχαιοῖσι 'will bring great glory to the Achaeans').
161 Cf. Vedic: *pitŕ̥ṣravaṇa* 'der für den Ruhm seines Vaters sorgt' (Tichy 1990: 132); cf. Nagy 1990: 94 'he who has the glory of the ancestors'.
162 Cf. Bouvier 2002: 368 (but he exaggerates a little in arguing that this sense reflects a hero's 'ultimate duty' and 'the essence of heroic identity', hence Patroklos is a 'nom parfait'; a hero's primary concern is his own *kleos*, as a type of immortality achieved through great deeds).
163 Proclus summarises this in one sentence (M. L. West 2003a: 112), but cf. Pi. *P.* 6.2 ff.

and Antilochos are said to be Achilles' dearest friends at *Od.* 24.76–81), and his death (like Patroklos') is avenged by Achilles who kills Memnon.[164] The *Iliad*'s dependance on the *Aithiopis* was a conviction of early neoanalysis.[165] However, the chronological priority of the *Aithiopis* is far from certain,[166] and it is possible that both poems drew independently on tradition, or that Patroklos' story in the *Iliad* was modelled on Achilles' story (which is of course the primary one), but in an earlier form than we have it in the *Aithiopis*.[167] If so, it is more likely that the friendship between Achilles and Antilochos was modelled on the friendship between Achilles and Patroklos, than vice-versa.[168] This does not leave much room to the possibility that Patroklos was modelled on Antilochos. It is equally hard to decide which of the two figures is 'older'. Patroklos can be seen as a 'young' hero, but it is impossible to know whether he had a pre-Iliadic presence.[169] Antilochos does not have a better claim to antiquity. It is perhaps significant that his main function in the *Iliad* is to bring the news of Patroklos' death (18.2–34), and otherwise his role is limited.[170] More importantly, it is not clear why the poet would have wished one of his heroes to function as a reflection of Antilochos

---

164 Mühlestein 1969: 88, n.21. Cf. Seaford 1994: 154–7 on similarities between the *Iliad* and the *Aithiopis*.
165 See e.g. Willcock 1997: 175–6, 179–83.
166 Willcock 1997: 181, cf. Kirk 1990: 27. The *Aithiopis* may offer an expanded treatment of the theme of Achilles' death, which was not included in the *Iliad*, but this was not necessarily an older version.
167 Patroklos' death and death ritual in the *Iliad* prefigure (or imitate?) Achilles'. Pestalozzi (1945) assumed a pre-existing poem that he called *Achilleis*. See M.L.West (2003b), with an overview of older scholarship (including neoanalysis) on the issue of the relationship between the *Iliad* and the *Aithiopis*. West argues that the Memnon episode in the *Aithiopis* is the result of a later effort to devise a death of Achilles that would suit the situation as left at the end of the *Iliad* (prolonging the tale of Troy was a fashion in the late 7th c. BC). The relevant arguments are that the poet of the *Iliad* was apparently unaware of a Memnon episode (nor could he have imagined a contingent of Aithiopians arriving at Troy, given their image in the *Iliad* 1.423, 23.205–7), and of course the prophecy that Achilles would die straight after Hektor. For a historical explanation of the development of the narrative tradition in the *Iliad* see Seaford (1994: 176–80), who argues that the ending of the poem with the death ritual of Hektor (not paralleled in the *Aithiopis*) reflects forms of integration within the *polis* and between city-states (Seaford implies the possibility that this ending replaced an earlier one).
168 This friendship between Achilles and Antilochos is only mentioned once in the *Iliad*, 23.556; see further M.L.West (2003b).
169 See *LfgrE* s.v. Πάτροκλος, Πατροκλ(έης) (H.W. Nordheider). Mühlestein 1972: 84 takes Patroklos to be a Homeric invention (cf. ibid.: 86, n.22 with bibliography, and 1969: 91); opposite view in Burgess 2001: 7 ff. M.L. West (2011a: 45) considers him 'an untraditional figure, introduced into the saga with Achilles.'
170 M.L. West (2011a: 63) notes that he is absent from the *Iliad*'s 'primary layer'.

in an epic of which Antilochos himself is part (he is notably also present in books 15–16 where Patroklos is prominent).

The name of Patroklos' father, Μενοίτιος, may express a quality of the son. Mühlestein extended the interpretation suggested by the proposed *Aithiopis* connection to the explanation of Menoitios' name as another reflection of Antilochos' actions (known from the already mentioned Pindaric ode): he stood up to death (μένειν + οἶτος).[171] But there is indeed no need to rely on the very uncertain connections between our poem and the *Aithiopis*. The meaning suggested for Menoitios' name[172] is suitable for Patroklos who bravely faced the blow of fate (death) when fighting for the Greeks. An allusion to οἶτος would also suit another Menoitios, a son of Titan Iapetos (Hes. *Th.* 51 ff.), who was thrown into Erebos by Zeus as a punishment for Hybris. The name could have an ambiguous meaning: on the one hand it would reflect the initial impression (illusion rather) that the name-bearer is master of his fate, on the other hand it would ominously allude to this fate, in the sense that he 'awaits fate (=death)'.[173] Such an ambivalence would suit both Patroklos as the son of Menoitios and the Hesiodic figure, as both are over-confident at first and then become victims of fate. The poetic value of these associations overshadows another potential etymology, from μένος and οἴσομαι, meaning 'he who carries force'.[174]

The discussion of Patroklos' name cannot ignore the very similar name Κλεοπάτρη, name of Meleagros' wife (*Il.* 9.561). In the Iliadic context, this name's similarity to Patroklos would perhaps attract attention for the following reasons: 1)

---

171 Mühlestein (ibid.) draws support for this from the assumption that the verb μένειν was present in the *Aithiopis* in the sense of standing up to death, at least judging by its use in Pindar (*P.* 6.31, 38). However, the use of οἶτος in Homer (perhaps especially in *Od.* 13.384, φθείσεσθαι κακὸν οἶτον 'perish by an evil fate') implies a possible source of Pindaric inspiration.
172 'Dem Schicksal standhaltend'; von Kamptz 1982 (1958): 33.
173 Cf. *LfgrE* s.v. Μενοίτιος (B. Mader). See von Kamptz 1982 (1958): 63 for a slightly different interpretation of the ambivalence: 'he who patiently awaits his fate', or 'he who fights against the mishaps of fortune'. M.L. West (1966: 308) notes that the name is appropriate to a man, not a god.
174 See Bechtel (1917: 346) on the similar name Μενοίτας, which he connected with Ἀλκοίτας: 'die Stärke und Mut bringen'; cf. von Kamptz 1982 (1958): 78. See also below, on the name Philoitios. This etymology may be encouraged by a couple of Iliadic lines: 16.602 (μένος δ' ἰθὺς φέρον αὐτῶν '[the Achaeans] carried their might straight on toward the foe') and 5.506 (οἳ δὲ μένος χειρῶν ἰθὺς φέρον 'the force of their hands they carried straight on'). A connection with μένος is assumed by Eustathius (113.4, on *Il.* 1.337), who does not however mention οἴσομαι as a second component.

there are some striking analogies between the two figures (both are connected with an angry hero who stays away from battle, and are the only ones capable of reversing his decision), made stronger if we accept that an erotic element existed in the relationship between Achilles and Patroklos.[175] 2) The element πατήρ was not very common in Greek onomastics, and two similar names containing it (the only two examples in Homer[176]) would therefore stand out. 3) The use of the same components in names was perhaps a deliberate play, used as help to memory and for convenience (cf. Ἑκαμήδη, Nestor's maid (11.624) and the sorceress Ἀγαμήδη, daughter of Augeias (11.740), appearing within a score of lines). Objections to associating the two names include the following:[177] 1) there are striking differences between the two characters; one is a wife, the other a fellow soldier. 2) Patroklos as an active figure becomes reminiscent of Kleopatre mainly at the point when he also attempts to bend Achilles' stubbornness, but that is 4160 lines later.[178] 3) Kleopatre's name is heard in the text only once; if the poet intended to create a pun between the two names, he would have made more use of the feminine name. 4) The components are in reverse order, which makes the etymological affinity less striking.

Could her name shed more light on his? Two possibilities are worth considering: that the name might be appropriate to Meleagros' wife in ways that could also suit Patroklos' name (e.g. if there was a suggestion that Kleopatre was named so because of the glory of her father); or that it might be an older name (for an older figure) and inspired the naming of Patroklos (called Patroklos and not Kleopatros for the sake of variety). The epic, however, does not hint at a meaning for the name Kleopatre. Could it have acted as a model for Patroklos? This possibility may seem initially encouraged by the many similarities that exist

---

175 There is support for this in ancient sources (though not in the *Iliad*), e.g. in Aeschylus' *Myrmidons* frr. 135–7 (Radt); Aeschin. *in Timarchum* 133. Cf. Swain 1988: 271–6; Morales – Mariscal 2003: 293–5. The Achilles – Patroklos relationship (which has been much debated) was perhaps based on oriental models (Gilgamesh – Enkidu), originating from the duplication of a hero in a heroic pair (cf. the greater Aias with the lesser Aias or Teukros); see *LfgrE* s.v. Πάτροκλος, Πατροκλ(έης), under 'Typologie der Freundespaare' (H.W. Nordheider).
176 Such names must have been rare also in Mycenaean (examples include Πάτρων? [Jorro-Adrados 1985 s.v. *pa-to-ro*]; *Philopatra*, similar to Kleopatre [Jorro-Adrados 1985 s.v. *pi-ro-pa-ta-ra*]). The masculine form Κλεόπατρος is attested at later times. Cf. ὀβριμοπάτρη, epithet of Athena (on which see also above, n. 155).
177 On these see mainly Kakridis 1949.
178 Kleopatre is not Patroklos' perfect counterpart, as M.L. West (2011a: 228) notes (persuasion of Achilles by Patroklos occurs at a later stage and does not produce quite the same effect as Kleopatre on Meleager).

between the stories of Achilles (of which Patroklos is part) and Meleagros,[179] and even more by the fact that Meleagros' story is addressed to Achilles as a paradigm in *Il.* 9.52 ff. Though the plot of this book raises numerous difficulties,[180] the substance of Meleagros' story is not doubted, and it can be assumed that one of the two stories influenced or inspired the other, and indeed that one of the two was older and its elements (including the names) were used as models for the other. The story of Meleagros apparently draws on a very ancient prototype,[181] and certain elements in the epic story are suggestive of great antiquity;[182] this has led to the assumption that the story of Meleagros is older, and hence also Kleopatre is likely to have provided the inspiration for Patroklos.[183] But is it possible to be sure that Kleopatre was part of the original, 'primitive' story? If so, her name may have had additional relevance which we ignore. If added later,[184] it is impossible to tell whether this was done by the poet of the *Iliad* or earlier.[185] The problem is made more complex by the presence of fluctuations in the story (e. g. differences in the naming of the brothers in later sources; there is only one in the *Iliad*, not named), which may suggest that no canonical form

---

179 Primarily the element of μῆνις, the hero's abstinence from battle, and his death coming soon after the taming of the anger.
180 See S.R. West 2001: 3 ff., and below, the discussion of the name Phoinix. The plot of Meleagros' story itself is problematic.
181 Traces are found in Phrynichus *TGrF* 1 fr. 6 (Snell) = Paus. 10.31.4, A. *Cho.* 60 ff., B. 5.9 ff., Ovid *Met.* 8.26 ff. These sources reflect a less rationalised version of the story, where the hero's life depended on a magic firebrand, burned by his mother to cause his death; in the epic version the hero's death results from the mother's curse (for his having killed her brother).
182 Cf. e.g. the preference for brother(s) over a son, and more importantly the presence of elements in the paradigm which do not suit Achilles' position (order of the embassies, the role of the wife, the presence of the mother) and which suggest an old, fixed story that the poet could not alter. Furthermore, Meleagros is two or three generations older than the Trojan war (cf. Hainsworth 1993: 131), and the story of Kalydon falls into one of the four epic cycles (cf. [Hes.] *Cat.* fr. 25 M–W).
183 Howald (1920/4: 405), who first made the connection between the two names, assumed that Patroklos was secondary to Kleopatre. He was followed by Schadewaldt 1966: 140.
184 This could have happened as part of the adaptation of an old folktale to the epic context, which gave importance to the hero's wife; a comparison between the two versions shows that many elements in the epic version (the anger of a goddess, a heroic achievement: the hunt of the Kalydonian boar, a war with a reason, the hero's anger, and finally a larger number of interacting figures) must be later additions, cf. Kakridis 1949. Bacchylides' Meleagros does not mention a wife.
185 There is a debate as to what the poet of the *Iliad* altered / added to the story to improve the parable; thus Willcock (1964: 141–54) argued that the χόλος of Meleagros and all that followed was the poet's invention; similarly M.L. West (2011a: 227): 'the wrath motif was ... transferred from Achilles to Meleager.' Opposite view in Kakridis 1949.

existed.¹⁸⁶ Thus even if we accept that the central theme of Meleagros' anger was older than that of Achilles, it is not easy to decide whether a detail such as Kleopatre is also pre-Homeric. Additionally, Patroklos' role is more vital, which provides support for his antiquity. It is perhaps preferable to view the name separately from the figure of Kleopatre: the name could be as old as the figure or a new name for an older figure, perhaps, punning on the (older name) Patroklos – it is always easier to add a name than a whole new figure.¹⁸⁷ As a new element in the Meleagros' story, Kleopatre's name would be more striking and therefore more noticeable for its significance.

The possibility of a later appearance of the name Kleopatre in the story could be encouraged by the digression concerning her double naming: her other name, Ἀλκυόνη, may be the primary one in the older tradition, and Kleopatre could have been the poet's own addition.¹⁸⁸ Alkyone's tradition indeed seems to have been more ancient: she is mentioned as a daughter of Atlas and one of the Pleiads in [Hes.] fr. 169 M–W, and as a daughter of Aiolos, wife of Keyx in fr.16.6 M–W; Alkyone as Kleopatre's eponym was perhaps inspired from the wife of Keyx, who experienced grief at the loss of her husband.¹⁸⁹ According to the Homeric passage, the name was chosen to reflect the pain of Kleopatre's mother, Marpessa;¹⁹⁰ but it was also potentially suitable to Kleopatre herself who experienced grief in the death of Meleagros, and who according to later sources suffered so much sadness that she died of it (Hyg. *Fab.* 174) or was led to suicide (Apollod. 1.73).

Kleopatre's husband, Meleagros, is also significantly named. His name was apparently at home in a lost Aitolian epos of great antiquity¹⁹¹ (cf. *Il.* 9.52 f.: Phoinix

---

186 Cf. Hainsworth 1993: 131. In another version ([Hes.] *Cat.* fr. 25 M–W, *P.Oxy.* 2075, and in the *Minyad* fr. 5 West, Paus. 10.31.3) Meleagros is killed by Apollo – apparently an effort to bring Meleagros even closer to Achilles.
187 According to Kakridis 1949 both name and figure are older. On the debate see also Willcock 1964: 150 n.4. See *LfgrE* s.v. Κλεοπάτρη (B. Mader) for further bibliography on the two opposed views.
188 Cf. Schadewaldt 1966: 140; Hainsworth 1993: 136; *HE* s.v. Kleopatre (M. Alden).
189 Thus Grossardt 2001: 37–8.
190 τὴν δὲ τότ' ἐν μεγάροισι πατὴρ καὶ πότνια μήτηρ / Ἀλκυόνην καλέεσκον ἐπώνυμον, οὕνεκ' ἄρ' αὐτῆς / μήτηρ ἀλκυόνος πολυπενθέος οἶτον ἔχουσα / κλαῖεν, ὅ μιν ἑκάεργος ἀνήρπασε Φοῖβος Ἀπόλλων· 'Cleopatra of old in their halls had her father and honored mother called Halcyone by name, because the mother herself, in a plight like that of the halcyon bird of many sorrows, wept because Apollo who works from afar had snatched her child away' (*Il.* 9.561–4).
191 A *Meleagris*? See Hainsworth 1993: 130–2 with bibliography and M.L. West 2011a: 226–7.

refers to the story as something he remembers from the distant past¹⁹²), which adds to the difficulty of explaining it. Still, it was clearly thought to be significant in antiquity, as a Euripidean fragment suggests: Μελέαγρε, μελέαν γάρ ποτ' ἀγρεύεις ἄγραν 'Meleager – malign indeed is the chase you've chosen' (*TGrF* 5.1 fr. 517 [Kannicht] [transl. Collard – Cropp]). This reflects the misfortunes that hunting has brought to the hero (*Il.* 9.54 ff.):¹⁹³ the killing of the boar proved pointless, as Artemis sent a new disaster, and in fact the hunt unlocked the chain of events that led to the hero's death (to which perhaps the epithet μελέαν in Euripides' fragment alludes). The lack of relevant puns in Homer, however, leaves the field open to alternative explanations of Meleagros, e.g. as a compound of μέλομαι + ἄγρα (cf. the use of μεμηλώς 'concerned for, caring about' at 5.708, 13.297) or μέλει ἄγρα.¹⁹⁴ This would suggest the meaning: 'who has a liking for / cares for hunting', making Meleagros a generic name for a hunter.¹⁹⁵ Other etymological efforts also link the name with hunting and weapons.¹⁹⁶ The names of his uncles (brothers of his father, Oineus), Ἄγριος and Μέλας (14.117),¹⁹⁷ probably emerged from the dismemberment of Meleagros' name.¹⁹⁸

---

192 It has been argued that the story of Meleagros has a special link with Nestor's reminiscence and his appeal to Patroklos in 11.78 ff. (cf. Swain 1988: 272), but it is impossible to establish genetic connections between such details.
193 Cf. *EM* s.v. Μελέαγρος; Mühlestein 1969: 84, n. 15.
194 See von Kamptz 1982 (1958): 62. Note a possible pun in Bacchylides 5.91–4 ("τὰ δέ που / Παλλάδι ξανθᾷ μέλει." / Τὸν δὲ προσέφα Μελέ/αγρος...).
195 Mühlestein (ibid.) argues that in that case the name should be Μέλ-αγρος; meanings of epic 'speaking' names, however, do not necessarily emerge from strictly correct etymologies.
196 See Watkins 1986b, who revived an old etymology (from a Greek word *Ϝαγρος) and supported it with evidence from formulaic analysis; cf. M.L. West 2007a: 251.
197 On the family see further *HE* s.v. Oineus (M. Alden). Meleager was a paternal uncle of Diomedes.
198 For further explanations of the name that were probably inspired from the hero's antiquity (e.g. as a god of thunders or of the Underworld), see *RE* s.v. Meleagros (Geffcken). His father's name, Οἰνεύς, has also been thought suggestive of a very ancient figure, alluding to an old god-protector of the vines (von Kamptz 1982 (1958): 31 see also below, p. 69). The mother's name too, Ἀλθαίη, may be etymologically significant (Hsch. ἄλθα· θεραπεία, suggesting the meaning 'healer'; this is appropriate to her initial role as guarantor of her son's well-being, but sounds ironic as she causes his death; ἄλθα is not a Homeric word).

2.2 Heroic Old Men

2.2.1 Nestor

Nestor's role and function in the *Iliad* are quite straightforward, but the same cannot be said of the meaning of his name, which is affected by complicated etymological problems; potential meanings may suggest different kinds of 'appropriateness'.

The widely accepted derivation from the root **nes-*[199] (the second part of the name is clearly an agent's suffix) is the only etymology that may trigger an acceptable meaning[200] and should imply a connection with the etymological group of νέομαι, νόστος. An agent-noun from νέομαι ('return home') should mean 'he who returns home'; thus already Kretschmer offered the meaning 'Rückkehrer' and similarly Pape-Benseler 'der Heimgekehrte' and Frisk 'der (glücklich wohin) gelangt'.[201] A connection with νόστος suggests a generic name, as the wish for safe homecoming is intrinsic to the heroic mentality.[202] However, the first part of the name can also function transitively, allowing the meaning 'he who brings (others) safely home', [203] as suggested by the attestation of the root **nes-* in the Mycenaean name Νεσέλαϝος (*ne-e-ra-wo* PY Fn 79.5), 'he who brings the war-folk safely home'.[204] There is clearly an analogy with names of the type Μενέ-λαϝος, Ἐχέ-λαϝος, Ἀγέ-λαϝος, with parallel forms Μέντωρ, Ἕκτωρ, Ἄκτωρ. Indeed a transitive interpretation of the name Nestor dates from before the Mycenaean evidence, as early as Curtius.[205] Palm-

---

199 See Frame (1978: 82, n.1) for the relevant bibliography.
200 Von Kamptz (1982 (1958): 38, 172) assumed another possibility, that the name is derived from the root **ned-* 'to roar', which may suggest a meaning 'Brüller'. But the use of such a root is unparalleled in Greek, and therefore improbable.
201 Kretschmer 1913: 30 f.; Pape-Benseler 1911: 992; Frisk 1960–72, s.v. νέομαι.
202 Mühlestein (1965: 157–8) thought that the presence of the root in other Homeric and Mycenaean names (*Φιλονέστας, Ἰφίνοος, Ἀλκίνοος) confirms the high appreciation of the notion of safe return in this society; but it will be shown below that the meaning of -νοος is controversial.
203 Note that Chantraine (1999 s.v. νέομαι) mentions both possibilities: 'qui rentre heureusement' or 'qui ramène heureusement son armée'. An example of transitive νέ(σ)ω would be given by Frame's conjecture at *Od.* 18.265 με νέσει θεός (Frame 1978: 99–102; 2009: 2 ff.).
204 Incidentally, the name appears in the company of the name Achilles. Notably the tablets seem to preserve a second name from the same root: Νεστιάνωρ (Cn 599.1 and Cn 40), which was read – not without some doubt – by Ventris-Chadwick (1973: 99). Palmer (1963: 80) is more confident.
205 Cf. his interpretation of Nestor's name: 'Heimführer' (1858: 315). The transitive meaning was also caught by Gruppe (1906: 643), who, however, strangely distanced himself from the sense of νέομαι in translating 'der Segner'.

er's[206] and Durante's[207] enthusiastic support of the identification of the Mycenaean name ΝεσέλαϜος with that of Nestor's father Neleus[208] was put forward in order to support the possibility that Nestor had the same meaning as ΝεσέλαϜος. Assuming that the reading of the Mycenaean name is correct, it is worth reminding that the names of members of the same family often contained common elements (e.g. Εὐρυσθεύς, parallel form of Εὐρυσθένης, son of Σθένελος, *Il.* 19.123).[209] In a similar spirit Mühlestein[210] connected Nestor and Neleus and interprets Nestor's name as meaning 'Heimführer', 'Retter'.

The safe homebringing of soldiers is of course a standard function of a hero who goes on an expedition. However, a more 'personal' demonstration of that function, which is related by Nestor himself and derives from his own experience, is found in the *Iliad* (11.732–61). Nestor tells the story of the war expedition against the Epeians which he led in his youth, noting that in the end he was able to bring his soldiers safely home. Nestor's story, generally thought to come from an older Pylian epos,[211] with its characteristic ending, has been seen as suggestive of the original meaning of his name, which was later blurred;[212] indeed the *Iliad* contains no relevant word-plays.

The connection of Nestor's name with νόστος, appropriate as it may be in a heroic name, and even though reflected in one episode of Nestor's life, does not express the prevailing function of the particular hero in the poem that concerns us here – the *Iliad*. Stories about his past achievements, including the safe home-bringing of war-folk, may form part of the poetic material of the *Iliad*, but Nestor's active contribution to the poem's plot mainly relies on his wisdom, that is, his mental abilities: his basic function is to give advice. It is therefore

---

206 1956: 8–9, with support from linguistics.
207 1967.
208 ΝεσέλαϜος > Νεhέ-λαϜος > Νηλεύς; *Ne(h)e-* from **nes-* with aspiration and loss of the intervocalic *-s-*, see esp. Palmer 1956: 8–9, n.4; cf. 1963: 80.
209 See further von Kamptz 1982 (1958): 37, Palmer 1956: 9–10, cf. 1963: 7 ff. and Durante 1967: 36.
210 1965: 158–9.
211 See M.L. West 2011a: 29–30. Cf. Vetta 2003.
212 Mühlestein 1965: 157–9, and n.22 for bibliography. The connection of an onomastic discussion with the effort to trace possible Iliadic sources is Mühlestein's concern also in the case of Patroklos' name (1972: 79–90), see below. He makes a weak case for a 'historical' Nestor (1965: 161–2) on the basis of alleged further attestations of the element **nes-* (or the notion of return) in the names of various Neleids (e.g. Melanthos, old king of Athens; Neileos, colonist of Miletus), which are known from various later Greek texts and which he connects with onomastic evidence from the Pylian tablets. The speculative character of the argument is not helped by the fact that the alleged later Neleids were apparently figures involved in foundation myths, the antiquity of which has been much doubted.

worth noting that the root *nes- has been connected also with νόος, though the etymological relationship is unconfirmed.²¹³ The Iliadic text offers some indication of a poetic association between Nestor, the 'wise counselor', and νόος 'mind': one speech of advice by Nestor to Agamemnon in book 9 (especially 103 – 9) contains a striking repetition of νόος-related vocabulary (104: νόον, νοήσει; 105: νοέω; 108: νόον). Nestor mentions *noos* once more at 14.62, again addressing Agamemnon. Similarly, in book 23 Nestor's instructions to his son Antilochos about chariot-racing are marked by the recurrence of the roughly synonymous term μῆτις (312 – 8). But although it is clear that an audience would make a connection between Nestor's function and the notion of 'mind', it remains uncertain that they would connect his name with *noos*, as the two are not phonetically close. On the other hand, Nestor's part in the *Odyssey* is just as expressive of the idea of safe homecoming (or home-bringing) as it is of his wisdom. He appropriately appears in a context centered on stories of return (he himself gives to Telemachos an account of the return of the Achaeans at 3.12 ff.). Nestor's own experience has fulfilled the ideal of safe return, as he apparently had a very easy journey back (3.182 – 3). As Nestor and Telemachos discuss Odysseus, the audience might have felt the lurking contrast between Nestor and his name, and Odysseus and his name: Nestor's name can reflect quiet wisdom and safe homecoming; Odysseus' name (as we shall see in the next chapter) echoes a tumultuous mind and the torments caused by the hero's wanderings and the long postponement of return.

The name's etymology has further been enlisted in speculations about the origins of Nestor;²¹⁴ these deserve a comment as they partly rely on the Homeric epics. The main lines of an elaborate argument, by D. Frame,²¹⁵ are as follows: the original meaning of the root *nes- may be seen as relevant to 'returning to life and light', and related vocabulary is used in contexts of sun-related symbol-

---

213 On the possible semantic development of the root see Ruijgh (1967: 371– 2) and Frei (1968: 48 – 57). For a different view see Heubeck 1987: 227– 38. For a summary of scholarly views on the issue see Stefanelli 2010: 217– 35.
214 Such speculations go back to Kretschmer (1913: 30 f.) who assumed that the name initially belonged to a vegetation figure characterised by yearly return, but without convincing arguments, such as the meaning of the suffix -τωρ (which for Kretschmer implied frequency or repetition, but this is not necessarily the case, see Benveniste 1948: 62), and the traditional, but far from uncontroversial connection of Nestor's home town Pylos with the Underworld. Meister (1921: 228, n.1) suggested that the name is of non-Greek origin (cf. also Page 1959: 215, n.91); this is unnecessary given the above discussion of the name's etymology.
215 Frame 1978.

ism, mostly involving the Sun's cattle.[216] The presence of that root in Nestor's name, as well as his involvement in an episode of the pre-Homeric age (the already mentioned expedition that he narrates in *Iliad* 11 as a story of his youth),[217] imply that behind the Iliadic Nestor hid an old, mythological figure whose original function was to release the Sun's cattle from the Pylos cave.[218] However, the argument largely depends on speculation regarding the meaning of the root *nes- and on metaphorical interpretations of episodes that are more easily understood without the intervention of the 'light' factor. In the story of the expedition against the Epeians (*Il.* 11.67 ff.), Nestor appears to 'save' his fellow-fighters in the sense that he brings them home safely after the fight against the Epeians. *nes- as the root of the name Nestor might indeed here mean 'save' or 'rescue',[219] but the case for a connection between Nestor and the Sun or the notion of 'light' is obscure. The case lies mainly in the episode of the cattle-raid in 11.681–2, where Nestor wins the herds and flocks of Pylos from the Epeians; but there is no need to see this as a reflex of a 'bring-to-light-and-life' act: the function of protecting property of one's home city and the responsibility for the safe return of war-folk are much more obviously connected with the heroic ideal than with the myth of the Sun.[220] The cattle episode, which is presented in the *Iliad* as part of standard heroic experience, and the doubtful hints to Pylos' connections with Hades[221] are not enough indication that Nestor's name held traces of an Underworld mythology.

---

216 See Frame (ibid.: 6 ff., 34 ff.) on the (rather speculative) linguistic and textual evidence, mainly from episodes of the first half of the *Odyssey*.
217 On Nestor's pre-Iliadic existence, cf. the famous 'Nestor's cup' from Pithekoussai in S. Italy, which dates back to the late 8th c. BC; see Graziosi 2002: 135.
218 Frame 1978: 8 ff.
219 With support from parallels from other Indo-European languages; see Pokorny 1959–69 s.v. *nes-*, Palmer 1956: 8–9; cf. Ruijgh 1967: 371–2. Frisk (1960–72, s.v. νέομαι) assumed a transitive verb *νέ(σ)ω 'save'.
220 According to Pausanias (4.36.2–3), Nestor's cattle were located in the Pylos cave; the cattle of the Sun are stationed in the cave of Tainaron (*h.Ap.* 411–3; Str. 8.5.1), a supposed entrance to the Underworld. Pylos' link with the Underworld is unclear, and perhaps only later than Homer, see next note.
221 Mainly the obscure line *Il.* 5.397 (see Kirk 1990: 102), where it is said that Herakles 'struck [Hades] among the dead'. Mühlestein (1965: 164, n.49) has further gathered some personal names connected with Pylos and the Neleids, that seem to allude to Hades – among which the name of Nestor's brother Periklymenos (cf. Klymenos, god of the nether world in *AP* and Paus.), but there is no allusion to him in the *Iliad*. He is only mentioned once in the *Odyssey* (11.286), where he is little more than a name, and receives more attention in [Hes.] *Cat.* (frr. 33a, 35 M–W), where he is killed by Herakles.

A similar sense for the name ('he who saves') is presupposed in Frame's most recent, lengthy discussion of the figure of Nestor.²²² He argues there that the Homeric Nestor reflects the Vedic hero *Nāsatyā*,²²³ who 'brings back to life' his twin brother; this implies an etymological connection between the Sanskrit name and νέομαι, which is far from uncontroversial.²²⁴ Nestor occasionally fails in the function of 'saviour': in the *Odyssey* (3.159–66), it is implied that he could not convince Odysseus to follow him on the return voyage (but he manages to bring his fellow warriors back safely in the war episode narrated in *Il.* 11). In Frame's argument, this failure is felt to be present in Homeric poetic consciousness, particularly in the *Odyssey* and in certain episodes relating to Odysseus' homecoming.²²⁵ But Nestor differs from *Nāsatyā* significantly: he did not have a twin brother (he had eleven brothers according to *Il.* 11.692, who had all perished). Moreover, the Vedic hero brings his brother back to life *literally*, while Nestor employs his wisdom to protect and save others (even if not always successfully). But Frame is right that Nestor's name should also bear a connection to *noos*, since wisdom can be seen as a vital trait in a saviour figure.²²⁶ He thus reconfirms the two basic possible etymological connections of the name (with *noos* and *neomai*). As we have seen, the Homeric epics include hints at the appropriateness of both these etymologies, but notably the latter (*neomai*) has greater poetic relevance. The name's association with pre-Homeric and / or non-Greek mythology may hold some charms, but is difficult to prove.

2.2.2 Phoinix

Phoinix is an important figure in the *Iliad*; he plays a crucial part in book 9, as a member of the delegation sent to Achilles in order to convince him to return to battle.²²⁷ Research in the meaning of his name is made compelling by the fact

---

222 Frame 2009: 9–94.
223 This is the pair corresponding to the Dioskouroi, the Aśvins; see M.L. West 2007a: 187.
224 See Beekes 2010 s.v. νέομαι.
225 See especially ch. 7, where he argues that the Phaeacians were created by the poet of the *Odyssey* to establish a correspondence to Nestor; but see also below, under 'Some Phaeacian names.'
226 Frame 2009: 93–4.
227 He appears also in *Il.* 16.196 and 19.311 (γέρων ἱππηλάτα Φοῖνιξ), in 23.360 as the ὀπάων of Peleus (see Edwards 1991: 271, Richardson 1993: 213), and 14.136a (line added by Zenodotus). Iris appears in Phoinix's form in 17.555, 561 (it must be our Phoinix, judging by the vocative γεραιέ). His personal history (9.43 ff.) is of particular interest: like in the story of Meleagros, which he narrates, the parent's curse plays a crucial role; see S.R. West 2001: 13. He has something in com-

that the presence of Phoinix in the embassy to Achilles is in all likelihood the poet's own addition to the story.²²⁸

The name is etymologically significant. Φοῖνιξ evokes the adjective or noun φοῖνιξ,²²⁹ a Homeric word: as an adjective 'red, dark red', it is used of a horse (bay) in *Il.* 23.454, and as a noun it means 'red or purple (as a pigment or dye)' (*Il.* 4.141, 6.219, 7.305, 15.538, cf. *Od.* 23.201); there is also φοινικόεις (only feminine, 'red or purple', *Il.* 23.717, 10.133) and the compound φοινικοπάρῃος ('red-prowed', epithet of ships in *Od.* 11.124, 23.271). φοῖνιξ comes from φοινός 'red';²³⁰ Phoinix could accordingly mean 'red-haired' or 'tanned, sunburnt, dark-skinned'. Notably Phoinix is the name of a stream in Herodotus (7.176, 200), identified by the red or rusty colour of its waters due to the presence of iron, and the name of the mythical bird of Egypt which had red wings (Hdt. 2.73 and Hes. fr. 304 M-W).²³¹

It is not clear how the meaning 'red' or 'red-haired' could suit our Phoinix. It could denote a physical characteristic associated with the hero, but no such hint is present in the epics. The name could alternatively be read as an ethnic, 'the Phoinician'.²³² Names of heroes sometimes denote provenance (another Homeric character with an ethnic name is Aigyptios, an Ithacan, *Od.* 2.15), and there are mentions of the Phoinician people in Homer (*Il.* 23.744, and more often in the *Odyssey*, where in fact all occurrences²³³ are of the ethnic, and none of the personal name). The ethnic has been thought appropriate for a paidagogue, in ad-

---

mon with Patroklos too: both came to Peleus' court in rather sinister circumstances. Griffin (1995: 44 ff.) further sees Phoinix's narrative 'almost like a burlesque of Achilles' story'.
228 See Page 1959: 297–304. This view is encouraged by the use of dual forms during the preparation of the embassy that seem to exclude Phoinix, and by the fact that he first appears in book 9 and on a few occasions *after* book 9. Cf. M.L. West 2011a: 13–4, 218–9. Note also that as Achilles' paidagogue he holds the place traditionally assigned to Chiron; cf. Burgess 2001: 85–6. But he was not necessarily *invented* for the *Iliad* (as Mühlestein thought, 1981: 90); see below.
229 See Chantraine 1999 s.v. φοῖνιξ (1). It should be accented paroxytone, not properispomenon, as the iota is long.
230 Chantraine ibid.; cf. Beekes 2010 s.v. Φοίνικες (he notes that the suffix -ικ- is probably pre-Greek).
231 The bird-name may be of foreign origin (Egyptian or Phoinician, with Greek adaptation of the pronunciation?) See Chantraine 1999 s.v. φοῖνιξ (5).
232 φοῖνιξ is believed to have been chosen by the Greeks as an ethnic for the Phoinicians because they had red, sunburnt skin (less likely because of their connection with purpura). See Chantraine 1999 s.v. φοῖνιξ (2). The etymological meaning, however, would gradually stop being noticed in an ethnic.
233 13.272, 14.288, 15.415, 419, 473.

herence with the habit of using ethnics as slave names[234] – though Phoinix is not a slave. The Iliadic Phoinix does not otherwise seem to have anything to do with Phoinike, but there is one namesake who does: the eponym and founder of the Phoinicians, brother of Kadmos, son of Agenor, king of Tyre, mentioned once in the *Iliad* (14.321, as the father of Europa; also mentioned in Apollod. 3.183 as the father of Adonis). The mythical founder of Phoinike, however, is by no means a strong presence in the *Iliad* and there is no reason why the name of a Thessalian hero would allude to him. None of the name's contexts suggest a particular significance.

It has been suggested that the name's appropriateness in the *Iliad* could be based on the close connection between Phoinix and the story he narrates:[235] his role is similar to that of Oineus, who in the parable approaches Meleagros just as Phoinix approaches Achilles (in an embassy, to plead for the hero's change of mind) and for a similar purpose (the hero's return to battle); Phoinix as a paidagogue is a parallel to Oineus as a father. The same formula, γέρων ἱππηλάτα 'old horseman', is applied to both: to Phoinix in 9.432 (cf. 16.196, 19.311) and to Oineus in 9.581; this formula only occurs in the *Iliad* in connection with these two and (perhaps not coincidentally!) with Peleus (9.438, cf. 7.125, 11.772, 18.331).[236] A possible implication is that the inspiration for the role of Phoinix was drawn from Oineus.[237] Mühlestein further thought that the two names (which are metrically equivalent) might be semantically close: the name of Οἰνεύς is clearly related to wine; wine plays an important role in the Phoinix discourse (cf. 9.489, 491, 469, 579), and Phoinix may mean 'Red', which could reflect the colour of red wine. However, the two names are not similar in sound, which certainly hinders any semantic correlation between them. Additionally, neither φοίνιξ nor φοινός are used for wine.[238] Mühlestein's argumentation would also presuppose that Phoinix's character is entirely or primarily dependent on the Meleagros story, which is not the case; he was clearly involved in other stories too, before and after he

---

234 See M.L. West 2011a: 219, citing an old source.
235 Mühlestein 1969: 83–6.
236 In the *Odyssey* the same formula (coming from an old Aitolian epos?) is used of Nestor (3.436, 444); in the *Iliad*, the metrically equivalent (and mysterious) Γερήνιος ἱππότα is used of him (2.336 etc.).
237 Thus Mühlestein 1969: 84–5.
238 This has led Mühlestein (1969: 86) to the far-fetched assumption that the name was suggested by the firebrand which turns red (the colour of blood) as Meleagros dies. A reference to the red firebrand with the desired vocabulary is found in Aeschylus (δαφοινὸν δαλὸν *Ch.* 607–8; δαφοινὸν is apparently etymologically connected with φοινός, cf. Chantraine 1999 s.v. φοινός), but there is no mention of the firebrand in the *Iliad*. His suggestion (1981: 91) that the name may be a compound of φοινός and ἱκέτης, is unconvincing.

became connected with Achilles.²³⁹ Even in the *Iliad*, the hero's presentation (9.168) and self-introduction suggest that he was a familiar character to the audience, and that his biography was not invented from scratch but adjusted to the Homeric narrative.²⁴⁰

Phoinix's odd self-presentation is perhaps a better place to look for clues regarding the name. He narrates how he left his home after having been cursed by his father for seducing his concubine, which he agreed to do in order to satisfy his mother's wish. S.R. West has suggested that this rather inconsequential story is an adaptation of an older, fuller version, where Phoinix was the victim of castration as a punishment by his father.²⁴¹ Could φοινός allude to blood and the wound caused by the punishment? (the adjective is used in *Il.* 16.159 in reference to blood). This is possible, especially if the reconstructed Phoinix tale was a well-known story among the Iliadic audience.

The meanings of the names in Phoinix's genealogy (*Il.* 9.448; cf. 10.266) sound generically heroic, but may also appear relevant to the narrative function served by Phoinix. The father's name Ἀμύντωρ means 'defender'; the grandfather's name Ὄρμενος (in the patronymic form Ὁρμενίδης) could be from ὄρνυμαι, a verb used of heroes rising to a call (commonly in the past ὦρτο, e.g. the games in 23.288 and *passim*, for the Phaeacians in *Od.* 8.111, cf. 7.162–3).²⁴² By an ingenious coincidence (?), both names could sound relevant to the purpose of the advice given by Phoinix to Achilles.²⁴³ The name Ἀμύντωρ evokes the hero's function as a defender of his people and country, and this indeed will be Achilles' duty when he returns to battle; ἀμύνειν is used in Phoinix's speech (between l.435 and 602) eight times. Phoinix wishes Achilles to rise up to fight, and this meaning would perhaps be 'read' in the grandfather's name. ὄρνυμαι is appropriately used in the preparation of the embassy to Achilles (8.474), where it is said that Hektor will not be stopped before Achilles ὄρθαι, and again in book 9 itself, where we hear that Achilles will fight again

---

239 Cf. *N.Pauly* s.v. Phoinix (2) (R. Nünlist).
240 See S.R. West 2001: 3 ff.
241 Ibid. 8 ff. This should explain some of the strange elements in the story (Amyntor's curse, the behaviour of friends and relations), while it suits the fact that Phoinix became Achilles' paidagogue despite his non-commendable acts; also Plutarch's testimony of the lines 458–61 (allegedly deleted by Aristarchus from Phoinix's speech) containing parricidal thoughts would make more sense as a reaction to a severe punishment. The fuller version of the story may have been present in the *Cypria* or the *Aithiopis*.
242 Grammatically the name amounts to the participle, which is only used in the *Iliad* twice in the neuter with πῦρ (17.737–8; 21.13–4) – apparently formulaically.
243 See Mühlestein 1969: 81–3.

when θεὸς ὅρσῃ (9.703) (but these references are not close enough to Phoinix's discourse).

Phoinix's personal story may add additional significance to the name Amyntor: Amyntor 'defends' himself against his son's conduct and retaliates with the curse. Phoinix's conduct may further imply the hero's attempt to overthrow his father,[244] in which case Amyntor defends his throne against the ambition of the son. The name is used only one other time, in *Il.* 10 as the name of the victim of the helmet's theft by Autolykos (10.267); an irony could be felt in the fact that the 'defender' by name failed to protect the item.[245] There is confusion regarding whether the two Amyntors were the same person or two different individuals;[246] the kingdom of Phoinix's father is Hellas (as opposed to Peleus' Phthie, see 9.447–8, 478–9), while the Amyntor of 10.266 comes from Eleon (in Boiotia, cf. 2.500). Finally, Phoinix's Thessalian provenance makes possible another interpretation for Ormenos: the name may be meant as an ethnic, from Ormenion in Thessaly (cf. *Il.* 2.734).[247]

2.3 Helen

Traditionally regarded as the cause of the Trojan war, Helen is a very important character in Homer and an object of uninterrupted scholarly interest.[248] She appears in both epics, while in the *Iliad* she is one of the few female figures in what is primarily a men's world.[249] However, the epic context does not suggest an ob-

---

[244] S.R. West (2001: 5) thinks it is possible that Phoinix's story was 'a trivialisation of an enterprise more worthy of a hero'.
[245] Thus Mühlestein 1969: 82–3.
[246] See Hainsworth 1993: 121–2; Scholia on *Il.* 10.266, Eust. 762.3 ff., Strabo 9.5.18; *LfgrE* s.v. Ἀμύντ(ωρ) (G. Steiner) assumes two different individuals. M. Finkelberg in *HE* (s.v. Amyntor) suggests 'uncertainty concerning Amyntor's whereabouts.' A simple explanation might be that the poet of *Il.* 10 made use of a name already at hand and in poetic memory, without much care for the details.
[247] Cf. von Kamptz 1982 (1958): 154 and *LfgrE* s.v. Ὄρμενος (V. Langholf). But note the uncertainty expressed in Kirk (1985: 234) about where exactly the Iliadic Ormenion was. Note also that the name is used for other heroes, two Trojans (8.274, 12.187) and the grandfather of Eumaios (*Od.* 18.414); von Kamptz 1982 (1958): 247 etymologised these from ὄρνυμαι.
[248] Cf. the two recent book-length contributions by Maguire (2009) and Blondell (2013).
[249] On *Iliad*'s women see Farron 1979, who identifies four significant female characters: Helen, Andromache, Hekabe and Briseis. This chapter discusses the names of the first three; Briseis' name (Βρισηΐς) is, like Chryseis' (Χρυσηΐς), a patronymic; see also Latacz 2000b: 85.

vious connection between her character's function and her name, and it may be futile to look for a 'scientific' etymology.[250]

Helen's name first gains an obvious significance in Aeschylus' famous pun (*Ag.* 681–9: τίς ποτ' ὠνόμαξεν ὧδ' / ἐς τὸ πᾶν ἐτητύμως– /... Ἑλέναν; ἐπεὶ πρεπόντως ἑλέναυς[251] ἕλανδρος ἑλέπτολις... 'Who was it that gave a name so utterly appropriate-... Helen? For in keeping with that name she brought hell to ships, to men, to cities...' [transl. Sommerstein]). Hekabe's warning to Menelaos about Helen's potential to cause destruction in Euripides' *Trojan women* (891–3) has a similar sense: ὁρᾶν δὲ τήνδε φεῦγε, μή σ' ἕληι πόθωι. / αἱρεῖ γὰρ ἀνδρῶν ὄμματ', ἐξαιρεῖ πόλεις, / πίμπρησιν οἴκους· (the use of ἕληι and αἱρεῖ echoes the Aeschylean pun) 'But whatever you do, don't look at her, don't look at her eyes: they ambush with desire, they snare the eyes of men, and as for her, she's hell for cities, burning hell for homes' (transl. Shapiro). Perhaps a pun was also heard between Ἑλένης and Ἑλληνίδ' (ἐς γῆν; the land of Greece) at 877–8 (at the start of two subsequent lines); similarly also in *Helen* 561–3 (Ἑλληνίς ... Ἑλένηι). These puns may imply the significant place of Helen's story in Greek myth.[252] Other possible post-Homeric puns on the name include a fragment of Sosibius (*FGrH* 595 F 20), of ca. 200 BC, which suggests an image of Helen as the 'corposant' hostile to ships;[253] on the other hand, Euripides (*Or.* 1637) introduces a Helen who is benevolent to sailors.[254]

A search for a possible Homeric meaning for the name might profit from exploring the content of the Aeschylean pun. The *Odyssey* has similar phrasing in the vicinity of the name at one point (11.438, Ἑλένης μὲν ἀπωλόμεθ' εἵνεκα πολλοί 'For Helen's sake many of us perished'), but it is hard to tell whether this constitutes a deliberate word-play: the element ἑλ- is repeatedly used in Homer in the past tense forms of αἱρέω 'destroy', which is a common verb; and the sound of the name Ἑλένη clearly involves more than this element. It can be argued, however, that the connection of the Homeric Helen with αἱρέω

---

250 Chantraine 1999 s.v. Ἑλένη.
251 'ship-destroying': Blomfield's emendation (ms: ἑλένας), not always favoured by editors, but adopted by Sommerstein in his recent Loeb edition of the play. The word-play indeed demands the reading ἑλέναυς.
252 As noted by Blondell 2013: 200, 218. She detects (ibid.: 133, 227–8) similar puns in Aeschylus (*Ag.* 429, though Helen's name is not mentioned) and Isocrates' *Encomium of Helen*. ἑλὼν / Ἑλλάδι, spoken of Helen in E. *Tr.* 1114–5, may also suggest a pun, if the MS reading is preferred to Wilamowitz's emendation ἔχων (adopted by Kovacs in the recent Loeb).
253 This may imply an old popular belief, possibly also reflected in the Aeschylean ἑλέναυς.
254 A function elsewhere attributed to her brothers, the Dioskouroi (Puhvel 1987: 142). This perception of Helen may be an *ad hoc* invention that reverses literary tradition to pleasantly surprise the audience, as Willink (1986: 352) argues.

has further support in the epic. The kind of action that the verb implies is not alien to Helen's characterisation, as the idea that she was the cause of much trouble is present in Homer. The *Iliad* includes references to her responsibility for the war (2.161, 9.339, 19.325, 22.114), and she is presented as aware of her guilt (e.g. 6.344). Notably the diction surrounding her name in the *Iliad* often suggests a dangerous and hated character (e.g. 'abhorred Helen' in Achilles' words, 19.325; the Trojan leaders wish her gone, 'not to be left here to be a bane', 3.159–60), and she sees herself this way: *Il.* 6.344 and 356 (Helen to Hektor: 'O brother of me that I am a dog, a contriver of mischief and abhorred by all'; 'Trouble [has] encompassed your mind because of shameless me'); similarly 3.180 ('shameless me'), 3.404 ('hateful me'), 24.775 ('all men shudder at me').[255] In the *Odyssey* too she seems 'morally trivial',[256] as she prepares a drink that causes forgetfulness of evils (4.221), thus symbolically posing a threat – even if a temporary one – to memory, the essential means of survival of epic *kleos* and poetry. In Homer αἱρέω is sometimes used of feelings and mental states (e.g. θάμβος δ' ἕλε πάντας 'amazement fell upon everyone', *Od.* 3.372), and it could thus allude to the power of Helen's beauty to control the feelings and behaviour of men (such an allusion is found in the above mentioned Euripidean excerpt: μή σ' ἕληι πόθωι).

Helen's responsibility for the war, however, is not the only (perhaps not even the main) element of her characterisation. In the *Iliad*, much emphasis is given on her dependence on Aphrodite (cf. 3.383–447), whose commands she is too weak to resist.[257] In the *Odyssey*, though there are still some references to her guilt (e.g. she is cursed by Eumaios at 14.68–9), the prevailing image of her is not negative,[258] and the emphasis is placed on her extraordinary experiences, which are already the stuff of legend, and for which she is not personally condemned (cf. 23.21 ff.). One might note that the central element in all that concerns Helen is her beauty (cf. *Il.* 9.140, 282, 3.14 ff.),[259] and it is reasonable to

---

255 Cf. Clader 1976: 17–8.
256 Thus Schein (1995: 23). She is seen as morally responsible for her actions (Katz 1991). On the history of the blame placed on Helen by posterity see Maguire 2009: 10 ff.
257 See *LfgrE* s.v. Ἑλένη (B. Mader). On Helen's familiarity with Aphrodite see also M.L. West (2011a: 136), who notes that she even shows a lack of respect towards the goddess by repenting her elopement.
258 Schein (1995: 23) rightly notes that this epic features a rather sympathetic treatment of the heroine. There are moments of sympathy for Helen in the *Iliad* too, when she shows remorse, is portayed in the same manner as a virtuous woman (doing a typical woman's work), and is ready to criticise Paris. See M.L. West (2011a: 130, 183), with references; he considers this view of Helen as 'possibly untraditional'.
259 See further Blondell 2013: 26 and *passim*.

ask whether her name could contain a relevant hint. One of the etymologies proposed sees it as a cognate of σέλας[260] – could the name connote the sense of 'light' and thus allude to the heroine's 'shining' beauty?[261] σέλας is a Homeric word (cf. *Il*. 19.366, *Od*. 21.246), but it does not seem to have been used in connection with beauty; its usual meaning is 'blaze, glow, brightness' (mainly of fire). Still it is significant that images involving light were used in the epic to express beauty, cf. *Il*. 6.401: Ἑκτορίδην ἀγαπητὸν, ἀλίγκιον ἀστέρι καλῷ 'the well-loved son of Hektor, like a fair star'. One difficulty is that σέλας is not close enough phonetically to Helen's name – at least in the form that we know it from the epics; nor does it occur in its vicinity.

The fact that the name is not easily explicable in the Greek language and within the epics allows room for the possibility that it originated from a different language, and that it may have been inspired or borrowed from foreign literature. It has been suggested that Helen's name may be explained with the help of Vedic literature.[262] This effort is compromised by the different attested forms (some include a digamma, some not), which make it difficult for us to pin it down to a particular Indo-European root. Skutsch attempts to overcome this difficulty by proposing two different roots, which should suggest two different names for two separate initial deities (each with a different meaning), and by speculating that the Homeric Helen is a fusion of the two. The first potential 'model' for Helen, the Vedic Saraṇyū, indeed shares similarities with Helen: she is associated with a pair of twin brothers (a parallel to the Dioskouroi),[263] but as their mother; she abandons her husband leaving an εἴδωλον. The meaning of the name in the Vedic, 'swift', is suitable for the concept of a runaway wife. The second possible prototype is associated with an etymology from a root *suel-* (this would cover the Greek forms with digamma), which should imply the meaning 'the shining one' (a similar meaning to what the σέλας etymology would imply).[264]

---

260 Von Kamptz 1982 (1958): 136.
261 Cf. references to her bright hair (πλοκάμους φαεινούς, *Il*. 14.176) and shining garments (ἑανῷ ἀργῆτι φαεινῷ, *Il*. 3.419). On the (rather scant) details of Helen's appearance found in classical authors see Maguire (2009: 45–9), who notes that Helen's beauty is largely demonstrated by its effect on others (see e.g. *Il*. 3.156–7), and by her visual similarities to goddesses.
262 Skutsch 1987: 189, Puhvel 1987: 141–3.
263 The Vedic Aśvins, see Puhvel 1987: 64, 142; M.L. West 2007a: 230–2.
264 De Simone 1978: 40–2; M.L. West ibid. This etymology was assumed by Puhvel (1987: 59, 142–3), who associated Helen with the Vedic Sūryā, the sun-maid daughter of the sun-god, wife of the Aśvins. Skutsch (1987) assumed a vegetation goddess; such a cult of Helen existed at Sparta (Hdt. 6.61) and at Rhodes (as Ἑλένα Δενδρῖτις, Paus. 3.19.9–10). Cf. Nilsson 1932: 252, but see recently Edmunds (2007: 1 ff.), who argues against the possibility that these rituals generated Helen's myth). Solmsen (1901: 105) suggested a goddess of light. M.L. West (1975: 7–13)

It is not impossible for an epic name to merge several sources of meaning, but the complicated two-deities hypothesis is supported by little linguistic and archaeological evidence (an Indo-European prototype is not to be denied, but the issue is impossibly complex).²⁶⁵ The Homeric Helen is certainly depicted as a very powerful female, akin to the divine;²⁶⁶ there is in fact a scholarly consensus that the origins of the figure were divine, even if the connection between goddess and heroine is obscure.²⁶⁷ However, as far as Homer is concerned, the view of Helen as a goddess must be secondary to Helen the epic heroine;²⁶⁸ possible 'theophoric' meanings for the name may be seen as re-interpretations of its epic sense. This includes efforts to explain the name with the help of ritual vocabulary: Ἑλένη as a semantic back-formation from ἐλενηφόρια,²⁶⁹ a feast in honour of one of the gods which could be (but is not certainly) Helen, is unlikely; none of the words that are phonetically equivalent to Helen (ἑλένη 'wicker-basket' for carrying the sacred utensils for the feast, ἑλάνη / ἑλένη 'torch' and ἑλένιον 'calamint', a plant²⁷⁰) have to be associated with ancient worship, and they may well be later usages which reflect different aspects of the heroine's associations: thus ἑλάνη / ἑλένη 'torch' may be the result of her association with light and may function as additional support to a light-related interpretation of her name, which suits both her basic characteristics, her beauty, and her di-

---

points out Helen's stay in Egypt, land of the Sun, and concludes by assuming a Sun-goddess (Daughter of the Sun). Notably Helen has also been connected with σελήνη 'moon' (which is the same root as σέλας, see Beekes 2010 s.v. σελήνη). E. *Or.* 1636–7 (she will be enthroned ἐν αἰθέρος πτυχαῖς 'in the heavens') may suggest a stellification of Helen.
265 Cf. Edmunds (2007: 2–11), who lists further potential parallels of Helen in Sanskrit literature and in the mythology of other Indo-European peoples (Lithuanian and Latvian). See also the previous note.
266 *Od.* 4.561–9 alludes to her divinity; it has often been noticed that the epic attributes unusual powers to her but never calls her a goddess. Higbie (1995: 127, 160) draws attention to the use of the epithet Ἀργείη for Helen (it is also used for the goddess Hera), and to the fact that her name appears in the naming pattern used for Paris (which also happens for Hera and Zeus); the reverse is the norm. She is also alone among mortals to recognise the disguised Odysseus during his exploration of Troy (a story she tells herself at *Od.* 4.24 ff.). Clader (1976: 53–62) suggested a typological affinity between Helen, Aphrodite and Eos (Dawn goddess).
267 See *OCD* s.v. Helen (A.L. Brown); Burkert 1985: 205. Edmunds (2007: 1 ff.) makes a strong case for Helen's myth as the explanation of her cults (which include the Attic cult at Rhamnus). See also Austin 1994: 88.
268 Cf. Farnell 1921: 32 ff. The emphasis on her human side serves the poet's artistic purposes and is in keeping with the rather rational treatment of folk-figures and elements; see Clader 1976: 39–40.
269 Thus Clader 1976: 6 ff.
270 Hsch., Chaerem. *TGrF* 1 fr. 14.12 (Snell), Thphr. *HP* 6.6.2, Dsc. 1.29.

vine side. It is perhaps significant that a relevant meaning would also be appropriate for the name of Ἕλενος, a son of Priam who had prophetic powers: he is described as 'far the best of diviners' (*Il.* 6.76 – a formula also used for Kalchas, 1.69); an allusion to 'light' in his name would suit his ability to foresee.[271]

2.4 The 'Greek' Trojans

Trojan heroes partake in the same heroic identity as the Greeks, and their naming mostly reflects this. 'Trojan' names can be just as rich in semantic power as those names that are used for the Greeks. Some names of Trojan heroes have obscure etymologies and meanings; others are perfectly understandable as Greek names – many are indeed also used for characters on the Greek side, or for Greeks in the *Odyssey*.[272] The Trojans are not presented as speakers of any language other than Greek, although the real language of Troy (mod. Hissarlik in Turkey) was definitely not Greek.[273] But poetic settings tend to ignore the linguistic difference (similarly every tribe and creature encountered by Odysseus during his travels speak Greek). Among names of the most prominent Trojans, Hektor and Andromache lack a foreign sound, while other names (Priam and Paris) are suggestive of an Anatolian origin and have obscure meanings. Such Anatolian echoes may be traces of an older tradition of referring to the Trojans by names appropriate to their foreignness; these names would later have been replaced by names of Greek origin or at least Greek sound, created by assimilation ('hellenisation') of non-Greek originals, either on the basis of existing Greek vocabulary or simply of word-building conventions. We should be cautious about resorting to foreign etymology for names of non-Greek sound: the ancient Greeks

---

[271] According to Eust. 626.25 (on *Il.* 6.73–101), Arrian recounted that he was originally called Skamandrios and changed his name to Helenos after the Thracian seer who taught him τὴν μαντικήν.
[272] For a list of these see Wathelet 1989: 29–30.
[273] The language of Troy was an Anatolian language (probably Luvian), see Watkins 1986a: 5 ff. (already Page 1959: 198–9 spoke of a non-Greek 'Trojan', but still Indo-European, language). Latacz (2004: 116–7) however questions that Luvian was the spoken language at Troy. The Trojan side in the war was marked by linguistic pluralism, given the presence of allies from various Anatolian cities, cf. *Il.* 2.803–6; 4.43 f. The name of Pandaros the Lycian (*Il.* 4) has a foreign sound, though another Lycian, Glaukos (famous as Diomedes' opponent and *xenos* in *Il.* 6) has a perfectly Greek name. The name of the Thracian Rhesos (*Il.* 6) must be foreign.

had limited access to foreign comparative material, and do not seem to have noticed similarities between their language and other languages.[274]

As is the case with many Greek heroes' names, several Greek names of Trojans may be entirely fictitious; this applies mostly to names of minor Trojan heroes that have an obvious significance. Lists of the slain mostly include Trojans, who receive names which sound like generic titles for soldiers, and which were perhaps invented for the occasion (e.g. the names of Lycians killed by Odysseus in *Il.* 5.677–8).[275] Some may be derived from Greek places (e.g. Ὄρμενος at *Il.* 8.274, 12.187, from Ormenon, a Thessalian place-name). One Trojan name seems to function as a joke: among the Trojan elders (*Il.* 3.146–8) we find one Οὐκαλέγων, 'Not-caring', who is not mentioned elsewhere (some rather insignificant information comes from Sch. T 13.42 f.), but he is remembered by Vergil (*Aeneid* 2.31 f.) because of his extraordinary name, obviously an invented mock-name for a counsellor.[276]

The names of the Trojan royal family are of primary interest, and the following sections explore their etymology and the view that the *Iliad* takes to their significance.

2.4.1 Priam, Hekabe

Lycophron (*Alexandra* 337–9) explains the name of the Trojan king Πρίαμος[277] by a story related to his youth: Priam was originally called Podarkes ('swift-foot'); when his brothers were killed by Herakles, he, being still a child, was in danger of enslavement, but was saved by Hekabe who *bought* him back: this adventure allegedly inspired the change of his name to Πρίαμος, from πρίασθαι 'buy'.[278] The story – which implies a 'hellenisation' of Priam – is nowhere alluded to in earlier literature and may well be a late invention inspired by the name's etymological sound. Priam's name in fact appears to be of very ancient origin; a very similar

---

274 In Plato's *Cratylus* (410a), Sokrates claims that he uses foreign etymology as a trick when other explanations are short (409d 3, 416a 4). See Szemerényi 1996: 2–3, Tsitsibakou-Vasalos 2007: 29–30.
275 'The Epic required nearly 200 Trojan victims', for which 'Greek names were invented in preference to bogus and probably uncouth barbarians' (Page 1959: 198). For more examples of naming of minor Trojans see Bowra (1930: 78–9).
276 On this name see also Kirk 1985: 283.
277 Perhaps a reflection of a real person (M.L. West 2011a: 41) – an unprovable assumption.
278 The story is repeated in one form or other in the ancient commentators and derivatives of Lycophron (Tz. *ad Lyc.* 34, 355, Apollod. 2.136 and Eust. 27, on *Il.* 1.18. Cf. Hyg. *Fab.* 76).

form (*pi-ri-ja-me-ja*, PY An 39, perhaps to be read *Πριαμείας[279]) is attested on the Mycenaean tablets. Scholars prefer to see it as Anatolian (from the Luvian *Pariyamuwas*),[280] rather than as a Greek name (Mycenaean records also preserve names of foreigners).[281] Another similar-sounding name, Παραμόας, attested in Asia Minor in the classical period, offers further support to the possibility of Priam's Anatolian provenance.[282]

In terms of Greek vocabulary the name Priam (in the form known to us) is closest to πρίασθαι; the pun on which Lycophron's story is based is the strongest Greek pun that the name might allow.[283] The effort to treat the name as a compound and examine possible components is not very rewarding: Πρί- and -αμος, though used in some Greek words, hardly mean anything in Greek and are probably of foreign origin.[284] A dialectic (Lesbian) variation of the name, Πέρ(ρ)αμος (used by Sappho and Alcaeus),[285] is glossed by Hesychius with βασιλεύς. The gloss might imply Priam's capacity as king of Troy, but it is much more likely that it simply explains πέρραμος as meaning 'king'. This may still create the impression that the name is etymologically associated with a term that is related to Priam's kingship – with *primus* /πρίν[286] or Πέργαμος (the highest part of Ilion, where Priam's house presumably was).[287] The epic, however, offers no relevant puns.

Ἑκάβη is hardly an easier name. Priam's wife is said to be the sister of a Phrygian man of the name Asios (*Il*. 16.717) – a name which is again mentioned (though now possibly belonging to a different Trojan) in connection with the probably Hittite Hyrtakos (*Il*. 13.759, 771).[288] All this may imply that the name Hekabe, like Priam, could be of Eastern origin;[289] but it cannot be excluded that it

---

279 See Chadwick-Baumbach 1963: 240 and Jorro-Adrados 1985 s.v. *pi-ri-ja-me-ja*. Cf. Page 1959: 199.
280 Laroche (1970/2: 126, n.32; 325; 364) thought Πρίαμος to be a contracted form of the Luvian name. Cf. Watkins (1986a: 56–8) and now M.L. West (2011a: 41).
281 On this see further Varias 1998/9: 35 ff.
282 Near Kaisareia in Cappadocia; see Zgusta 1964: 417.
283 Note that there are hardly any personal names from this verb (one Ἀπριάτη is noted by Beekes 2010 s.v. πρίασθαι [2nd-1st c. BC, *LGPN* IV]).
284 Cf. Wathelet 1988: 910 with bibliography.
285 Sappho fr. 44.16 Voigt; Alcaeus fr. 42.2 Voigt.
286 Beekes 2010 s.v. πρίν.
287 Cf. Wathelet 1988: 909. On Pergamos see Kirk 1985: 393.
288 See Watkins 1986a: 54–5.
289 Cf. von Kamptz 1982 (1958): 140. The name Ϝεκάβᾱ is attested on two Korinthian vases of the 6th c. BC; see Wachter 2001: 365 (Index s.v. Ϝεκάβᾱ), cf. Bechtel 1921–4, v.2: 217, 237 – but this is of course the Trojan queen.

acquired some sense in Greek. It has in fact been etymologised as Greek name from ἑκαβόλος (ἑκηβόλος) 'who strikes from afar',²⁹⁰ a common epithet of Apollo (Il. 1.438 etc.; cf. ἑκατηβόλος, 16.711 etc.). The first part of the name evokes also another standard epithet of the god, ἑκάεργος 'who works from afar' (Il. 15.243 etc.). One might be tempted to think that Troy's queen has a name that alludes to the god who is a chief supporter of her people, but the phonetic similarity is not strong enough to guarantee the connection. The only other Homeric personal name starting with ἑκα-, Ἑκαμήδη (name of a captive slave girl from Tenedos, Il. 11.624, 14.6),²⁹¹ seems equally unconnected.

In fact, the first part of Hekabe's name may evoke anything from ἑκάς 'far' and ἑκών ('of one's own will') to the number ἑκατό(ν) 'a hundred'. This last possibility seems better suited to the second part of the name, more plausibly etymologised as a contraction from βοῦς 'ox' (cf. ἑκατόμβη 'sacrifice [of a hundred oxen]') than as a contracted feminine form of -βόλος.²⁹² Puns are absent in Homer, but incidentally Hekabe's name was connected to the animal world in a different context: according to an ancient Scholium on Euripides (Hec. 3), the name was used in Orphic poetry as a metonymy for a sow because of its fecundity, and Hekabe was called Χοιρίλη (from χοίρα, feminine of χοῖρος 'sow') by the historian Philochorus.²⁹³ The *Iliad* tells us that Hekabe was the mother of 19 sons (24.496). Perhaps the name was seen – already in the Homeric context – as a designation of the womanly and motherly functions that Hekabe represented. *Iliad*'s Hekabe is otherwise a rather passive character,²⁹⁴ whose action is dependent on one of her children, her favourite son Hektor (cf. 6.251–311, 24.193–227).

---

290 Bechtel 1914: 116; Chantraine 1999 s.v. Ἑκάβη.
291 On which see below, under 'Minor' speaking names.
292 Cf. Meister (1921: 228, n.2) who connects the name with female names of the type Σθενέβοια, Ἠρίβοια, Ἀλφεσίβοια. There is also Ἑκατόμβιος, an epithet of Apollo (e.g. SEG 38, 665; ca. 100 BC) and a personal name (one attestation from Thrace (4ᵗʰ c. BC, LGPN IV) and two from Asia Minor (Ionia, 5ᵗʰ–4ᵗʰ c. BC, LGPN VA); cf. Ἑκάτομβος / Ἑκάτονβος (two attestations from 3ᵗʰ c. BC Thessaly, LGPN IIIB).
293 Φιλόχορος μὲν γὰρ ἐν τῶι Περὶ τραγωιδιῶν συγγράμματι Χοιρίλην αὐτήν φησι καλεῖσθαι, ἴσως δὲ διὰ τὸ πολύπαιδα γεγενῆσθαι· ἡ γὰρ χοῖρος πολλὰ τίκτει, καὶ ἐν τοῖς Ὀρφικοῖς αἱ χοῖραι ἑκάβαι προσαγορεύονται (FGrH 328 F 90; fr. 402 Bernabé). This is not the only connection between Hekabe and the animal world: in E. Hec. 1265–6 it is predicted that she will be turned into a bitch (cf. Apollod. 5.23).
294 See also OCD s.v. Hecuba (A.L. Brown).

2.4.2 Hektor, Astyanax, Andromache

Hektor, the premier Trojan warrior, is very important for the part of the Trojan saga that involves Achilles, but as has been suggested already,[295] this part is not necessary for the story of the Trojan war. Indeed Hektor, unlike his brother Paris, does not do anything essential to the story of the Trojan war and has been seen as an invention for the Iliadic plot.[296] His origins, however, may lie outside the *Iliad* in a very old tradition.[297] The form of his name may suggest that his heroic role had evolved in a Greek context;[298] Ἕκτωρ is a normal Greek formation, attested as early as Mycenaean.[299] As a compound it has many parallels (e. g. Ἄκτωρ from ἄγω), and its main element occurs in numerous personal names, among which also some heroic names (e. g. Ἔχεκλος, *Il.* 16.694; Ἐχέπωλος, *Il.* 23.296).

The name clearly suggests the meaning 'he who has and / or holds together', which is suitable for a leader of a city, who is a king's son and the greatest Trojan defender. This etymology, which was attributed to the name already in antiquity (Plato *Cra.* 393a-b; cf. Sch. T *Il.* 24.730 *ex.*), lurks also in Homer: Andromache's use of ἔχω in 24.730 (ἔχες δ'ἀλόχους κεδνὰς καὶ νήπια τέκνα 'you who kept safe the noble wives and little ones [of Troy]') sounds as a pun on her husband's name. Hektor's function as Troy's mainstay, as well as the prop of his immediate family, is emphasised in the *Iliad* (cf. his encounter with his wife in book 6, 39 ff., especially 6.403 οἷος γὰρ ἐρύετο Ἴλιον Ἕκτωρ 'for only Hektor guarded Ilion'). Notably a common noun ἕκτωρ appears at 24.272 as a *varia lectio* of ἔστωρ, apparently an object with the function of holding fast.[300]

---

295 See above, p. 30.
296 See M.L. West 2011a: 45. Different view in Burgess 2001: 63–5 (with bibliography), who notes Hektor's presence outside the *Iliad*, most prominently as the slayer of Protesilaos in the *Cypria* (M.L. West, however, finds good reason to consider this tradition as 'no doubt secondary', ibid.: 120).
297 Janko 1982: 92, M.L. West 1988; together with Paris, they may be seen to form a pair reflecting the Indo-European brother pair. Burgess (2001: 63–5) refers to artistic depictions drawing on non-Homeric myth (cf. *LIMC* s.v. Hektor [O. Touchefeu-Meynier]) and argues that Hektor's wife and son also have an old presence in the tradition (ibid: 65–6).
298 Hektor is associated with Thebes in later sources. According to Pausanias (9.18.5), the Delphic oracle had ordered the transfer of his remains to Thebes. On the view that he was originally a mainland hero see e. g. Dowden 1992: 67.
299 See Jorro-Adrados 1985 s.v. *e-ko-to*; cf. the adjective *e-ko-to-ri-jo* =*Ἑκτόριος (probably a patronymic).
300 ἔστορι, with *v.l.* ἔκτορι. The latter term (acc. plur., ἔκτορας) is used of anchors in Lyc. 100; cf. Hsch. s.v. ἔκτορες· πάσσαλοι ἐν ῥυμῷ. The word is finally found in an obscure Sapphic fragment (fr. 180 Voigt: ἔκτορες, 'holders' ... the name Sappho gives to Zeus (?) [transl. Campbell]).

The above is not the only possible explanation of the name. It would be hard to disregard the fact that the king's son and first warrior is in *possession* of material goods and power, and it is not impossible that ἔχω was meant to contain a relevant allusion. The name may be loaded with a touch of irony or tragic feeling, as the audience was well aware that all of Hektor's efforts to protect his family and his countrymen would eventually fail, and that everything he possessed and fought for would eventually be lost: his city, his wife and child, his very life. The poet of the *Iliad* seems to allude to this in the following pun: at 5.472–3, Sarpedon worries that Hektor, his people's mainstay until now, may be losing force (Ἕκτορ, πῇ δή τοι μένος οἴχεται, ὃ πρὶν ἔχεσκες; / φῇς που ἄτερ λαῶν πόλιν ἑξέμεν ἠδ' ἐπικούρων... 'Hektor, where now is the force gone that before you had? You thought, I suppose, that without men and allies you would hold the city alone...').[301]

The name of Hektor's son bears no etymological similarity to the name Hektor, but expresses a similar notion. A passage from the *Iliad* demonstrates this clearly: Ἀστυάναξ, ὃν Τρῶες ἐπίκλησιν καλέουσιν· / οἶος γάρ σφιν ἔρυσο πύλας καὶ τείχεα μακρά 'Astyanax, whom the Trojans call by this name since, Hektor, you alone saved their gates and their high walls' (22.506–7; cf. Pl. *Cra.* 392b-e); notably ἔρυσο is the same verb that is used for Hektor at 6.403. The passage suggests that the name was felt to express a capacity of the child's father; but it is also an appropriate name for the little boy who would have been king, had it not been for the Trojan war. However, this was not the child's only name; Hektor used an entirely different one, Σκαμάνδριος (*Il.* 6.402–3: τόν ῥ' Ἕκτωρ καλέεσκε Σκαμάνδριον, αὐτὰρ οἱ ἄλλοι / Ἀστυάνακτ'·). This name was probably of Anatolian origin (a Trojan hunter killed by Menelaos in *Il.* 5.49 is also called Skamandrios – perhaps an Anatolian stock name?) but reflected the Greek habit of naming children after rivers.[302] Conversely, the name Astyanax is unique to Hektor's son.

The double naming of Hektor's son may imply the character's age and firm presence in the tradition;[303] it can also be paralleled with that of the river Skamandros, which also has two names: Skamandros is the name used by men, a name which sounded foreign and insignificant to Greek ears. On the other

---

301 This outcome is prepared by Hektor's military deficiencies (cf. especially his combat with Achilles, where he is turned to flight), a noticeable element in his characterisation, as Farron (1978) argued; he saw Hektor as a carefully constructed character, whose devotion to his family and sense of duty, in combination with his martial shortcomings, bestow him with a tragic touch.
302 See further under 'Minor' speaking names.
303 As Burgess thinks (2001: 66).

hand, gods use the name Ξάνθος, a Greek name of potentially appropriate meaning[304] (cf. *Il.* 20.74). This falls within the recognised pattern of 'language of gods vs language of men':[305] the names used by gods should be seen as the original, 'true' names. The name preferred by gods in this case, insofar as it is significant, may imply the poet's inclination to regard significant names as 'superior'. This superiority is further implied in the case of the naming of Hektor's son, where the name Astyanax is given more prominence (it is heard a total of three times in two different books) than the comparatively less meaningful alternative, mentioned only once in the epic.

The name of Hektor's wife, Ἀνδρομάχη, is another genuinely Greek name: it is rarely attested,[306] but there are plenty of attestations of the male form in the archaic, as well as the classical period. The name's meaning has been explained as 'she who fights against men'.[307] The name seems to presuppose an adjective ἀνδρομάχος, but the latter only occurs in later poetry, in *AP* 7.241 (χερσὶν ... ἀνδρομάχοις) and *AP* 11.378 (ἀλόχου τῆς ἀνδρομάχης). These examples reinforce the usual explanation of the Homeric name, while the adjective in the second poem, designating a wife who is hostile to her husband, is identical in form to the Homeric name – perhaps the adjective was inspired by the name. The sense of the name has a certain 'Amazonian ring',[308] but Andromache's characterisation is not reminiscent of an Amazon: a meaning 'fighter' is not relevant to her character in the *Iliad*, where she is presented as extremely fearful of the war's possible outcome and entirely dependent on Hektor (cf. especially their meeting in book 6).[309] Her portrayal further emphasises her performance of typical female duties (8.187–9, cf. 6.490–2). Her attitude may even seem to contradict the sense of her name at 6.433–9, when she advises Hektor to take a defensive stance in the war in order to stay safe – advice that Hektor declares he would be too ashamed to follow, as it would be a sign of cowardice. Andromache eventually deplores her husband's military prowess that led to what she sees as a sad end

---

304 The adjective ξανθός 'yellow, blond', is mainly used of horses (a proper name for one of Achilles' horses, *Il.* 16.149) and men's hair; but here it may express the colour of the water when light reflects on it. Cf. the definition of the colour in Pl. *Ti.* 68b (λαμπρόν τε ἐρυθρῷ λευκῷ τε μειγνύμενον ξανθὸν γέγονεν). Xanthos is also a common proper name for a man (a Trojan, *Il.* 5.152), perhaps intentionally chosen to pair with a father's name Φαίνοψ ('bright'?).
305 On which see mainly Lazzeroni 1957: 1–25. Cf. Kraus 1987: 27–30 and M.L. West 2007a: 161. See further Kim (2010: 99–100) on the reception of this distinction in Dio Chrysostomus' *Trojan Oration*.
306 See Appendix.
307 Cf. Wathelet 1988: 275. See also von Kamptz 1982 (1958): 32, 72.
308 Thus Burgess 2001: 66.
309 Cf. Farron 1979: 22–5, with bibliography.

(*Il.* 24.725–45). Her name indeed suits *him* more than her:[310] it is a designation of Hektor's chosen path of action – to fight and risk his life in war. The name may well reflect her dependance on him, and it is certainly significant that she is mostly referred to as 'Hektor's wife'.[311]

2.4.3 Paris-Alexandros

The most intriguing specimen of Trojan onomastics concerns a hero who does not have a great share in the action, Priam's son Paris / Alexandros. Though not the only case of double naming,[312] the two names of Paris are of exceptional interest since, unlike other instances, they are related to a major hero and are mentioned numerous times (though never together in Homer[313]). The question why the Trojan prince should have two names is inevitably linked with the effort to establish whether any significance was meant for them.

Alexandros is the most commonly used of the two, with 45 occurrences in the *Iliad*, against 11 of Paris (or 13 if we include Δύσπαρις). Despite its perfectly Greek sound and easily understandable meaning, Ἀλέξανδρος has been involved in much controversy and has often been seen as alien to Greek name-formation and inexplicable in Greek, mainly due to the element –ανδρος: Greek compounds of this type usually have -ηνωρ as a second component.[314] However, examples such as ἘτέFανδρος, Ἡγήσανδρος, Τέρπανδρος are apparently very old,[315] and a form *a-re-ka-sa-da-ra* (read Alexandra) is attested in Mycenaean.[316] There is no Mycenaean Alexandros, but one early attestation of the name (ca.1280) is for the Hittite ruler *Alakšanduš* of the kingdom of *Wilusa*; this must be a foreign interpretation of the Greek name, and not the original form

---

310 Cf. Neumann (1991: 316) who noted that the name belongs to the male value system. The name's components might suggest the alternative meaning 'she with a warrior husband', which would suit the heroine better, but other Homeric names in –μαχος (gathered in von Kamptz 1982 [1958]: 72) do not offer support to this possibility; they seem to suggest a different semantic correlation between the first and the second part of the compound.
311 She is also referred to as the daughter of Eetion (*Il.* 6.395–6, 414–6); the sack of his city, Thebes, by Achilles (on which cf. *Il.* 2.690–3), may well have belonged to an old, established tradition (see M.L. West 2011a: 119). However, this potentially pre-Homeric background (cf. Burgess 2001: 66) does not throw further light on Andromache's character.
312 For a list of these cases see von Kamptz 1982 (1958): 33–5.
313 They are only used together by imperial authors (Plin. *Nat.* 34.77, Hyg. *Fab.* 92.2).
314 Wackernagel 1919: 6 f., followed by Sommer 1932: 370 and von Kamptz 1982 (1958): 94–6.
315 Chantraine 1999 s.v. ἀνήρ.
316 Cf. Jorro-Adrados 1985 s.v. *a-re-ka-sa-da-ra* (MY V 659.2).

of the name.³¹⁷ The possibility that the name originates in the Greek language is encouraged by the mention of the place-name *Wilusa*, which is usually identified with the Homeric (W)Ilios = Troy.³¹⁸ The Hittite Alexandros predates the sack of Troy by two or three generations, hence the Hittite evidence cannot mention the Homeric Paris-Alexandros. The epos clearly made use of a name which was already at hand, while it is possible that in the use of Alexandros 'the bards remembered a historical ruler'³¹⁹ – perhaps the name 'speaks' about the poet's sources.

It seems rather certain that, whether Greek (most probably) or Anatolian (less likely), historical (probably) or invented, the name was understood by the Iliadic audience to mean something like: 'he who stands up against his enemies and keeps them away'. The verb ἀλέξω (also in the middle voice, ἀλέξομαι) is common in Homeric poetry and can mean either 'ward off' or 'help, defend'.³²⁰ The latter meaning is cited by the Scholia, representing the grammatical tradition.³²¹ A meaning along these lines is suggested also by a story (Apollod. 3.150; Hyg. *Fab.* 91.3), according to which the hero was raised by shepherds:³²² he was originally called Paris, but was given the name Alexandros as he matured, on grounds of his strength and ability to defend herds against raiders (Ἀλέξανδρος προσωνομάσθη, ληστὰς ἀμυνόμενος καὶ τοῖς ποιμνίοις ἀλεξήσας, Apollod. 3.150.6–7). However, a verse from the *Iliad* containing the expression ἀλέξασθαι ἄνδρας (13.475), a perfect equivalent to the name, supports the former interpretation, as there the verb definitely means 'ward off' (αὐτὰρ ὀδόντας / θήγει, ἀλέξασθαι μεμαὼς κύνας ἠδὲ καὶ ἄνδρας 'and he whets his tusks,

---

317 See already Luckenbill 1911; cf. Kretschmer 1924. An Anatolian origin was favoured by Sommer (1932: 370; cf. von Kamptz 1982 [1958]: 94–5); but see now Beekes 2010 s.v. ἀλέξω. The Mycenaean attestation of the feminine form proves that the Greek name can be as old as its Hittite equivalent; cf. Niemeier 2012: 154.
318 Sommer 1932: 37 f. For a different opinion see Bowra 1930: 179; recent opinions favouring the initial identification include Watkins' (1986a: 48–49), who also takes *Alakšanduš* as Greek, and Starke's (1997). For a concise presentation of the problems surrounding the Hittite connections with Troy and several Homeric names see Güterbock 1986: 33–44.
319 Güterbock 1986: 43–4; cf. M.L. West 2011a: 40.
320 There is also ἀλεξητήρ (μάχης) (a 'warder off' of battle; of Demoleon, Antenor's son, *Il.* 20.396) and the compounds ἀλεξίκακος (μῆτις) (a device 'to ward off evil', *Il.* 10.20) and ἀλεξάνεμος (χλαῖνα) (a cloak 'to keep off the wind', *Od.* 14.529). ἀλέξανδρος later occurs as an epithet of πόλεμος (μνᾶμα τ' ἀλεξάνδρου πολέμου, epigr. ap. D.S. 11.14).
321 Sch. AB 12.93: ὅτι τῇ πατρίδι 'ἀλέξησεν' ὅ ἐστιν ἐβοήθησε, πολεμίων ἐπελθόντων. Cf. *EM* and *Et.Gud.* s.v. Ἀλέξανδρος.
322 This story was probably dramatised in two plays called *Alexandros*, by Euripides (*TGrF* 5.1 frr. 41a-64 [Kannicht]) and Sophocles (*TGrF* 4 frr. 91a-100a [Radt]).

eager to ward off dogs and men', of the boar to which Idomeneus is compared).[323]

The question that now arises is whether the meaning suggested above has any particular relevance to the name's Iliadic context and to the character who bears it. The name is obviously good for a fighter, and the earlier mentioned Scholium hastens to make a connection between the name and the bearer's alleged contribution to the war – but this is certainly not the prevailing impression that the poem creates of Paris: the prince is more attracted to the pleasures of love than to fighting. Early in the *Iliad* he is scared away by Menelaos (3.21 ff.), which earns him a reprimand from his brother Hektor (3.38 ff.). Though he ventures to fight Menelaos, he is saved by Aphrodite from imminent death and is taken back to the pleasures of love by the side of Helen.[324] The name might imply that the earlier (pre-Homeric) presentation of Paris was perhaps more heroic. This possibility is encouraged by the role played by Paris in causing the Trojan war, which suggests that he must have been a primary character in the story, later displaced by Hektor. If so, it can be assumed that the hero's role in the story developed in a way that no longer did credit to the name, which perhaps even ended up sounding ironic. However, occasional glimpses of a fighting Alexandros are not entirely absent, and at some point (*Il.* 11.36 ff.) he wounds a few Achaeans with his arrows. In this context the name might suggest the hero's particular manner of fighting, as he who fights by keeping other warriors at a distance; notably archery was regarded as a less honourable and courageous practice;[325] indeed Diomedes, struck by one of Paris' arrows, humiliates him by comparing his strike to that of a woman (11.384–95).

The hero's other name, Paris, is clearly non-Greek. Watkins indicated a possible Luvian attestation of it and related it to the name of his father Priam, which is allegedly of the same etymology (Luvian: *Pariyamuvas* 'supreme in force', from *pari(ya)-*, which is contracted in the case of Priam).[326] It may thus seem that the name Paris is equivalent in sense to Alexandros. However, it is very doubtful that the poem appreciated the meaning of a name in a foreign language, and perhaps

---

323 Cf. Kassandra's alternative (though non-Homeric) name, Alexandra 'warding off men'.
324 His weakness may also be suggested by the fact that he is occasionally referred to as his wife's husband (e.g. *Il.* 11.369, Ἑλένης πόσις) – as is the norm generally for women, not for men.
325 See also pp. 54, 108.
326 1986a: 56–8, cf. Laroche 1970/2: 325, 364 and now M.L. West (2011a: 41). Von Kamptz 1982 (1958): 35 considered it Illyrian. Carnoy (1956: 122) unconvincingly associated Paris with personal names in –πορις (found mostly in Thrace, e.g. Μουκάπορις, Αὐλούπορις, but not present in Homer) assuming derivation from the root *per- and a meaning 'combattant' (but the main sense of the root is 'pierce', 'pervade', as in the verb πείρω).

Paris had no more than the exotic touch which is appropriate for a Trojan, i.e. a foreign and eastern character. Paris might be a more recent name for Alexandros, brought upon the character as he developed from the generic function of the warrior-hero to the love-prone figure for whom fighting is by no means a priority; the apparently older and better developed formulaic system that is applied to Alexandros may be an indication of the precedence of this name over Paris.[327] Similarly the use of Δύσπαρις (by Hektor at 3.39 and 13.769) bears the signs of flexibility associated with the treatment of a more recent element than of an old, traditional one, which has a well-established position in the poem.[328] Dysparis is of course significant in its own right: it suggests that Paris is a miserable man in Hektor's eyes; similarly Telemachos addresses his mother with δύσμητερ 'unhappy mother' (Od. 23.97), and Thetis calls herself δυσαριστοτόκεια 'who bore to her sorrow the best of men' (Il. 18.54).[329]

The alleged development of Alexandros – Paris' characterisation and its possible reflection in the two names can fit the reality of epic composition well. It cannot, however, be excluded that behind the two separate names hide two originally separate heroes,[330] for whom each name had a particular significance and who were later amalgamated. But even if true, these origins should lie in a long and distant past and should not have affected antiquity's view of Paris / Alexandros as a single hero with two names.[331]

---

327 Suter 1991b: 8 ff. She further alleges (ibid.: 25; cf. 1991a) that the double naming conforms to the convention of language of gods and language of men, where Paris appears to be the divine name, and is used in a way that indicates connections of the character with the divine; this has seemed to encourage a link between Paris and the figure of the 'abductor' in Vedic narratives that parallel the story of Helen's abduction (Edmunds 2007: 6–7). Other efforts to explain the double naming include de Jong's narratological approach (1987: 124–8) and Lloyd's attempt to attribute the two names to different name-givers (1989: 76–9). These theories are very speculative; also the issue of potential significance of the names is limited by de Jong to the contrast between Greekness and non-Greekness, while Lloyd neglects this issue completely.
328 But Δυσαλέξανδρος would have created metrical difficulties.
329 Examples of δυσ- compounds collected in Edwards 1987: 122.
330 Thus HE s.v. Paris (J. Griffin). For relevant bibliography see LfgrE s.v. Ἀλέξανδρος (M. van der Valk).
331 Dionysius Thrax mentions the names Alexandros and Paris as an example of a διώνυμον (37.3), which he understood as the use of a second name for one and the same person. Cf. Sch. Il. 20.40 b and Eust. 1197.48 (on Il. 20.74) on the διωνυμία Skamandros / Xanthos. The term is used by Eustathius and the Scholia several times.

2.4.4 Aineias

Outside Troy's first family, the name that mostly attracts attention is that of Αἰνείας. Aineias is probably not integral to the story of the Trojan war,[332] but he is given considerable importance by the poet of the *Iliad* (and he clearly acquired a central role in later myths about the Troad).[333] He is labelled as one of Troy's best men (cf. 17.513); he and Hektor are named together as the most valiant Trojan fighters on the battlefield (e. g. 17.754; the two are often mentioned together), and even Achilles is frightened of him at one instance (20.262). His heroism is not immaculate: he is repeatedly defeated by Achaeans (e. g. 5.29 ff., 20.8 ff.), and needs often to be rescued by deities (though these rescues make his character all the more memorable). His name, heard in the *Iliad* about a hundred times, is the most frequently mentioned Trojan name after Hektor's. It is reasonable to wonder whether it too was seen as a Greek name and whether it was thought to be significant. Its etymology may lie in the place-name Αἶνος, a city in Thrace (cf. *Il.* 4.519–20), or Αἴνεια, foothills close to Potidaia (Hdt. 7.123). The *Iliad* also mentions the very similar personal name Αἴνιος, for a Paeonian slain by Achilles (21.210).[334] Even if the geographical names are of foreign origin,[335] the use of the personal name Aineias was firmly established in Greek onomastics: attestations of the almost identical form Αἰνέας date from the archaic period.[336]

Whatever the name's true etymology, poetic word-play favours a connection with αἰνός 'terrible'. Idomeneus' cry 'δείδια δ' αἰνῶς / Αἰνείαν' ('and dreadfully do I fear Aeneas', *Il.* 13.481–2) is an obvious pun on the name. The poet of the *Homeric hymn to Aphrodite* (19 ff.) explains the name as a result of the αἰνὸν ἄχος that Aineias' mother, Aphrodite, felt for having slept with a mortal man. αἰνὸν ἄχος 'terrible sorrow' is found frequently in the *Iliad* (19.307 etc.), where αἰνός also occurs with μόρος ('fate', 18.464) and emotional terms such as τρόμος

---

332 See M.L. West's convincing arguments (2011a: 63): the rise of Aineias was probably a way of honouring the Aineiadai of Troad, with whom the poet was acquainted.
333 See *LfgrE* s.v. Αἰνείας (M. van der Valk).
334 On which see von Kamptz 1982 (1958): 284. Cf. also the Thracian Αἰνιεῖς mentioned by Hipponax as the people of king Rhesos (fr. 72 W). According to the hellenistic mythographer Conon (*FGrH* 26 F 1.46), Aineias founded a city, at first called Aineia and later Ainos, on the Thermaic gulf (see also Nagy 2010: 201, who infers from this story an Aeolian identity for the Aineiadai).
335 Thus Wilamowitz (1916: 83), who regarded Aineias as a non-Greek name.
336 This form (found once in the *Iliad*, 13.541) is attested on Korinthian vases from the 6th c. BC, see Wachter 2001: 363 (Index s.v. Αἰνέᾱς), 262, and *LGPN* IIA. The different forms seem to have emerged from the 'mutation' of the original diphthong, cf. also Αἰνίας. See Meister 1921: 156–7 and Schulze 1892.

('fear', 11.117).³³⁷ It is not found as an epithet for heroes, though in the superlative form it qualifies divine names (αἰνότατε Κρονίδη 'most dreadful son of Kronos', 4.25; αἰνοτάτη, of Athena, 8.423). The phonetic similarity of Aineias to αἰνός may have activated an allusion to the notion of 'terrifying warrior' (cf. his depiction at 13.482–3, especially that he is 'very mighty to slay men in battle'). Additionally, Aineias is phonetically close to αἶνος, also a Homeric word, used in the *Iliad* in the sense of 'tale' (23.652), but also of 'praise' (23.795).³³⁸ Both etymologies ('terrifying warrior' and 'much-praised') are cited in the ancient tradition;³³⁹ they are both generically suitable for an epic hero.

Aineias is the son of a famous father, Anchises (Ἀγχίσης); he admittedly has no part in the Iliadic story,³⁴⁰ but the several mentions of his name in the poem and the obscurity of its etymology invite a comment. The –s– element of the name has been thought to indicate pre-Greek origin.³⁴¹ The name further sounds similar to the place names Ἀγχίση, a mythical city in Italy (D.H. 1.73), and Ἀγχισία, a hill in Arcadia and a supposed burying-place for the hero (Paus. 8.12.8).³⁴² Both of these places, however, are attested much later and were most likely named after the hero. Perhaps it is preferable to assume an Anatolian connection: Anchises, as a lover of Aphrodite (*Il.* 2.820, 5.312–3), might originate among the young male figures (the most famous one is Adonis) of Eastern origin, who get involved with the goddess. Some names from the hero's genealogy (which goes back to Zeus), such as Kapys (his father) and Assarakos (his grandfather) also have an Anatolian echo and probably originate in a different language.³⁴³ A pun on the name, based on the story of Anchises' sexual encounter with Aphrodite, is suggested in lexicography: Παρὰ τὸ ἄγχι (τὸ ἐγγὺς) γενέσθαι τῆς Ἀφροδίτης (*EM* s.v. Ἀγχίσης). No such pun is found in Homer; however, a parallel for a significant use of ἀγχι- in Homeric onomastics is found in Ἀγχίαλος (*Od.* 8.112), 'close to the sea' – one of a number of sea-related Phaeacian names.³⁴⁴

---

337 See further *DGE* s.v. αἰνός.
338 Note that αἶνος and αἰνέω have produced numerous historical names (see Bechtel 1917: 25–8). Janko (1992: 106) interprets Aineias as a possible derivative of αἰνέω; cf. Nagy 1979: 274.
339 *EM* s.v. Αἰνείας.
340 For an explanation of this see *HE* s.vv. Anchises and Aeneas (B. Currie).
341 Cf. Χρῦσα/Χρύση, Μάρπησσα/Μάρπησσος, Βρῆσσα /Βρήσσης; see von Kamptz 1982 (1958): 156–8.
342 One of the many traditions about Anchises' burial place, cf. *N.Pauly* s.v. Anchises (F. Graf).
343 On Κάπυς see Zgusta 1964: 214. For Ἀσσάρακος cf. Ἀρδάρακος (ten attestations in *LGPN* IV).
344 On these see below.

3 Names from the *Odyssey*

> 'On the one hand, a simple pathos of heroic life and death;
> on the other, greater complexity and a nearer approach to sentimentality.'
>
> (Griffin 1980: 111, comparing the two epics)

The differences between the *Odyssey* and the *Iliad* in content and spirit are reflected in the use of personal names. In the *Iliad*, transparent names usually express the action and aspirations of heroic warriors in a rather fixed setting of wartime conditions; these names often sound like generic compliments to their bearers (admiration for heroes is a vital element of the Homeric view of the world, cf. *Il.* 5.305 about the superiority of the heroic generation).[1] Some main heroes' names are obscure, but most appear relevant to the heroic nature of their bearers in one way or another. There is a certain uniformity in the meanings of Iliadic names and the underlying naming motives; names used for Odyssean characters are more diverse than for Iliadic characters in terms of significance, and the motives for their choice vary extremely – this explains the greater scholarly attention attracted by Odyssean than by Iliadic onomastics. The *Odyssey* presents a wider range of characters, including a number of women, whose presence is much stronger here than in the *Iliad*; and character identities are more subtle and distinct:[2] many belong to the world of heroic epic, but embody a different notion of heroism, as the opposition between the main heroes, Achilles and Odysseus shows.[3] Some of the *Iliad*'s poignant figures return (e.g. Menelaos, Nestor, Helen), but with much less pronounced roles – and many new figures appear, both human and non-human. The variety of Odys-

---

1 See also above, 'Introductory notes' p. 4.
2 On *Odyssey*'s emphasis on characterisation, already noticed in antiquity, see e.g. Saïd 1998: 214 (with references) and now M.L. West 2014: 56. For an overview of *Odyssey*'s female characters see Schein 1995.
3 Achilles to Odysseus: 'For hateful in my eyes as the gates of Hades is that man who hides one thing in his mind and says another' (*Il.* 9.312–3). This opposition is encapsulated in the different core elements of their characterisation: Achilles' anger at Agamemnon's insult to his heroic identity (μῆνις) and Odysseus' resourcefulness (μῆτις); these elements may be felt to express two distinctly different views of heroism (discussed at length by Edwards, 1985). For further comparisons between the two heroes see also Saïd 1998: 304–306 and below, 'Afterword'; and between the two epics (now commonly believed to belong to separate authors, cf. above p. 2 n. 8), Rutherford 2001, with bibliography (who suggests that the *Odyssey* is not to be seen – as often in the past – as the inferior epos, but as offering another view of human society that complements the Iliadic view; Austin [1975] and Edwards [1985] take a similar perspective). See also M.L. West's comparison (2014: 1; 44–5).

sean characters is a direct consequence of the complexity of the world of the *Odyssey*, which derives from numerous heterogeneous sources, encompassing various epic traditions as well as folktale-like adventures – a completely different world to that of the *Iliad*. Odyssean characters are further often set against a background which appears closer to the poet's own world (offering a reflection of mundane daily life in peace) and which includes figures that represent less the heroic race and more the everyday human level;[4] but some characters are thought to originate in folktale.[5]

The question of sources of Odyssean motifs and characters is clearly relevant to the interpretation of personal names. The purposeful use of names in the *Odyssey* (made more explicit there than in the *Iliad*) is equally connected with the more self-conscious literary character of this epic, suggested by the fact that the hero narrates part of the poem, and two of the characters, Demodokos and Phemios, are poets.[6] A striking manifestation of the epic's literary self-consciousness, as well as of the complexity of its world, concerns Odysseus' name – the starting point of this chapter. Discussion of the hero's name will be followed by the presentation of names of members of his immediate family. The remainder of the chapter will discuss significantly named characters that appear in the two main fields in which the hero's action is divided: his travels and the events on Ithaca.

3.1 Odysseus

Odysseus is the only major Homeric hero whose name receives an explicit (and in fact quite elaborate) justification within the story. Strikingly, this justification largely depends on a realistic account of how Odysseus got his name as a baby.

---

4 Cf. Clarke 2004: 86–90. According to the pseudo-Herodotean *Vit.Hom.* (347–52 West), some characters (Mentor, Phemios, Mentes) were named after people who were friends of the poet, and to whom he owed a debt of gratitude (see Nagy 2010: 40).
5 A definition of folktale is hard to form (cf. Page 1973: 117 n.2 with bibliography). Its essence is a tale repeated for its intrinsic entertainment value and not tied to a particular place or time, and it often concerns creatures of grotesque form and supernatural powers, living in an imaginary world. In Homer, folktale is blurred with saga, which concerns persons believed to be historical and represented as behaving realistically in the actual world. When a similar plot is shared, legend must derive from folktale rather than the opposite (Hansen 2002: 15–6). The theme of the *Odyssey* itself, the return of the husband after many years, has its origins in folktale (cf. Davies 2009; the theme of the hero's disguise is also folkloric). The poet of the *Odyssey* modifies supernatural elements to make them seem more credible (Page 1973: 4), cf. below under Polyphemos.
6 Cf. Segal 1994: 85–6; see also Rutherford 2001: 135.

According to *Od*. 19.407–9 (part of a digression from the scene where Eurykleia washes her master's feet, who is yet unrecognised and in the disguise of a beggar),⁷ the name was chosen by his grandfather Autolykos, and it was inspired by Autolykos' own experience: πολλοῖσιν γὰρ ἐγώ γε <u>ὀδυσσάμενος</u> τόδ' ἱκάνω,/ ἀνδράσιν ἠδὲ γυναιξὶν ἀνὰ χθόνα βωτιάνειραν·/ τῷ δ' Ὀδυσεὺς ὄνομ' ἔστω ἐπώνυμον 'Inasmuch as I have come here as one that has willed pain (*odyssamenos*) to many, both men and women, over the fruitful earth, therefore let the name by which the child is named be Odysseus'. The intentionality of the naming, made clear by the pun ὀδυσσάμενος – Ὀδυσεύς,⁸ is emphasised by the term ἐπώνυμον, used in Homer for names that are well suited to their bearers.⁹

Clearly on a first level the name appears to be ἐπώνυμον not in respect to Odysseus, but to the name-giver. There are not many explicit examples of this kind in Homer, but this naming motive is certainly implicit in quite a few other names, which reflect the habit of naming children after a characteristic of a parent or relative.¹⁰ Still, the story of Odysseus' naming contains some startling elements: the inspiration for a name usually comes from a paternal characteristic (cf. the name of Odysseus' son, to be discussed later on; another example from the *Odyssey* is the name of Menelaos' son Μεγαπένθης, 4.11, from the great grief caused to Menelaos by Helen's desertion).¹¹ But in Odysseus' case neither of his parents seem to be involved in the naming, and it is, strangely, the *maternal* grandfather who is asked to name the child,¹² while the only other person who has any role in this process is the old nanny Eurykleia¹³ (who may seem to suggest a different name, as we shall see in the course of the discussion).

---

7 On the ambivalent interpretation of the narrative technique used to unite main scene and digression see Köhnken 2009.
8 Ὀδυσ(σ)εύς too, like Ἀχιλ(λ)εύς, is spelled with a single or double consonant according to the metre.
9 Cf. *Od*. 7.54 about the name Arete (see also below, under 'Some Phaeacian names').
10 Cf. the name of Meleagros' wife Kleopatre – Alkyone: the name Alkyone was chosen by her parents to express metaphorically her mother's grief (*Il*. 9.561–4); or Astyanax, whose name was chosen by the Trojans to reflect his father's function as lord and protector of the city (*Il*. 22.506–7). See also above, pp. 61, 81.
11 A 'gloomy' speaking name, see also Alden 2000: 55, n.22. The name also accentuates Megapenthes' second-class status as a bastard.
12 The fact that the father is not involved in Odysseus' naming may suggest uncertainty about the paternity of the baby; notably quite a few post-Homeric sources (mainly Sophocles in his *Philoctetes*) name Sisyphos as Odysseus' real father. See Ussher 1990: 125 and *N.Pauly* s.v. Sisyphos (R. Nünlist).
13 But her prominence in this account must have to do with the poet's need to coordinate the digression with the main narrative, in which she plays a significant part (thus Köhnken 2009: 55–6).

Another striking element is Autolykos' own name: αὐτο-λυκος must have implied a meaning such as 'the wolf himself' or 'the very wolf'.[14] The wolf element seems to suit Autolykos' brief self-characterisation, which emphasises his animosity towards others and his habit of selfish gain. An element of egotism may also be detected in his wish to project an expression of his own personality in the naming of his grandson. Notoriety for deceit was perhaps the main element of Autolykos' traditional depiction,[15] and it was probably reflected in his wolf-name (notably wolves are regarded as particularly intelligent animals[16]). These associations may have suggested him to the poet as an appropriate name-giver for Odysseus: not only is he significantly named, but his name further expresses a personal characteristic which may account for a similar trait in Odysseus' character (the negative aspects of his trickery, perceived as Odysseus' 'Autolykan' nature).[17]

It has long been noticed that the relevance of the name's etymology is not restricted to the grandfather. The Autolykos passage is not the only place where the verb ὀδύ(σσ)ομαι occurs in connection with Odysseus. A pun between name and verb is found as early as 1.62 (in Athena's words to Zeus): τί νύ οἱ τόσον ὠδύσαο, Ζεῦ; 'Why then did you will him such pain, O Zeus?' The verb is then used several times to denote the gods' hostility towards Odysseus: in Ino Leukothee's words at 5.339–40 (κάμμορε, τίπτε τοι ὧδε Ποσειδάων ἐνοσίχθων / ὠδύσατ' ἐκπάγλως 'Unhappy man, how is it that Poseidon, the earth-shaker, has so astoundingly willed your pain'), by Odysseus himself at 5.423 (οἶδα γὰρ ὥς μοι ὀδώδυσται κλυτὸς ἐννοσίγαιος 'For I know how the great Earth-shaker wills me pain'), and at 19.275–6, which follow after the Autolykos

---

14 *Comm. on Od.* v.3: 96 (Russo), cf. Peradotto 1990: 128–9. Similarly von Kamptz 1982 (1958): 93 translates (with doubt) as 'leibhaftiger Wolf'. For further etymological discussion see *LfgrE* s.v. Αὐτόλυκος (W. Beck). A derivation from the root *λυκ- 'light' (cf. lat. *lux*) is made less likely by the fact that λυκ- 'wolf' is indisputably a stronger element in Greek (and other Indo-European) onomastics, and there are examples where no other interpretation of the root is possible, e.g. Λυκοφόντης 'wolf-killer'. See Eisler 1951: 140 ff.
15 Cf. *Il.* 10.266 which presents him as a thief, and [Hes.] *Cat.* fr. 67b M-W; cf. also his special relationship with Hermes, patron of thieves: *Od.* 19.394 ff., [Hes.] *Cat.* fr. 66 and fr. 65 M-W, where Autolykos is Hermes' son.
16 They hunt with intelligence (X. *Eq.Mag.* 4.18–20) and act intelligently when they catch prey (Arist. *HA* 612b). See further *RE* Suppl. 15 s.v. Wolf (W. Richter), on the animal's character, in particular its cunning and thieving nature.
17 Cf. *Comm. on Od.* v.3: 96 (Russo). Odysseus' potential for deceit is intrinsic to a personality marked by the (in itself not negative) characteristic of cleverness; cf. the frequent use of formulaic epithets such as πολύμητις for Odysseus in both the *Odyssey* and the *Iliad*. See *LfgrE* s.v. Ὀδυσ(σ)εύς (G. Markwald).

story (ὀδύσαντο γὰρ αὐτῷ Ζεύς τε καὶ Ἥλιος 'For Zeus and Helios willed pain to him').[18] The poem implies that the ὀδυσσάμενος feature is transferred from the context of Autolykos' self-characterisation to the field of Odysseus' experience. The fact that Odysseus is given a name which is proven appropriate in later life implies the concept of *nomen omen*; the poem wishes to suggest that, by naming him, Autolykos 'programmed' his grandson's fate. [19]

However, the exact implications of the above puns for the meaning of Odysseus' name are not immediately clear. *ὀδύσ(σ)ομαι is grammatically obscure (it occurs only in the aorist and perfect, in what voice it cannot be decided), and its sense (despite the above translations) is not precisely known. It occurs in the *Odyssey* only in connection with Odysseus;[20] it is also found once in the *Iliad* (8.37, notably in Athena's words to Zeus, and in relation to divine wrath, cf. *Od.* 1.62): ὡς μὴ πάντες ὄλωνται ὀδυσσαμένοιο τεοῖο '[but counsel we will offer to the Argives which will benefit them] so that they may not all perish because of your wrath'; and once in Hesiod (*Th.* 617): Ὀβριάρεῳ δ' ὡς πρῶτα πατὴρ ὠδύσσατο θυμῷ 'When first their father became angry in his spirit with Obriareos...'[21] (transl. Most; it is worth a reminder here that the *Theogony* may be earlier than the *Odyssey*).[22] In the Autolykos passage, ὀδυσσάμενος seems to denote a hostile relationship between him and society. Stanford[23] must be right that the meaning of ὀδύ(σσ)ομαι was 'wide enough to imply either anger or hatred', but it is not altogether clear whether Autolykos hates / angers himself against

---

18 A further possible pun is found in Hermes' address to Odysseus at 10.281, ὦ δύστηνε; cf. *LfgrE* s.v. Ὀδυσ(σ)εύς (G. Markwald).
19 The relative importance of Odysseus and Autolykos in the tradition may suggest that Odysseus' naming constitutes a kind of reversal of roles for poetic purposes. Odysseus is the primary figure in the epic and Autolykos is arguably assimilated to him (rather than the opposite), in a manner which would be comparable to the function of paradigmatic figures elsewhere in Homer): Autolykos' κλεπτοσύνη is conceived in terms that are reminiscent of Odysseus' famous guile; his 'anger' (*odyssamenos*) may reflect his grandson's emotional state on his return to Ithaca. See Köhnken (2009: 56–8), with references to the text (Autolykos is portrayed as a 'doppelgänger' to Odysseus). A famous example of mythological paradigm from the *Iliad* is Meleager and his story, on which see above under 'Patroklos'.
20 It has been thought that the word is a later insertion in the text to create a pun; notably all occurrences of the verb in the *Odyssey*, as well as the Autolykos passage itself, have been suspected by later commentators (as early as Arist. *Poet.* 7.1451a) not to be genuine; see Rank 1951: 54 ff. But the pun gains strength from its recurrence and from the presence of plenty of other similar puns on names. For a justification of the Autolykos passage see Peradotto 1990: 125.
21 The only instances of the term in later literature are Hom. *Epigr.* 6.8, *AP* 9.117 (epic context), and in a Sophoclean fragment (*TGrF* 4 fr. 965 [Radt], on which see below).
22 M.L.West 1995; 2014: 32–4.
23 1952: 209.

or is hated by / has incurred the anger of 'many men and women'; linguistic evidence may favour the former,[24] but is not ample enough to be conclusive. The puns concerning Odysseus make use of the active verb instead of the participle: the gods direct their anger towards him, therefore he could be seen as 'the hated'; but if the name retains the active sense of the verb, then it should mean 'hater' (this meaning would suit him especially in connection with his treatment of the suitors).

Poetic etymology may appear confusing, but clearly discussion of the name does not end with the explanation of puns: it needs to be deciphered as a symbol of the hero's identity.[25] This is because first, it is embedded in a narrative (about a wild boar hunt on mount Parnassos) that resembles an adolescent rite of passage or coming-of-age tale;[26] this provides the context where Odysseus lives up to his name for the first time (he both causes harm and is harmed in his encounter with the boar). Second, the name is withheld or revealed in the contexts of the hero's different adventures, which has implications for the way his identity is perceived by himself and by the people he comes in contact with. For instance, in an ingenious (if rather far-fetched) way Odysseus contrives to conceal his name[27] from the Phaeacians until 9.19 (this becomes even more striking in the light of 8.550–4 and of the fact that Alkinoos has after all offered him Nausikaa without knowing his name; see 7.311–4).[28] Perhaps the sense of the name was not limited to a particular episode in the hero's adventures, but specific contexts and episodes would remind of one or both senses of *odyssomai*; and overall as a reflection of the hero's character, the name might generally allude to the wrath,

---

24 Marót (1961) took ὀδυσσάμενος as a passive; see Köhnken (2009: 57, n. 40) for bibliography that follows this view – which, according to Köhnken, lacks linguistic support. See Peradotto 1990: 129 ff. with an account of the views on the subject.
25 Cf. Higbie 1995: 5.
26 Thus Dimock 1956: 52–5, cf. Peradotto 1990: 94 and Cook 2009: 115. Significantly, the Sch. *Od.* 19.410 glosses ἡβήσας with ὀδυσσάμενος.
27 See further Goldhill 1991: 1, 24–36. It may be felt that the name is sometimes avoided because of its ill-omened sense (note that Penelope and the goddess Athena have used *keinon* to refer to Odysseus, avoiding naming him, 4.832–7), and at times out of caution about 'the orderings of the structures of society' (thus Goldhill 1991: 28), e.g. at *Od.* 14.145–7, where Eumaios declares that he is ashamed to pronounce his master's name. The delayed mention of the name, at the end of Eumaios' speech, produces a climactic effect (M.L. West 2014: 237).
28 For a detailed treatment of this point see Austin 1972: 3 ff. and Fenik 1974, esp. 53 (who rightly notes that the delay in the mention of Odysseus' name in the Phaeacian episode is in harmony with the poem's general tendency to delay identifications); cf. Peradotto 1990: 101–2 and Goldhill's analysis (1991: 30–6) of withholding the name as 'an essential dynamic of the narrative of the *Odyssey*'. Cook (2009: 124) suggests that Odysseus reclaims his name (as a symbol of his true identity) by exiting the 'enchanted realm.'

confrontation and torment that were involved in Odysseus' homecoming. The hero was responsible for causing some of these negative experiences, but in other cases he was the innocent victim. He offends the divine world, and attacks and hurts some of the fantastic beings he encounters (even if not always willingly); he hates but is equally hated by the suitors, as well as members of his own household (the hostile servants). This is what Peradotto[29] defines as 'notion of character in the middle voice', an interpretation suggested already by the ancient Scholia (Sch. V. *Od.* 19.407 ὀδυσσάμενος] μισηθείς· ἢ ὀργὴν ἀγαγών· ἢ βλάψας). An intentional ambiguity in Odysseus' name would suit the versatility of his nature, and the often folklore-like character of the *Odyssey*. Odysseus is reminiscent of the 'trickster' figure in folklore and mythology, who is both a deceiver and a victim of deception, who both causes and suffers pain.[30] The Homeric character may well have evolved from a pre-epic trickster figure and have been adapted to a heroic setting in epic poetry.[31]

Having established the flexibility of the name's sense, it is now worth asking whether, as far as the epic is concerned, certain nuances of the name's significance are stronger or more prevalent than others. In order to answer this question, we need to look more carefully at the hero's characterisation. It is important that among the different aspects of Odysseus' personality and adventures, the epic places the emphasis on the pain he suffered during his return. Significantly, this is the only aspect brought out in the proem (which makes no mention of the hate for or the killing of the suitors). Pain has rightly been identified as a core element of heroic identity – more so than hate; as noted earlier, Odysseus' connection with pain (both as a perpetrator and a sufferer) is a feature he shares with Achilles (his anguish is even described as *achos* at one instance, 18.346–8, 20.285–6 – the suitors are incited by the goddess Athena to more outrageous behaviour in order to cause the hero more *achos*).[32] Moreover, Odysseus'

---

29 1990: 115–6, 119.
30 Radin 1956: 23; cf. *Comm. on Od.* v.3: 97 (Russo), Cook 2009: 116 (with n. 15 on the use of the term 'trickster'). A similar perception of Autolykos, as a folklore figure with magical powers, is possible; see Marót 1961: 24–30, who argued that the figure of Autolykos may bear testimony to the influence of pre-Homeric traditional poetry.
31 Clay 1983: 68 ff., following Maronitis 1973: 150–96. See now also M.L. West 2014: 9–11.
32 But Cook (2009: 113–4) rightly notes that Odysseus' heroism is defined in rather more moralising terms (his men bear responsibility for their sad fate and the suitors are punished for their crimes – unlike the Achaeans of the *Iliad* whose suffering is caused by Achilles' anger and is not their own fault; even the Cyclops, whom he blinds, is part of a society that has no respect for ethical norms). Cook further suggests (ibid.: 116) that the inclusion of the story of the boar hunt, to which Odysseus' naming is subordinated, implies superiority of the heroic warrior iden-

survival during the majority of his adventures seems mostly to depend on what has been termed as 'passive heroism' (endurance of mental and physical pain, often with the employment of trickery in the place of active heroic force); the image of the 'suffering wanderer' prevails in his self-presentation to the Phaeacians.[33] The *Odyssey* is mainly a tale of a tormented homecoming, and its very title has become synonymous with a long and tantalising adventure, in which 'the principal hero is the principal sufferer'. Pain was more prominent in the *nostos* than hate.[34] This pain concerns not only Odysseus, but is also present in the emotional reactions to Odysseus of people he is related to or whom he meets in his adventures.[35] This could make the name lean more often towards the 'passive' meaning.[36] The poem's diction seems to favour this interpretation: in the *Odyssey* there are 85 occurences of adjectives such as πολύτλας 'much enduring' and others in the same semantic range (δύστηνος, ταλασίφρων etc.).[37] The use of formulaic epithets for Odysseus is not exclusive to the *Odyssey*; they are found in the *Iliad* too (some 8 examples),[38] which implies that the seeds of this perception of Odysseus are present in the older poem.[39]

The 'passive' interpretation (as 'victim of hatred') also offers a more dignified meaning. The active sense 'he who caused anger / hatred to others' would

---

tity over that of the 'trickster' (a view which is suggested also in the *Iliad*, e.g. in Achilles' words at 9.312–3: 'hateful is that man who hides one thing in his mind and says another').

33 See esp. 7.211–25 and cf. Odysseus' pain at the memory of the sack of Troy (8.536–86), with Cook 2009: 121–7 (and earlier Schein 1995: 20–21, who distinguishes between 'warrior heroism' and the 'heroism of *nostos*', based on cunning intelligence).

34 Thus Dimock 1956: 52–70.

35 The point is emphasised by Dimock, 1956: *passim*, esp. 63. Dimock (ibid. 57) has made the only attempt known to me to translate the name into English: 'Trouble'.

36 Also the end of Eurykleia's account of the story of the hero's naming (19.474–5) has been thought to imply such a passive meaning: ἦ μάλ' Ὀδυσσεύς ἐσσι, φίλον τέκος· οὐδέ σ' ἐγώ γε πρὶν ἔγνων, πρὶν πάντα ἄνακτ' ἐμὸν ἀμφαφάασθαι. 'You verily are Odysseus (= the hated one), my child, since not even I recognised you immediately' (de Jong 2001: 477–8), but this interpretation is not necessary.

37 Note that πολύτλας and ταλασίφρων are not free from ambiguity: forms of *τλάω were commonly used in Homer to express courage, fortitude, or boldness; both adjectives are thus appropriate, not only for the much (or courageously) suffering, but also for the bold, daring and adventurous – these too are characteristics of Odysseus.

38 See *LfgrE* s.v. Ὀδυσ(σ)εύς (G. Markwald).

39 Where, however, instances of 'active' heroism prevail (with emphasis on his quality of mind – the Iliadic hero, after all, took Troy by trickery); see also Cook 2009 *passim*. Apparently the exploitation of Odysseus' name in the manner described in this chapter is the work of the *Odyssey* poet.

not be ethically appropriate for the name of a respectable Homeric hero.[40] Finally, the meaning 'hated' may suit one other, latent aspect of Odysseus' character: apart from being persecuted by gods, he seems to have been somewhat unpopular among men ('man-hated?'), perhaps because of his unusual cleverness. We get this feeling from the *Iliad* a few times (cf. Agamemnon's abuse of him in 4.336 ff., Achilles' reply to his speech in the embassy in 9.307 ff.), as well as from the *Odyssey* (cf. his companions' mistrust in the Aiolos episode, 10.34 ff.; his poor judgement in the Cyclops' episode could not conduce to good relations with his men).[41] A relevant interpretation of the name is suggested by Sophocles in a lost (untitled) play; ὀρθῶς δ' Ὀδυσσεύς εἰμ' ἐπώνυμος κακῶν· / πολλοὶ γὰρ ὠδύσαντο δυσμενεῖς ἐμοί 'I am rightly called Odysseus, after something bad; for many enemies have been angry with me' (*TGrF* 4 fr. 965 [Radt]; transl. Lloyd-Jones).[42] This aspect of Odysseus' personality would be in keeping with his 'Autolycan nature', and perhaps the sense of the name evolved accordingly from 'trickster who causes and receives trouble' to 'suffering hero'.[43] Indeed negative views of Odysseus in the epic are balanced by positive ones: he is chosen as particularly suitable for the embassy to Achilles, and Diomedes regards him as an ideal partner (*Il.* 10.242 ff.).[44]

The association of *nostos* with pain and suffering possibly activates a further word-play. ὀδύνη 'pain'[45] and ὀδύρομαι 'lament' are similar in sound to the name Odysseus. In the *Iliad*, *nostos* is connected with ὀδύρομαι, referring to the grief caused by the heroes' long absence from home: ἀλλήλοισιν ὀδύρονται οἰκόνδε νέεσθαι 'they wail to each other in longing to return home' (*Il.* 2.290). This verb is used in relation to Odysseus a few times in the *Odyssey*: 1.55, 5.160, 9.13, 11.214, 13.219 (9.13 and 11.214 imply a formula).[46] Admittedly, none of the references to Odysseus as *odyromenos* shows any allusion to his name, and clearly *odus-* (of *ὀδύσ(σ)ομαι) is phonetically closer to the name than *odun-* or *odur-*. It is noteworthy, though, that all uses of the latter vocabulary for Odysseus are

---

40 See Stanford (1952: 211), who collected other examples of etymologies of heroic names, such as Pentheus, Aias, where the emphasis is on suffering rather than doing.
41 See Stanford 1952: 211–3.
42 Risch (1947: 83) proposed both a passive and an active meaning ('verhasst' or 'grollend'), with a preference for the former; see also Danek 1998: 44. The active meaning was preferred by Rank (1951: 52–60), who, however, recognised the passive sense as a possibility in *Od.* 19.407. See further Austin 1972: 2, 3 and n.6.
43 Cf. Clay 1983: 70.
44 See now M.L. West (2014: 5–6) for the highlights of Odysseus' role in the Trojan saga.
45 A Homeric word, cf. *Il.* 11.398, 5.417 and *Od.* 1.242, 2.79.
46 Cf. Risch 1974: 85. It is not clear whether ὀδύνη and ὀδύρομαι are cognates (see Chantraine 1999 s.v.), but they may well be.

placed before the naming episode of book 19; we might assume that this episode confirms the poet's decision on the name's 'primary' etymology.

The meanings implied by the Autolykos episode do not exhaust the name's significant potential; it will be shown below that Odysseus' name can lead further into other directions, as expected of the name of a very old and very complex hero. From antiquity to the present day, there is no shortage of explanations of how the name Odysseus emerged, though not all are equally convincing.[47] Conversely, it is worth exploring epigraphical evidence on the development of the name's form, which may suggest that the initial perception of Odysseus' name (and figure) was not identical with the image of the hero of the *Odyssey*. There are different spellings of the name, some of which have λ instead of δ: Ὀλισεύς, the standard spelling of the Korinthian form, appears on vase inscriptions since the late seventh century BC, and there follow the Attic form Ὀλυτ(τ)εύς in the early sixth century, and the Boiotian Ὀλυσεύς in the late sixth century.[48] The 'standard' form Ὀδυσ(σ)εύς is not epigraphically attested until the mid-sixth century, but it certainly was dominant by the mid-fifth, when the form with λ became extinct in Greek (it was preferred in Etruscan and then in Latin). The greater antiquity and diversion of the forms with λ may indicate that the original form of the name had a λ.[49] Some effort has been made to provide etymologies which would suit this form, most notably a connection with οὐλή (*Οὐλυσσεύς),[50] from the scar on Odysseus' knee (acquired during a wild boar hunt), by which Eurykleia recognised the hero. However, it is the scar that provides the trigger for the account of the *ὀδύσ(σ)ομαι etymology, and thus seems to be treated here as another manifestation of suffering.[51] The importance of οὐλή in the story may still

---

[47] Cf. the attempt to explain the name through a story about Odysseus' birth (ἐπεὶ κατὰ τὴν ὁδόν ὗσεν ὁ Ζεύς), Sch. *Od.* 1.75 (this seems to ignore the pun a few lines above, at 62: τί νύ οἱ τόσον ὠδύσαο, Ζεῦ;). Cf. *EM* s.v. Ὀδυσσεύς. Recent efforts to re-etymologise Odysseus include Palmer's (1980: 36) ὁ + *deuk- (cf. lat. *ducere*), meaning 'he who succeeds in fulfilling a purpose'. Palmer thought that this etymology would agree with 'the pre-dominance of martial themes in the name-giving, natural in a heroic context', while Peradotto (1990: 164 f.) suspected a generic hint at the hero's leadership. But the assumed reconstruction *Odyk-j-eus is difficult and the closeness in sound not strong.
[48] See Wachter 2001: 265–8, Immerwahr 1990: 45.
[49] See Brommer 1983a: 18, against the earlier view (Solmsen 1909b: 207 ff.) that the form with δ is older. See now M.L. West (2014: 6–7) for a summary of the situation.
[50] Marót 1960: 1–6; cf. Peradotto 1990: 146.
[51] Cf. Cook (2009: 115), who sees the scar as 'an emblem and record of physical pain', thus suggesting a common feature between this name and the torment expressed in *odyssomai* – Odysseus.

imply that a relevant etymology could have held a central place in an older narrative, which used the version of the name with λ,⁵² and where οὐλή perhaps served as a source of puns. Another possibility would be to relate Ὀλυσσεύς to ὄλλυμι 'destroy' (or *Οὐλυσσεύς to the adjective οὖλος / οὔλιος 'destructive'⁵³); this would denote the appropriate sense that the hero 'caused the death of many', but also that 'he brought misery upon himself'.⁵⁴

As far as 'scientific' etymology is concerned, the forms with λ suggest a strong case for a pre-Hellenic origin of the name.⁵⁵ Ὀλυ- (Olympos, Olynthos) and -σσ- are thought to be pre-Greek elements.⁵⁶ Linguistic evidence reinforces the possibility of a proto-name for Odysseus, which suits the hero's alleged great antiquity. As Odysseus clearly had an already long history behind him when he became part of the epic stories, it is not impossible that the alternative dialectal forms of the name are traces of different stages in the development of the figure.⁵⁷ It is probably fair to say that the exact etymological meaning of the name 'is lost in antiquity.'⁵⁸

Finally, as is the case with nearly all major Homeric heroes, Odysseus too has been thought to have a divine aspect, possibly as a pre-Greek god.⁵⁹ Even if true, divine origin finds no echo in the epics: Odysseus blatantly denies any relation to the divine world in his meeting with Alkinoos (7.199–203, where he empasises his human suffering), and passes up the opportunity to be made immortal by Kalypso. Unlike the cases of Achilles, Aias and Nestor, the treatment of

---

52 Cf. Peradotto 1990: 146 – an attractive speculation.
53 An epithet of Ares and Achilles in the *Iliad* (5.461; 21.536). Note the historical name Οὐλιάδης / -ας (*LGPN*).
54 Note that Eustathius (289.39, on *Il.* 2.569–80) records both forms: ὁ Ὀδυσσεύς δέ που Ὀλυσσεύς καὶ ἡ Ὀδύσσεια Ὀλύσσεια. For more etymological efforts see *LfgrE* s.v. Ὀδυσ(σ)εύς (G. Markwald).
55 There is evidence that the sound *d* replaced *l* in the pronounciation in words borrowed from the pre-Greek language; see Bosshardt 1942: 139, cf. Chantraine 1999 and Beekes 2010 s.v. Ὀδυσσεύς. Kretschmer (1896: 280–1) thought that the form Ὀδυσσεύς was the product of a folk-etymological interpretation of an original name with λ.
56 Bosshardt 1942:139, Heubeck 1961: 25.
57 See above, p. 95. Latacz (1996: 136) saw him as an old seaman figure, originally in the sagas of the pre-Greek people. See also M.L. West (2014: 8–9) on local traditions about Odysseus and on the old view that he was an indigenous figure from north-west Greece (perhaps a seer). Cf. *LIMC* s.v. Odysseus (O. Touchefeu-Meynier).
58 Thus M.L. West 2014: 7. Kretschmer's suggestion (1940: 253) that the form 'Odysseus' was a creation of the *Odyssey* poet to suit his poetic etymology from *odysomai*, is highly unlikely.
59 See *RE* 17 s.v. Odysseus (Wüst), esp. 1910–3 (who bases the argument mainly on the evidence about later cults of Odysseus). Philippson (1947) assumed (unconvincigly) a pre-Homeric chthonic figure connected with Hermes through the Autolykan background.

the question whether Odysseus' figure might have divine roots cannot easily involve the hero's name.⁶⁰

Aside from the name Odysseus, the poem identifies its hero in other ways, by alternative proper names and also by adjectives which sound like potential names (and may have been momentarily thus interpreted). These alternative appellations are offered in the place of Odysseus' true name at various instances of the poem's plot, which employs 'a strategy of ironies' in order to conceal the hero's identity;⁶¹ they appear not to be random choices but carry meaning, and they function, each in its own way, as further instalments to the hero's characterisation.

First, there is the Polyphemos episode and the much-discussed name Οὖτις, used by Odysseus to trick the Cyclops. Outis, 'no-one', is a paradoxical name; the sense 'no-one' implies 'no-name', but the context clearly suggests a personal name ('Outis is my name', 9.366; cf. the accusative οὖτιν, not οὖτινα), one with comic overtones; its primary function is as a joke, at the centre of a *paronomasia*. The resulting pun on μῆτις – μή τις (9.408–15) even seems to suggest an alternative name for the hero, 'Mr Cunning-Intelligence' (note that πολύμητις is a common epithet of, and is almost exclusively used for, Odysseus⁶²); the ways in which he conceals or reveals his name are a distinctive aspect of his cunning.⁶³

Outis sounds appropriate in further ways: first as a name for someone who is of much smaller size and has less strength than his opponent, which is how Odysseus compares to the Cyclops (note that he calls the hero οὐτιδανός 'of no account', 'worthless' [LSJ], 9.515). But it may also function as an allegory; on a deeper symbolic level, Odysseus is a Mr Nobody (οὖτις), in the sense that he suffers from a loss of homeland and status,⁶⁴ and more specifically of his traditional heroic identity, as in his encounter with the Cyclops the trickster takes over: Odysseus fights Polyphemos with trickery (δόλος), not with force (βίη; cf. 9.408 and 9.299–305, where he explicitly states that his heroic *thymos*

---

60 It might be possible to see a linguistic connection between Ὀλ-υσσεύς and Ἀπ-όλ(λ)ων, the latter name being also supposedly pre-Greek, but further assumptions about the type of Odysseus' 'divine' existence would be entirely speculative.
61 See further Goldhill 1991: 1, 24–36.
62 Cf. its use for Bdelykleon in Aristophanes' *Wasps*, Kanavou 2011: 86–7.
63 Cf. Cook 2009: 118–9. As Goldhill notes (1991: 32), 'his name *outis* and its synonym *mētis* ... is itself a *mētis*.' On the possible association between this nickname and folktale see Edwards 1987: 120–1.
64 Cf. Austin 1972: 15–7 and Segal 1994: 90–5 (more specifically on the connection between heroic name and *kleos*).

could not prevail in this instance).⁶⁵ Of course, the poetic treatment of his life and days ensures that the hero never really becomes a 'nobody'. His epic personality has not faded; his *kleos* clearly endures, and it is acknowledged during his travels.⁶⁶

Self-introduction by false identities becomes a systematic practice of Odysseus as soon as he arrives at Ithaca. There are no fewer than four instances: to Eumaios, to the suitors, to Penelope and finally to his father Laertes. In each case Odysseus tells a false story about his provenance and parentage, but does not always reveal a personal name; he does so only in the latter two instances. In the story told to Eumaios, the hero identifies Crete as his place of origin (14.199) and names an adopted father (Kastor Hylakides, 14.204).⁶⁷ He presents himself to Eumaios⁶⁸ as a beggar, and he does the same with the suitors (17.415 ff.), again avoiding naming himself.

---

65 See Cook (2009: 117–21), who, however, finds that the identities of trickster and hero converge in the scene of the Cyclops' blinding (perhaps seen as reminiscent of a warrior's *aristeia*) and in the appropriation of 19 rams by Odysseus (reminiscent of a heroic cattle raid). Odysseus' heroic identity resurfaces completely as he takes leave from the Cyclops and reveals his name (at the expense of the trickster's nature), thus reasserting his *kleos* (cf. Segal 1994: 97 and Higbie 1995: 164). On the interpetation of Odysseus' contact in the Cyclops' episode as *hybris* see Cook ibid.: 120 (and n. 24), with bibliography. For a recent extant study of Odysseus' dual nature (as 'avenger hero' and 'trickster') see Van Nortwick (2009).
66 Other interpretations of Outis include Photius' (citing Ptolemaeus Chennos) 'big ears' (οὖς), and the unconvincing assumption that Outis and Odysseus share phonetic similarities (Austin 1972: 14, n.20). A phonetic similarity has been noted between Outis and the vocabulary used for the wounding of Odysseus in the account of the boar hunt (οὐτάμεναι 19.449, οὐτῆσε 19.452), which belongs to the context of the story of Odysseus' naming (Peradotto 1990: 146, and earlier Ziegler 1962: 396–8), but a connection between the two episodes seems unlikely. Outis has further been seen as an expression of the failure of the personal name to contain the totality of the bearer's personality: the name refers to a nobody in that it annihilates the individual by inevitably placing him in a more or less generic semantic category (Peradotto 1990: 152 ff.). This is hardly relevant to the Homeric context, but reflects a modern philosophical point about the nature of personal names (cf. Ong 1986: 130–1 on name and individuality). Interestingly, Outis was used as a historical name, though the evidence is scarce and late (one attestation from Thespiai, Boiotia, 2ⁿᵈ c.AD), and it may have been inspired from the Homeric use.
67 On this remarkable name and patronymic combination, see *Comm. on Od.* v.2: 207 (Hoekstra). ὑλακτέω 'howl' occurs in Homer (*Il.* 18.586, of dogs, cf. κύνες ὑλακόμωροι 'baying dogs' *Od.* 14.29), and if κάστωρ is also relevant to dogs (cf. X. *Cyn.* 3.1, καστόριαι, one of two breeds of dogs), then indeed a pun may be intended.
68 Eumaios' use of οὔ τις (14.122) perhaps echoes Odysseus' self-introduction to the Cyclops (cf. Dougherty 2001: 64, Goldhill 1991: 38).

On the other hand, his introductions to Penelope and Laertes both include personal names; these are deliberately significant. He introduces himself as Αἴθων (ὄνομα κλυτόν 'a famous name'[69]) to Penelope at 19.183, shortly before Eurykleia's story of how he got his (real) name. The name Aithon is etymologically significant, and perhaps not an accidental choice. An adjective αἴθων is used in the epics for a variety of animals and metallic objects, though its exact meaning is hard to determine. One possibility is 'shining' (perhaps from αἰθός).[70] Another possibility is that it functioned as a colour term: 'tawny' for a lion and 'sorrel', 'brown' for horses;[71] in the case of metals, it could allude to the reddish-brownish colour of bronze. The personal name would then mean 'dark-complexioned'; the common understanding of the ethnic Αἰθίοψ and the various instances of darkness as a male physical trait encourage this meaning.[72] A different use of αἶθοψ, which was probably interchangeable with αἴθων (αἶθοψ was used in Homer for wine, bronze or smoke), might suggest another appropriate sense for the name: the adjective is used for hunger (λιμόν; Hesiod *Op.* 363,[73] perhaps with the meaning 'fiery' = 'intense'?)[74] More significantly, it is used as a proper name for Erysichthon, who suffered from insatiable hunger.[75] Hunger is relevant to the identity assumed by Odysseus as Aithon, which is that of a beggar. We may conclude that the name had an ambiguous sense that reflected the double implication of the beggar disguise for Odysseus' character, as a trickster and as a man who suffers.[76]

Odysseus' self-introduction to his father involves no fewer than four false names: εἰμὶ μὲν ἐξ Ἀλύβαντος,... / υἱὸς Ἀφείδαντος Πολυπημονίδαο ἄνακτος· / αὐτὰρ ἐμοί γ' ὄνομ' ἐστὶν Ἐπήριτος· 'I come from Alybas... and I am the son of Apheidas, son of lord Polypemon, and my name is Eperitos' (*Od.* 24.304–6). It is

---

[69] An ironic designation, cf. Pucci 1987: 197 n.19.
[70] Cf. πάναιθος at *Il.* 14.372, 'gleaming all over'. See *LfgrE* s.v. αἴθω and αἴθοπ- (H.J. Mette). The passive participle αἰθόμενος has the middle sense 'burning, blazing' (e.g. *Il.* 4.485, 6.182, cf. *Od.* 1.184, 428). The active form αἴθω ('to set on fire', 'kindle') is post-Homeric.
[71] For lions: *Il.* 10.24=178 (so, too, of oxen and eagles); for horses: *Il.* 2.839 = 12.97. Thus Edgeworth 1983: 31–40, followed by *Comm. on Od.* v.3: 86 (Russo).
[72] E.g. *Od.* 16.175, 19.246. Cf. *Comm. on Od.* v.3: 86 (Russo).
[73] M.L.West (1978: 248). Notably, Bergk chose to replace the mss reading αἴθοπα (preferred by West) with αἴθωνα.
[74] 'fiery famine' (transl. Most). Cf. [Hes.] *Cat.* fr. 43a M–W, 'Simon.' (Page 1981: 257–9), Call. *Cer.* 66–7.
[75] [Hes.] *Cat.* fr.43a, b M–W and Hellan., *FGrH* 4 F 7 etc. (τὸν δ' Αἴθων' ἐκάλεσσαν ἐπ]ών[υ]μ[ο]ν εἵνεκα λιμοῦ / αἴθωνος κρατεροῦ). See also M.L.West 1978: 248.
[76] On this function of the beggar identity see Cook 2009: 129. Hunger is also very relevant to Odysseus' self-presentation at 7.215 ff.

surprising that Odysseus has to invent a different false identity for Laertes, and the scene further alerts us to the very problematic character of the Epilogue of the *Odyssey*, whose authenticity has been strongly debated.⁷⁷ Still, the chosen names suit the plot of our *Odyssey*; although Laertes does not react to them, the audience would notice that they are all significant (even if not wholly easy to explain). The alleged father's name, Ἀφείδας, is from the root φειδ-⁷⁸ with the prefix α-, which can denote either deprivation or quantity. In the latter case it would appear synonymous with Πολυφείδης (*Od.* 15.249, 252). The meaning of the verb φείδομαι ('let live', 'abstain from harming, save from injury or inconvenience, be solicitous for, spare'⁷⁹), however, is more sensibly combined with the notion of deprivation,⁸⁰ in which case Apheidas should mean 'he who did not spare'; this may refer to property ('rich, generous') or to the suitors (before going to meet his father, Odysseus had killed = 'not spared' the suitors).⁸¹ The grandfather's name, Πολυπημονίδης, also encompasses different possibilities.⁸² It may evoke πῆμα: 'he who has suffered much', or it may conceal Πολυπάμων (cf. Hom. πολυπάμων 'owning much property' *Il.* 4.433, and the name Πάμ(μ)ων *Il.* 24.250).⁸³ The context allows a *double entendre:* papponymic and patronymic combined would suit the designation of Apheidas as ἄναξ (cf. 24.305) – an *anax* is expected to own wealth; they would also suit the nature of a noble character who suffered and who was not spared from misfortune.

---

77 See further *Comm. on Od.* v.3 (Heubeck) and S.R.West 1988: 113–43. There is good reason to believe that this Epilogue was a later addition to the epic, while the details of the meeting of Odysseus with his father are better explained if in a different version of the story it happened earlier on after the hero's homecoming (see S.R.West 1988: 126–7). On the case for an original ending of the poem shortly after Odysseus' and Penelope's reunion on their marriage bed (23.299), see M.L.West 2014: 294–5.
78 Homeric names with this root are gathered in von Kamptz 1982 (1958): 224; e.g. Φείδας *Il.* 13.691, Φείδων *Il.* 14.361.
79 Cf. *Il.* 24.158=187, 20.464, *Od.* 22.54, 16.185 and *Il.* 5.202 as an explanation of the name Φείδιππος (*Il.* 2.678). The precise meaning of the verb eludes us; von Kamptz 1982 (1958): 248–9 included the sense 'take care of'.
80 This is probably what the initial Ἀ- meant in other Homeric names (cf. Ἀδάμας *Il.* 12.140, Ἀκάμας *Il.* 2.823 etc.).
81 Cf. *Comm. on Od.* v.3: 395 (Heubeck).
82 For an account of these see Heubeck (*Comm. on Od.* v.3: 395, with bibliography). Note also the form Πολυπαμονίδαο, suggested by Cobet – perhaps preferable in view of *Il.* 4.433 and 24.250.
83 From πᾶμα 'property', πέπαμαι 'I own', cf. Hom. Πολυκτήμων, κτῆμα, κτάομαι. See von Kamptz 1982 (1958): 80–1.

Regarding the name that Odysseus adopts for himself, Ἐπήριτος, two distinct explanations have been proposed:[84] the name could be connected either with ἔρις ('man of strife'), or, more likely, with the archaic adjective ἐπάριτος 'picked', 'chosen', which is strikingly close in sound.[85] This etymology would suggest the meaning 'the chosen one': chosen to suffer, or chosen as a member of a social elite? If the name is associated with suffering or strife, and Πολυπήμων is taken to mean 'much-suffering', they would both fall within roughly the same semantic field as ὀδυσσάμενος.[86] If the combination of Ἀφείδας and Πολυπημονίδης is heard to imply class and wealth, Eparitos can join in as part of a genealogy that reflects the name-bearer's alleged high-class origin (implied by ἄνακτος); thus the man who was introduced to Penelope earlier as a beggar would now become, by name, a rich aristocrat. The name perhaps also includes a self-conscious poetic hint: under his disguise, he is a man chosen for greatness, to be sung and glorified by poetry.

The place-name Ἀλύβας continues the *double entendre*:[87] it may suggest ἀλάομαι 'to wander, rove' or ἀλύω ('to be beside oneself from pain or grief', *Il.* 5.352, 24.12 or from exultation, *Od.* 18.333–393). This would suit the interpretation of Odysseus' false name and genealogy as relevant to the meaning of ὀδυσσάμενος. However, it could be simply meant to evoke South Italy (because of Σικανίη mentioned at 24.307; other place-names in Magna Graecia were formed with –αντ–, e.g. Taras, Acragas).[88]

The semantic ambiguity of Odysseus' self-introductions was in all probability, as already implied, deliberate: all possible meanings constitute good (false) introductions, which are not only convincing but also playful, with disguised references to aspects of the hero's self.

As mentioned earlier, some adjectives associated with Odysseus are close in form to onomastic labels. This is particularly true for πολυάρητος – another ambiguous term: it appears in Eurykleia's plea to Autolykos just before the naming of the child (19.404), and it has been seen as a discreet suggestion for a proper name.[89] It was

---

84 See Heubeck *Comm. on Od.* v.3: 395, with bibliography.
85 This is from the root ἀρι- 'count' (as in ἀριθμός), found in Hom. εἰκοσιν-ήριτος ('twenty times the normal, twenty-fold', *Il.* 22.349). Cf. ἐπάριτοι, used in X. *HG* 7.4 for the Arkadian troups (= ἐπίλεκτοι in D.S. 15.62); cf. also lacon. Πεδάριτος (Th. 8.28.5) and νήριτος ('innumerable') ὕλη (i.e. 'immense forest' Hes. *Op.* 511 [transl. Most]); see von Kamptz 1982 (1958): 57, 82. Ἐπάριτος is attested as a historical name (Aiolis-Kyme, 350–250 BC, *LGPN* VA).
86 Cf. Peradotto 1990: 144.
87 Again I rely mostly on Heubeck (*Comm. on Od.* v.3: 395) for the distillation of the possibilities.
88 Cf. also the similar place-name Ἀλύβη (*Il.* 2.857) and personal name Ἀρύβας (*Od.* 15.426).
89 See Dimock 1956: 54, Peradotto 1990: 128.

definitely used as one for historical people.⁹⁰ As a choice for Odysseus, it could mean 'much prayed for' (LSJ), which is suitable in a name suggested by his dedicated and loving nanny. On the other hand, the extant use of ἀρή and ἀρητός within the semantic field of 'curse' implies a different, negative meaning: 'much cursed'; this would be roughly synonymous with ὀδυσσάμενος.⁹¹ The one other occurrence of the epithet in the poem (6.280) alludes to Odysseus and is equally ambivalent: Nausikaa nearly mistakes him for a god and a husband-to-be, someone who has come as an answer to her prayers – in reality he will only cause pain, and not only by not fulfilling Nausikaa's wishes: Poseidon is angry with the Phaeacians for helping Odysseus and curses them (13.146 ff.).⁹²

Another adjective, πολύτροπος 'of many ways', 'resourceful', is also strongly associated with Odysseus; significantly, it is otherwise only used for Hermes (*h.Merc.* 13 and 439), a god characterised by guile, and with whom Odysseus' grandfather Autolykos seems to have had a connection; the adjective is thus an integral part of Odysseus' trickster identity.⁹³ *Polytropos* has a prominent place in the proem, where the hero's name (first mentioned at 1.21) is notably absent.⁹⁴ The adjectival nature of *polytropos* is not very strong, as it is only used twice (*Od.* 1.1, 10.330), and only in connection with Odysseus; the adjective is used alongside Odysseus' name at 10.330, but not in the proem, where it may have been interpreted almost as an alternative name by some among the audience.⁹⁵

No onomastic example from the *Iliad* can rival the importance attributed to Odysseus' name(s). The ambiguous false names or potential names are reflections of the temporary shapes assumed by the hero's personality (cf. again Peradotto's concept of 'man in the middle voice'), marking steps on the way to the

---

90 Πολυάρητος is attested as early as the 6th c. BC (Paros), while the form Πολυάρατος is very common in the Aegean region from the 4th c. BC onwards (*LGPN* I).
91 Peradotto 1990: 138–9. Cf. also the discussion of the name Arete (Ἀρήτη) below.
92 See Dimock 1956: 64–5. Note that in the middle of this description of the harm caused because of Odysseus there is a reminder of the sufferer hero: 13.131–2, 'For I just now declared that Odysseus should suffer many woes before he reached his home' (Poseidon's words).
93 Cf. M.L. West 2014: 10. See also above, pp. 95, 97.
94 For a detailed analysis of this absence, in relation to the epithet *polytropos*, see Pucci 1998: 22–9. Peradotto (1990: 116) saw it as a semantic opposite to the name Kalypso (to be discussed later on), which is usually understood to imply the notion of constraint, while the flexibility – versatility implied by *polytropos* can be associated with freedom; but the lack of direct verbal hints makes these associations too complex for the audience.
95 Note also that Polytropos occurs as a personal name, for the man who directed a Spartan invasion of Arkadia in 369/8 (X. *HG* 6.5.11–13; cf. D.S. 15.62.1).

reestablishment of Odysseus' original epic identity. They further reflect the various 'mutations' that this identity underwent in the long poetic tradition. The poet of the *Odyssey* connects the naming of his hero with the deepest aspects of this identity; it might seem as though the hero suffered loss of it because of the fate implied by his name, but the identity problem is then solved through the name: the recovery of his identity is signalled by means of the return to this name (cf. *Od.* 19.474; 22.45; 23.209; 24.328).

3.2 Odysseus' Family

As we have seen, Odysseus' name, that expresses the essence of his identity, and each of the alternative names and appellations, hold clues to the hero's personality. We shall see in this section that aspects of this uniquely versatile character may be reflected also in the names of members of his immediate family.

3.2.1 Laertes, Antikleia

The name Λαέρτης is usually analysed as a compound from λαός and the root **er-* 'set in motion, pull'.[96] Laertes is similar to a Mycenaean name, Ertilaos (or Etilaos?[97]), which seems to consist of the same components in the reverse order. On account of its etymology, Laertes should mean 'he who sets the men (λαός) in motion'.[98]

This significance does not suit the Laertes of the *Odyssey*, an old man retired to the countryside,[99] living alone, with no public function. His humble way of life is poignantly described at *Od.* 11.187–96 by the ghost of his wife: he sleeps in the slaves' quarters and has no proper bed; and he is utterly consumed by grief (cf. the image of him dressed in poor, dirty clothes, worn down by old age, that so moves Odysseus at 24.226–34). Aside from the memorable reunion with his

---

[96] See e.g. Chantraine 1999 (followed by Beekes 2010) s.v. Λαέρτης. Words from this root are part of Homeric vocabulary: ὄρνυμι, ὀρίνω and ἔρνος 'young tree, sapling' (e.g. *Il.* 18.56; cf. Hsch. ἔρετο· ὡρμήθη). Cf. the phrase ὄρνυθι λαούς 'urge on the men' (*Il.* 15.475), which seems to reflect the name's etymology.
[97] See Jorro-Adrados 1985 s.v. *e-ti-ra-wo*.
[98] 'Mannenantreiber', von Kamptz 1982 (1958): 33, 77. Similarly Chantraine 1999 s.v. Λαέρτης 'l'homme qui met en mouvement le peuple'.
[99] Though a former king and the father of a king, his Odyssean existence may reflect the class of 'non-elite farmers', see Raaflaub 1997: 635.

son and his small participation in the final battle in book 24 (226 ff.), he has a surprisingly limited role in the *Odyssey*, while in the *Iliad* there is no indication that he is still alive (it is unusual for a hero's father to be alive so long, when a third generation – Telemachos – has reached adulthood). There is good reason to suspect that his footing in our *Odyssey* is not that strong.[100] He further seems to have played no independent role in saga (the poem mentions only one heroic deed by Laertes, as king of Kephallenians taking Nerikos, *Od.* 24.377 ff. – notably the speaker there is Odysseus).[101] Perhaps the name was used as a generic heroic name, deriving from Mycenaean stock. We might assume that a further motive for its choice was that it suited Odysseus, who is very much a public figure (he is perhaps seen most emphatically so in the action he undertakes in *Il.* 2) and a leader of men.

The name of Odysseus' mother Ἀντίκλεια is not very prominent in the poem either. It is only mentioned once (11.85), and already its bearer is dead and is visited by her son in Hades (still she is given importance by the fact that Odysseus' encounter with her ghost occupies more lines than his interview with Teiresias). Her role, like Laertes', seems to have been entirely dependent on her son: her main characteristic is her love for Odysseus, and she died of the grief caused by her son's long absence (*Od.* 11.202 ff., 15.356 ff.). Her name does not express a personal characteristic but is rather generic, to be explained in connection with the large group of Homeric names with *kleos*. As noted earlier, this element was most likely understood as 'heroic glory' (rather than as a general word for 'hearing' or 'reputation');[102] the name Antikleia should mean 'equal to / worthy of glory' and thus express a notion which is central in heroic poetry and to her son's characterisation as the epic's hero.

3.2.2 Telemachos

Like the names of his parents, the name of Odysseus' son appears to reflect the hero's own life and experience. The name has two possible meanings that would

---

100 S.R.West (1988: 115–8) has argued convincingly in favour of a seemingly late integration of Laertes in the plot. M.L. West (2014: 23) describes him as 'an embellishment to the Returning Husband story'. See also above p. 103 on the problematic character of the *Odyssey*'s last book.
101 *LfgrE* s.v. Λαέρτης (W. Beck).
102 See above, on Patroklos' name. Peradotto (1990: 138) read in her name the meaning 'opposed to *kleos*' – an allusion to the unheroic traits of her father's (Autolykos') character. This is difficult, given the absence of a pun and the occurrence of the masculine form Antiklos, a generic heroic name (*Od.* 4.286).

suit Odysseus: 'a fighter far away' and 'one who fights from a distance = a master bowman'. Telemachos' name should thus reflect the known practice, also encountered elsewhere in the epics,[103] of naming children for some characteristic of the parent.

Of the two aforementioned meanings, other linguistic and onomastic evidence seems to favour the sense 'archer'. The similar formation Τήλεφος (Τηλεφίδης *Od.* 11.519, for Eurypylos, son of Telephos) is probably a parallel form of Τηλέφονος,[104] which must mean 'killing from afar': this suggests a good analogy with Telemachos' name as 'fighter from a distance'. The very similar Homeric adjective ἀγχέμαχος 'fighting at close quarters / hand to hand' (cf. *Il.* 13.5, 16.248, 272, 17.165) points to an original adjective *τηλέμαχος, which should mean the exact opposite: 'fighter from afar'.[105]

Regardless of etymology, the *Odyssey* encourages both possible meanings at different points. The context of the first mention of Telemachos' name (*Od.* 1.113 ff.) refers to his father, that he is a warrior, and that he is away from home, while a later reference (21.126–9; Telemachos in connection with the stringing of his father's bow) may relate to the second meaning. References to archery as Odysseus' characteristic method of fighting in the *Odyssey* are found at various places: 8.215 ff., 21.393 ff., 22.1 ff.[106] The only two mentions of Telemachos in the *Iliad* (2.260, 4.354) are part of Odysseus' self-presentation, when he notably introduces himself as his son's father and not by reference to

---

103 See further under 'Minor' speaking names.
104 Cf. Von Kamptz 1982 (1958): 71. Telemachos is the only name with τηλε- in the *Iliad*. Other similar names in the *Odyssey* include Τήλεμος (9.509), the name of the prophet who foretold to Polyphemos that Odysseus would one day blind him – perhaps a short form of Telemachos (von Kamptz 1982 (1958): 138); and the obscure Τηλέπυλος (10.82, cf. 23.318), either 'the Laestrygonian town Telepylos' or an epithet for Λαιστρυγονίη as the name of the town (Heubeck *Comm. on Od.* v.3: 48; 'with gates far apart' (LSJ); more likely 'distant portal' (M.L.West 1997: 406), alluding to the folktale nature of the place) – unlike -*machos*, the second component of Telepylos cannot function verbally.
105 Von Kamptz 1982 (1958): 32, n.28. This analogy is encouraged by the Arkadian form Τηλίμαχος, apparently influenced by ἀγχίμαχος (Chantraine 1999 and Beekes 2010 s.v. τῆλε). Cf. *Comm. on Od.* v.1: 91–2 (S.R.West). Note also the treaty inscription supposed to date from the Lelantine war, with the provision μὴ χρῆσθαι τηλεβόλοις 'not to use long-range weapons' (Str. 10.1.12).
106 But not in the *Iliad*, which does not show much appreciation for archery (see also above, pp. 54, 85); cf. S.R. West (2012: 538–9), who argues that the *Odyssey*'s interest in the use of the bow (seen also in the archery contest towards the end of the epic) reflects central Asian nomadic practice (whose poetic depiction is found in the epic of *Alpamysh*), and that the *Odyssey* in that respect relies on a poetic ancestor from that region. Cf. M.L. West 2014: 99.

Laertes. These instances may be felt to increase Telemachos' importance,[107] but may equally indicate that the meaning of his name is to be connected with Odysseus. At *Il.* 4.353–5 (ὄψεαι, ἢν ἐθέλησθα καὶ αἴ κέν τοι τὰ μεμήλῃ, /Τηλεμάχοιο φίλον πατέρα προμάχοισι μιγέντα / Τρώων ἱπποδάμων· 'You will see, if you wish and if you have any interest, the dear father of Telemachos mingling with the foremost fighters of the horse-taming Trojans'), Odysseus seems to be saying:[108] 'Although my son's name is Telemachos, and truly in keeping with this I am a distance fighter, I will now throw myself on the front line and fight against the first of the Trojans'. A pun on προμάχοισι may be intended, gaining force from the fact that Odysseus refers to himself as the father of Telemachos, which is not only unusual, but also happens just as he announces his intention to fight as a πρόμαχος from then on.[109]

The association of Telemachos' name with his father and not with himself[110] may suggest a character whose poetic conception did not endow him with a strong personality or with striking individual characteristics[111] – a lesser man than his father, as often sons of great heroes are[112] (in the words of Athena-Mentor at 2.276–7, addressed to Telemachos). Indeed Telemachos shows (at least at the beginning) a lack of initiative and self-confidence in his handling of the situation (he is practically pushed into action by Athena-Mentes in book 1). His most important function lies apparently in his association with his father, which is vital even when he becomes more self-reliant in the latter part of the *Odyssey*; his action then does not merely reflect a potential inherited from his

---

107 Perhaps also suggest that the hero had a notable poetic pre-history; thus M.L. West 2014: 98; see also below, n. 111.
108 Cf. Howald 1947: 87.
109 See, in similar lines, Martin 1989: 70–1. Cf. M.L. West 2011a: 145–6. The other time when Odysseus identifies himself as the father of Telemachos (*Il.* 2.260) is in the context of his attack on Thersites. The two instances perhaps share a passionate tone, but otherwise the use of a paidonymic is odd, as Higbie notes (1995: 159–60).
110 Another possible meaning, 'far from the fighting' (Chantraine 1999 s.v. τῆλε), might seem appropriate for Telemachos as the young son who did not experience the Trojan battles – but etymology does not encourage this sense, which is, further, little relevant to Telemachos' function in the *Odyssey*.
111 Higbie (1995: 149) assumed that Telemachos had a secondary status in traditional Trojan epic stories, based on the naming patterns used for him. S.R. West (*Comm. on Od.* v.1: 51–2) suggested that Telemachos' role developed in the *Odyssey*, and he rose to a more prominent part, because of the length of Odysseus' *nostos*. M.L. West similarly alleges that his role was a secondary development, but probably earlier than our *Odyssey*, though no Telemachy could have existed as an independent poem (2014: 2, 95, 98–9).
112 Cf. M.L. West 2007a: 440.

father,[113] but is derived from Odysseus' very presence and is centered on helping him. Such a depiction of Telemachos is necessary in order to preserve Odysseus' protagonistic status: Telemachos must not rival his father, but depend on him (for handling the suitors), and this dependence is reflected in his name.[114]

3.2.3 Penelope

Later poetry once refers to Penelope as a wife and mother whose husband and son are both significantly named: Οὐδενὸς εὐνάτειρα Μακροπτολέμοιο δὲ μάτηρ (Theocritus, *Syrinx* 1; Makroptolemos is Telemachos as the son of 'far-fighting', and Oudeis of course equals Odysseus' famous appellation Outis).[115] In keeping with the rest of the family, Penelope too was traditionally thought to carry a significant name. Her name, however, differs from the names of Odysseus' parents and son in that – as we shall see – its significance does not reflect on the hero; its focus is Penelope herself, who is perhaps thus singled out for her poetic importance – an importance that is echoed in all possible explanations of her name.

The common folk-etymology of the name Πηνελόπη sees it as a compound of πήνη 'woof, thread' (*Il*. 23.762) and ὀλόπτω 'to tear out' or λέπω 'to strip off' (only aor. ἔλεψεν, *Il*. 1.236).[116] The first part derives from the common female sphere (the craft of weaving, cf. *Od*. 2.93–110), but the second part suggests a twist – the trick played by Penelope on her suitors: the weaving of the shroud for Laertes by day, which she kept undoing by night, so that she could prolong the wait for the return of her husband. This is an essential theme and is mentioned several times in the *Odyssey*: 2.93–100; 19.139–156; 24.128–49.[117] Its ori-

---

113 As pointed out by the disguised Athena (2.279: 'nor has the wisdom of Odysseus wholly failed you', cf. 3.22–8).
114 Telemachos' name probably provided inspiration for Τηλέγονος, the name of Odysseus' son by Kirke (Hes. *Th.* 1011–14), easily understood to mean 'the one born far (from Ithaca)'.
115 Part of a group of poems known as the *Technopaignia*; the riddle-like names are explained by the Scholia there. See further Gow 1952 (vol. 2): 552 ff. and now Kwapisz (2013: 138 ff.).
116 Also λεπτός, λοπός 'a husk or skin', *Od*. 19.233, and notably λώπη 'covering', 'robe', *Od*. 13.224. See von Kamptz 1982 (1958): 70; Mactoux 1975: 233 (her study of Penelope is of seminal importance for later interpretations of the heroine's name and character).
117 It is important enough to form part of Penelope's artistic representation, see Buitron-Oliver & Cohen 1995: 44–7. Notable examples include an Attic vase painting of the classical period that depicts Penelope together with the famous loom; and a Melian relief of the same period depicting a seated Penelope with a wool basket beneath her seat (she is similarly depicted on an early imperial Roman relief).

gin may lie in the sphere of folktale and is therefore potentially of great antiquity.[118] Perhaps the name is intrinsic to this story, which might explain the fact that its relevant significance is not made explicit in the *Odyssey*, and corresponding puns are absent. Still, the importance of this story in the long epic affirms that the possible connection of the name Penelope with 'loom' would create a strong tie between the name and a key symbolic object of the Odyssean plot.[119]

The poet of the *Odyssey* arguably creates further links between this etymology and the heroine's characterisation. As expressive of trickery, the name is further reminiscent of Odysseus' main character trait: *mētis* (cunning) – a characteristic apparently also shared by Telemachos (who prepares to deceive his mother in *Od.* 2.373–5). It has often been noticed that the depiction of the characters of Odysseus and Penelope shares common elements.[120] She has been seen as the most important character for the poem's plot after Odysseus (her faithful wait and her actions in the last books of the *Odyssey* set in motion her husband's reestablishment in his position),[121] and she too, like Odysseus, wins *kleos* (for her strength of character and for her wifely virtue).[122] Penelope is not the typical female character, as her circumstances demand of her more initiative than normally expected of her sex.[123] Her power of mind is further displayed in the poem's penultimate book, in her dialogue with Odysseus (where she asks of Teiresias' prophecies about the future of Odysseus, 23.257–62) and her testing of Odysseus' knowledge of their marriage bed (23.176–80). The adjectives περίφρων ('very thoughtful', 'very careful'; LSJ) and ἐχέφρων ('sensible', 'prudent'; LSJ), used for Penelope repeatedly,[124] confirm her depiction as a woman of wisdom and good sense. Perhaps Penelope would further strike the audience as sharing

---

118 Peradotto 1990: 107–8, cf. 46. Inconsistencies in the relation of this tale to the plot of our *Odyssey* also suggest an old story which the poet could handle in various ways; Laertes' shroud may have replaced a wedding garment that Penelope would make in view of her forthcoming wedding to one of the suitors. See S.R. West 1988: 116–7; M.L. West 2014: 105.
119 On symbolic objects see also Zeitlin 1995 and for the *Iliad*, Griffin 1980: 1 ff.
120 See Murnaghan 1986: 103 and the bibliography gathered in n. 2 there. Cf. Schein (1995: 22–3), who stresses the mental similarity between the two.
121 On Penelope's importance see Murnaghan 1986: 103. However, Clayton's feminist view (2004, esp. ch. 3) of Penelope as the prototype of *mētis*, whose weaving and reweaving mirrors Odysseus' cunning (and not vice versa), is rather far-fetched.
122 *Kleos* is ascribed to her by the dead Agamemnon at 24.196–7 (cf. 18.215–25). See further Foley 1995: 95–6, 105. This is feminine *kleos*, which requires a different type of achievement to the male *kleos* acquired by Odysseus (through his *nostos*).
123 Thus Raaflaub 1997: 639–40. On ancient belief in the moral inferiority of women see Foley 1995: 93–4 (the main source is Aristotle *Politics*).
124 περίφρων is the most frequent of the two. It is applied exclusively to women, but rarely to others than Penelope. See Higbie 1995: 130–2.

with Odysseus also a figurative bardic function – she too, like Odysseus, tells stories (she repeats the story of Laertes' shroud) and has a distinct voice in the poem. If weaving can be seen as a metaphor for song-making, as assumed by some scholars, then her name might mirror this association too.[125]

However, both Penelope's characterisation and the form of the name leave room for another, entirely different etymology: from πηνέλοψ 'duck'.[126] This etymology is not only linguistically easier but also ancient (Arist. HA 593b23, Sch. Ar. Aves 1302). It seems also to account for another Homeric name, Πηνέλεως, of a Boiotian leader (Il. 2.494 etc.).[127] πηνέλοψ is not found in Homer, but it occurs in archaic lyric poetry (Alc. fr. 345 Voigt, Ibyc. fr. 317a PMGF). In the ancient world women's names were often related to bird names,[128] and ducks are significantly monogamous,[129] which makes an association with πηνέλοψ particularly appropriate for Penelope's name. Indeed, references to her faithful waiting for her husband are frequent in the Odyssey: she receives praise for this by Odysseus' mother and Agamemnon in the Nekyia (11.177–9; 181–3; 444–6) and later by Athena (13.190–3; 333–8; 379–81, 20. 33–524) and by Agamemnon's shadow (24.191–202). True, it has been felt that both Penelope's cunning and fidelity lose strength in the books leading to Odysseus' victory over the suitors (the encouragement she offers to the suitors in book 18 and the setting of the bow contest are particularly problematic),[130] but these details do not obscure the prevailing image of the faithful wife. Penelope certainly is the paradigm of the faith-

---

125 On the debatable connection between 'weaving' and poetry see Nagy 1996b: 64–5 (with bibliography); M.L. West 2007a: 36–8. Clayton (2004, esp. ch. 2) has argued in favour of an association between weaving, mētis and poetry in the character of Penelope.
126 Chantraine 1999 s.v. Πηνελόπεια and Beekes 2010 s.v. πηνέλοψ,-οπος; cf. Comm. on Od. v.1: 103 (S.R.West), Broadbent 1968: 307, Peradotto 1990: 107–8, Mactoux 1975: 233–6.
127 Von Kamptz 1982 (1958): 120, 376; Beekes 2010 s.v. πηνέλοψ,-οπος.
128 For examples see Bechtel 1902: 92–4. Cf. also the interpretation (presented below) of Kirke's name as 'hawk'.
129 On this notion (admittedly not attested in Greek) see further S.R. West's note (Comm. on Od. v.1: 103).
130 Murnaghan (1986) suggested that these 'failures' are down to the social pressures and restrictions faced by the female sex (cf. Foley 1995, esp. 107–8; also down to the lack of trust that accompanies wives in the ancient tradition, partly because of the behaviour of Helen and Klytaimestra). It is unnecessary to resort to interpretations involving e.g. a subconscious recognition of Odysseus and female intuition (see Murnaghan's note 21 and Schein 1995: 27 n. 16 for further bibliography on this issue). For a reading that justifies the bow contest and presents Penelope's actions as moral and socially responsible in the narrative framework where they belong, see Foley 1995, esp. 102–4. M.L. West (2014: 68) accounts for Penelope's changing attitude from the pressure from the needs of the story as a whole, of changing contexts and from the possible existence of different versions.

ful wife in later Greek tradition (see e.g. Ps.Arist. *Oec.* 3.1). Finally, heroines with names of water-birds (e.g. Alkyone) may point to deities of a pre-Hellenic belief;[131] perhaps Penelope originated in such a deity.[132] She was later given semi-divine status in her homeland Arkadia, where she was believed to be the mother of Pan by Hermes or Apollo (Pi. fr. 100, Hdt. 2.145).[133]

Could the above suggested meanings and connotations be combined in the name of one and the same figure? A certain Russian folktale, where a bird turns into a maiden who then has a carpet woven, allows us to imagine that the name could have combined both meanings (bird and woman who spins) in a folktale context.[134] Penelope perhaps had a career in popular pre-Homeric poetry and folklore, which might explain the above implied inconsistencies in her epic character as traces of older versions of stories surrounding her;[135] as far as her name is concerned, we might assume that each story activated a different meaning. Regarding the Homeric Penelope, it seems likely that the audience was encouraged to think of one meaning at certain points, then of the other: of the sense of weaving at references to the heroine's trick, and of the duck *penelops* where her fidelity is stressed.

3.3 Odysseus' Travels

The *Odyssey*'s onomastic diversity peaks in this section, as the world of epic merges with the world of folktale, and easy-to-interpret names coexist with dark and exotic ones.

3.3.1 Kalypso and Kirke

Kalypso and Kirke are apparently part of a common tradition: both are divine figures who live on islands on the edge of the world and possess some sort of magical powers; both fall for Odysseus and increase his plight at first, but end up

---

131 Fick 1905: 140. Birds and goddesses were closely linked in Minoan representations (see Carter 1995: 290).
132 See the various speculations of Mactoux (1975: 236–9) – some rather far-fetched.
133 See also Larson 1995: 58–9. The connection between Penelope and Pan may have emerged from the similarity of the first part of her name to his; cf. Mactoux 1975: 233.
134 See Hölscher (1989: 325, n.6).
135 This is a plausible alternative to the psychological explanation summarised above, n. 130. See further Mactoux 1975: 7–27.

offering help; they both give a taste of folktale. Their exact origins and development are difficult to determine, but they may be of Eastern inspiration.[136] Perceptions of their place in the epic and other mythical contexts are interconnected with interpretations of their names.

Of the two figures, Kalypso is clearly the most important one for the plot. Her name is mentioned in several books of the *Odyssey*, but primarily in 5. Outside the epic, it belongs to a known tradition of names for the Oceanids, as suggested in Hesiod's *Theogony* (358). A Kalypso is said to be the daughter of Okeanos in Hesiod (*Th.* 362, cf. *h.Dem.* 423), and the daughter of Atlas in the *Odyssey* (1.52, 7.245; in Apollod. 1.12.2 a Nereid – this may suggest that the name was shared by different nymphs).[137] The name is from the verb καλύπτω[138] and is clearly significant. It is similar to feminine names inspired by the veil worn as head-cover by women, e.g. Καλύπτρη (*AP* 9.240). The *Theogony* passage includes the epithet κροκόπεπλος 'with yellow dress', used for one of the Oceanids (though not for Kalypso herself), while *Od.* 5.232 (κεφαλῇ δ' ἐφύπερθε καλύπτρην 'and on her head she placed a veil'), which refers to Kalypso, was perhaps meant as a pun on the name.[139] A meaning such as 'the veiled one' may be encouraged by the similarities between Kalypso and the divine alewife Shiduri of the epic of Gilgamesh, who is introduced as 'veiled with a veil'.[140]

The above do not suggest a particular connection between Kalypso's name and the Odyssean plot. Still, it is widely thought that Kalypso and her name were deliberately inserted in the story by the poet of the *Odyssey*;[141] this insertion was meant to suit a plot necessity, that wanted its main hero to stay away from home for ten years, and had to provide a cause for this late homecoming. If so, the choice of name may well be intentional. Does the epic imply a connection between the sense of 'covering' or 'hiding' (καλύπτω) and the heroine's character and action? Ancient explanations of the name see it as an expression of Ka-

---

136 Crane 1988: 31, cf. M.L.West (1997: 404–5; 2014: 126–7) who thinks that they both correspond in nature and function to the divine alewife Shiduri of the Gilgamesh epic. Wilamowitz (1884: 115 ff.) thought that Kirke has an older tradition and Kalypso is an imitation, but the Kalypso of the *Odyssey* has clearly influenced the figure of Kirke.
137 M.L.West 1966: 267.
138 A short form of *Καλυψάνειρα according to Heubeck 1965: 143.
139 Thus Richardson 1974: 289.
140 See M.L.West 1997: 410; 2014: 127 n.67. An old (and rather unconvincing) mythological interpretation connected Kalypso with Hestia (from ἀμφι-έννυμι 'to cover with clothes'), and further to the tradition that the fire goddess should not be viewed by men uncovered (Gruppe 1906: 1402).
141 Cf. *Comm. on Od.* v.1: 249–50 (Hainsworth); Peradotto 1990: 102; M.L. West 2014: 127 n.67 (with references).

lypso's tendency to hide her thoughts: Ἡ μὴ ἁπλῆ, καλύπτουσα δὲ τὸ διανοούμενον (*EM* s.v. Καλυψώ, citing the Homeric epithet for Kalypso, δολόεσσα 'guileful' [*Od.* 7.245]). The Scholium at 7.245 explains *doloessa* by the fact that she deceived Odysseus and deprived him of *nostos* (αὐτὸν ἦγεν ἐξαπατῶσα καὶ ἀφῄρει τὸν νόστον). Kalypso is indeed not entirely honest with Odysseus, as she could have indicated tools and materials for the boat-building rather sooner, and she does not reveal that she is obliged to let Odysseus go; she seems to want the credit for her generosity. In this light her words at 5.143, αὐτάρ οἱ πρόφρων ὑποθήσομαι οὐδ' ἐπικεύσω 'But with a ready heart will I give him counsel, and hide nothing', sound as an ironic pun on her name. On the other hand she cannot be seen as entirely deceitful, as she does not conceal either her own intentions or Odysseus' options (when these emerge). The prevailing impression of her is not that of a fraudulent person, but that of a woman in love who is desperate to keep her man.

It is perhaps more fitting to see Kalypso as 'she who hid' Odysseus from the world by keeping him on her island.[142] This is the theme of a whole book (5), and several puns relate to it. It is perhaps particularly significant that in the context of the first mention of the name (1.14), we encounter the phrase ἔρυκε ... ἐν σπέεσι γλαφυροῖσι 'she kept [Odysseus] prisoner ... in her hollow caves'.[143] This concealment of Odysseus has been seen as a way 'to rob him of fame and memory', by tempting him to give up his homeland for an immortal paradise (see in particular 1.235–43, 1.55–6, 9.97, 102, 10.236, 472).[144] In this light, the name's meaning may acquire a moral relevance to Odysseus, as it would suggest a moral interpretation of Odysseus' character and adventures.

The often-cited association between Kalypso and death[145] finds no support in her name:[146] καλύπτω (often used in the *Iliad* of burying, e.g. 5.553, 13.580)

---

142 Cf. *LfgrE* s.v. Καλυψώ (M. Schmidt): 'die Verbergerin'; Peradotto 1990: 102–6; Schein 1995: 20 ('concealer'). Note also that the Hesiodic context may imply an analogous meaning, inspired from the waves which hide quickly and wholly the men who get caught in them. This finds support in the fact that the majority of the forty-one names of Okeanos' daughters suit waves (Dornseiff 1956: 109). Kalypso is further the mother of two sons with sea-related 'speaking' names (Nausinoos, Nausithoos) in *Th.* 1017–8, see also under 'Some Phaeacian names'.
143 The same verb is used again in connection with Kalypso in 9.29, 23.334 (κατέρυκε). Also the diction of 5.491–93, which is close to the sound of Kalypso's name, has been seen as a relevant pun (Peradotto 1990: 102–3); this is somewhat difficult, as at that stage the hero has made his escape, and there is no reason why the audience should think of the nymph.
144 Cf. Rutherford 1986: 146, n.6.
145 Louden 2011: 132 (with references); Crane 1988. Her island, Ogygia, indeed has eschatological features (Louden ibid.). A mural painting in a tomb at Kertsch (Ukraine), dating from the 1st

may have been influenced by κρύπτω,[147] but its predominant sense in Homer is 'to cover for protection or concealment' (cf. also the derivatives κάλυμμα, καλύπτρη 'veil').[148] Therefore Kalypso as 'the personification of all that καλύπτει man',[149] can hardly be a metaphor for death.

Kirke is a remarkable and indeed unforgettable figure to the reader, mostly for causing the magical (and strangely unmotivated) transformation of Odysseus' comrades to pigs – but on the whole she is clearly less important for the plot than Kalypso. She shares with Kalypso the formula δεινὴ θεὸς αὐδήεσσα 'dread goddess of human speech' (10.136, cf. 12.449).[150]

Kirke's not very transparent name may imply her antiquity,[151] as well as a foreign origin. It does not appear immediately relevant to the Odyssean plot or to the character. Κίρκη is probably derived from κίρκος, 'falcon', a word that occurs in Homer a few times.[152] In mythology, Kirke is surrounded by significantly loaded names: the island Αἰαίη, her brother Αἰήτης, her niece Μήδεια, with whom she also has in common the practice of magic (the name is not mentioned in Homer) – and she is, of course, a daughter of Helios (Od. 12.3–4). All this implies Argonautic associations (cf. Od. 12.70)[153] and a connection with Sun-related mythology: the falcon may be seen as a solar symbol; in Egyptian iconography the Sun-god is represented as a falcon. It has been assumed that the name Kirke suggests a sort of goddess-falcon;[154] this semantic connection appears to have

---

c. AD, shows Kalypso together with Hermes in a way that may indicate a pair of θεοί ψυχοπομποί (see *LIMC* s.v. Kalypso [B. Rafn]); but this is much later than the *Odyssey*.
146 Güntert (1919: 31 ff., 250) unconvincingly associated Kalypso's name with names for Indo-European goddesses that are derived from verbs of the sense καλύπτω or κρύπτω (e. g. the Skandinavian goddess Hel, from germ. *Helan* 'hide').
147 See Chantraine 1999 s.v. καλύπτω.
148 Despite Dyer (1964: 32): 'καλύπτω is a religious verb, closely bound to contexts of the gods, death, sleep and sorrow'.
149 Dyer 1964: 32.
150 See *LfgrE* s.v. Κίρκη (B. Mader). Cf. *Od.* 5.334 ἣ πρὶν μὲν ἔην βροτὸς αὐδήεσσα (for Ino Leukothee).
151 Perhaps significantly, Kirke (along with Skylla and the Sirens) is one of the first female characters of the *Odyssey* represented in Greek art, see further Buitron-Oliver & Cohen 1995: 36–8.
152 Chantraine 1999 s.v. κίρκος; a name of bird in *Il.* 17.757, 22.139, *Od.* 15.526, and an epithet of ἴρηξ in *Od.* 13.87; the feminine Kirke appears as a bird-name in Ael. *NA* 4.5.
153 See Meuli 1921: 84–6, 97 ff., and now M.L. West (2014: 30, 119), who suggests that Kirke was imported to the *Odyssey* from Argonautic adventures.
154 The ornithological etymology is favoured by Yarnall (1994: 28). See also *LIMC* s.v. Kirke (F. Canciani); M.L.West 1997: 408. West further suggests that Aia is close in form to the name

been strong enough to allow puns: on a Korinthian aryballos of the sixth century BC, Kirke is depicted along with the Sirens and Odysseus' ship, over which hovers a bird with the appearance of a falcon – this may well be intended as a pun on Kirke's name.[155]

A different meaning is proposed in the pseudo-Plutarchian *Vita Homeri* (126 Kindstrand), where it is claimed (in neo-Platonic fashion) that Kirke is the name for the circular moving of everything in the universe (τὴν τοῦ παντὸς ἐγκύκλιον περιφοράν, ἣν Κίρκη προσαγορεύει). κίρκος can mean 'circle',[156] which could refer to a circle of reincarnations implied by the transformation of humans into animals by Kirke (but this idea was unknown to Greeks at the time of the *Odyssey*); it could also refer to the concept of conversion of forms and essences,[157] or more generally to the universe.[158] This meaning may be brought to mind by the famous archaic representation of Kirke on an Attic black-figure cup, where she is depicted nude, mixing her magic brew, surrounded by the half-metamorphosed companions of Odysseus.[159] This interpretation suits Kirke's Odyssean context, but the absence of specific puns would make it hard for the audience. The same is true for the following possible allusion: κίρκιος occurs in later literature as an alternative name for the north-northwest wind.[160] Wind plays an important part in Odysseus' adventures, most strikingly because of Aiolos and his bag, but also during the hero's voyage to the Underworld: Kirke predicts that Boreas, the north wind, will take him there (*Od.* 10.507); and she sends a wind behind Odysseus at 11.6–8 and again at 12.148–50.

---

of the Babylonian goddess *Aya*, wife of the Sun-god; the name is similar to the Hebrew word for falcon *ayyāh*, which may have existed also in Aramaic. Thus it is possible that the name of *Aya* was interpreted as 'falcon' by Aramaic speakers, in which case the name Kirke could be a Greek translation of *Aya* understood in this way. On the name Aia see also M.L.West 2007b and above, p. 41 n. 72.

155 Brilliant 1995: 172, following Darcy 1985. The Sirens were depicted as woman-headed birds in Greek art since the early 6th c. BC, see Buitron-Oliver & Cohen 1995: 30–4.
156 LSJ; examples are rare – the main form is κρίκος (found in Homer only once, *Il.* 24.272, for the ring by which a mule yoke is tied to a peg).
157 Brilliant 1995: 171.
158 *LIMC* s.v. Kirke (F. Canciani). If the personal name puns on the 'circle of fate', then perhaps also Αἰαίη, which is said to be from αἰάζειν, alludes to the suffering caused by the men's death.
159 On artistic depictions of Kirke see further Buitron-Oliver & Cohen 1995: 36–8.
160 More commonly: θρασκίας (LSJ). The word κίρκιος is found in Agathem. 2.7 (citing the earlier geographer Timosthenes); κιρκίας or κέρκιος (uncertain reading) in Arist. *Mu.* 394b31.

3.3.2 Polyphemos

The Cyclops is the main focus of one of Odysseus' most striking homecoming adventures, but his importance for the plot of the *Odyssey* goes far beyond that. He lies in the heart of the main obstacle to Odysseus' *nostos*; and he is the centre of an episode which is vital for perceptions of the hero's identity, self-presentation and evolution of character in the poem.[161]

The involvement of the Cyclops in an all-famous episode has, not surprisingly, provided inspiration for the prevailing explanation of his name, 'much-famed'.[162] Significantly, this interpretation seems also to suit the one other bearer of the name in Homer, the Lapith Polyphemos, who is mentioned in *Il.* 1.264; in his case, too, the name may allude to the fame of a story. Though this Polyphemos does not have as much personal fame as the Cyclops, the tribe of the Lapiths from Thessaly, to which he belongs, was famous in myth and art, mainly for the war against the Centaurs – a story alluded to also in *Il.* 2.742–4 and *Od.* 21.295–304.[163]

Polyphemos is certainly not a name in 'mainstream' mythology. He does not share the same origins as the Cyclops figures of Hesiod, Brontes, Steropes, Arges ('Thunder', 'Lightning', 'Bright' [transl. Most]), who make Zeus his thunderbolt (*Th.* 139–46, 501–6). The Homeric Cyclops must originate from the world of folktale and literary fiction.[164] He appears to be a version of the figure of the 'one-eyed ogre';[165] the story of his encounter with Odysseus may well predate the composition of our *Odyssey* and may have been present in pre-Homeric poetry, which recounted the encounter of Odysseus with the one-eyed, cannibalistic monster.[166] As a character in the poem, Polyphemos is thus probably not the

---

161 See Schein 1970: 83.
162 Cf. Bakker 2002: 135, n.2.
163 The omission of the tribal name in *Il.* 2.742–4 may be suggestive of the audience's familiarity with the story; see Kirk 1985: 235. Note also that the same formula, ἀντίθεον Πολύφημον, is used for both name-bearers, the Cyclops in *Od.* 1.70 (start of line), and the Lapith in *Il.* 1.264 (end of line).
164 His most famous other literary context is Theocritus *Idyll* 2, that presents a young and lovesick Cyclops.
165 Cf. Mondi 1983: 17 ff.; on the folktale character of the episode see Burgess 2001: 94 ff.; M.L. West 2014: 12–3.
166 What must have been the autonomous tale of the triumph of Odysseus the trickster over a folktale monster was transformed by the poet of the *Odyssey* in an exploit of the heroic warrior Odysseus, as S.R.West argues (1998: 74–5). She further draws attention to potentially very old poetic accounts of voyages recounting stories about a foreign population with characteristics

poet's invention.¹⁶⁷ The fact that a basic characteristic of his, his single eye, is never mentioned by the poet, suggests that he was already a familiar figure to the audience, notably one who had long been associated with Odysseus.¹⁶⁸ The meaning 'famous' for his name is encouraged also by this relevance to folktale – in which case we might assume that the name sprang from the poet's spontaneous desire to allude to the Cyclops' already acquired fame (κύκλωψ πολύφημος = 'the very famous Cyclops' or 'the Cyclops Polyphemos'; similarly for the Lapith Polyphemos – the Lapith 'of the famous story'). Significantly, he starts off as a nameless being, and the name is only used three times during the story (9.403, 407, 446), and in all its occurrences (including the one at 1.70) it could be an epithet.

The etymological connection of the name with φημί and φήμη might suggest subtler nuances of the meaning 'famous'. As a compound of πολύ and φημί, it would imply the meaning 'on whom much is said'. πολύφημος occurs as an adjective in the *Odyssey*, at 2.150 as an epithet for ἀγορά ('voiceful') and at 22.376 for the singer Phemios (perhaps as a pun), apparently with the meaning 'rich in songs'.¹⁶⁹ Given that a basic element in the description of the Cyclops' homeland is the lack of the refined kind of civilisation enjoyed by the Greek cities (the Cyclops do not have an *agora*, nor, presumably, singers), it is not impossible that the name had an ironic tone towards the savage character of the Cyclopian 'civilisation'.¹⁷⁰ Of course, 'rich in songs' remains an appropriate meaning for the name of a figure who has been widely sung, and is therefore well-known in poetic tradition. The few occurrences of the adjective outside Homer mostly suggest the meanings 'famous' (in a positive way) or 'rich in songs' (which can be relevant to 'famous'): Pindar seems to have used the doric form πολύφαμος as a synonym of πολύφατος¹⁷¹ (θρῆνον ... πολύφαμον *I.* 8.58, 'famous' or 'excellent' dirge or 'of many voices'); the meanings of πολύφημον ὁδὸν of Parmenides, as well as

---

similar to those of Polyphemos. Presumably the fame of these tales contributed to the fame of Polyphemos.

167 Though his promotion to the poem's start (essential for the poem's economy) must be; see S.R.West 1998: 68–9. Rather than assuming that the Cyclops impersonates Poseidon's destructive force, his link with Poseidon is better seen as the poet's way of integrating the Cyclops in the Odyssean plot.
168 S.R.West 1998: 71–3; M.L. West 2014: 199.
169 Cf. the similar name Εὔφημος (the leader of the Kikones, *Il.* 2.846), '(speaking words of) good omen'. See von Kamptz 1982 (1958): 88. –φημος became more common in later onomastics and was combined with various different first elements (Ἀντί-, Θεό-, Λυσί-, Χαρί-).
170 See Gera 2003: 8 n. 30.
171 *O.* 1.8 πολύφατος ὕμνος, *P.* 11.47 ἀγώνων πολυφάτων, *N.* 7.81 πολύφατον θρόον ὕμνων; all these usages can be explained with 'famous' or 'rich in songs'.

the ὁ πολύφημος... καὶ πολυώνυμος σοφός (Philo *De ebrietate* 92.2) must lie within the range of 'famous' or 'much-speaking'.

The semantic range of πολύφημος may also include other notions of 'famous'. One of these may be relevant to φῆμις (six occurrences in the *Odyssey* and one in the *Iliad*), which had a negative connotation: not good fame, *kleos*, but unwanted publicity, resulting in a bad reputation. It has been argued[172] that this could suit Polyphemos in two different ways: firstly, he gains negative attention from his fellow Cyclopes when he cries out that he was blinded by 'No-man' (9.407–8); he then becomes the cause of disastrous fame for Odysseus: when the hero, proud of his achievement, finally discloses his name to the Cyclops with the expectation that this will bring him *kleos* (9.502–5), it only brings him unwanted publicity when the news of the Cyclops' wounding reaches Poseidon. But φῆμις occurs together with the adjective χαλεπή 'harsh' (e.g. 14.239), which implies that it is not necessarily negative.[173] Secondly, φήμη can mean 'speech that serves as on omen' (cf. *Od.* 2.35, 20.100, 105). Polyphemos may be seen as an utterer of a *pheme* of this sort: in pronouncing his curse to Poseidon, he foretells the hero's subsequent plight.[174] However, this would leave the name's first component (Poly-) unexplained. It seems that other potential connections between the name and the Cyclops' character and role in the plot are not equally compelling and do not overshadow the name's primary function as an expression of the fame of the Cyclops' story.

3.3.3 Some Phaeacian names

The Phaeacians and their world arguably stand between the folktale imagination of Odysseus' preceding adventures and the reality of Ithaca.[175] The names of

---

172 Bakker 2002.
173 Bakker (2002: 142) thought that φῆμις may be used to explain the name Phemios negatively as 'market poet', for a singer who had been betraying his master by singing for the suitors (but see 22.331 ἤειδε ... ἀνάγκῃ 'he sang perforce'), or who has gained a bad name. It is not easy to see, however, how the patronymic Τερπιάδης could fit this interpretation. The two names combined clearly stress the function of a poet.
174 Bakker 2002.
175 Notably their name may be derived from φαιός, 'grey', 'misty' – an allusion to the 'legendary mist' that covers them? (cf. Segal 1994: 61). Alcaeus reportedly attributed their origins to the drops of Ouranos' blood (fr. 441 Voigt). On the Phaeacians see further *Comm. on Od.* v.1: 289–92, 341–46 (Hainsworth). Sergent (2002) may be right to argue that their origins need to be sought in pre-Homeric mythology; cf. M.L. West 2014: 84–5.

Phaeacians are mostly normal Greek formations[176] and constitute a fine way of self-introduction to the stranger Odysseus; they advertise to him – and to the poet's audience – their bearers' strengths and abilities.[177] More specifically, the names of the Phaeacian youths at the assembly (8.111 ff.) can be arranged and explained from an etymological point of view as follows:

Ἀκρόνεως, Ναυτεύς, Ἀναβησίνεως,[178] Ναυβολίδης,[179] Κλυτόνηος (8.111–3, 116, 123): these names are all compounds with ναῦς 'ship'. Nausikaa too belongs here.

Further ship-related names: Πρυμνεύς, Πρῳρεύς (8.113; from πρύμνη and πρῷρα, the back and front side of the ship respectively), Ἐρετμεύς (8.112; from ἐρετμόν 'oar') and Ἐλατρεύς (8.113), probably a cognate of ἐλατήρ ('driver', Il. 4.145), here possibly synonymous with Eretmeus.[180] The two are heard at the end of two consecutive lines and have an alliterative effect.

Ποντεύς (8.113); also the name of the herald Ποντόνοος (7.179 etc.), from πόντος 'sea', which may imply that in fulfilling his duities he also undertook sea travel.

Ἅλιος 'of the sea' (adj. ἅλιος, e.g. Od. 4.365), Ἀγχίαλος, Ἀμφίαλος, Ὠκύαλος, Εὐρύαλος (8.111–2, 114–5, 119). The second component –αλος is obscure,[181] but with the exception of Euryalos, these names are all etymologically connected with sea-related vocabulary: adj. ἀγχίαλος 'near the sea' (Il. 2.640, 697; Od. 1.401);[182] adj. ἀμφίαλος 'sea-surrounded', of Ithaca (e.g. Od. 1.386); adj. ὠκύαλος 'swift-moving', used as an epithet of a ship (Il. 15.705; Od. 12.182,

---

176 Note that two of the names (Amphialos and Ponteus) are attested in Mycenaean (Ventris-Chadwick 1973: 104–5; also Elatreus as an occupational name, García Ramón 2011: 241). Some appear to be recycled names, as e.g. Ἀγχίαλος, which also occurs for an Achaean (Il. 5.609), and for the father of Mentes (Od. 1.180).
177 Cf. Higbie 1995: 7. Higbie thought the the names 'may underscore the image of the exotic, otherworldly Phaeacians' – but the names are plausible Greek concoctions and not particularly exotic.
178 An odd name, from ἀναβαίνω and ναῦς (cf. Od. 15.284); see von Kamptz 1982 (1958): 65.
179 The meaning of the name is perhaps suggested by Il. 13.628–9: νῦν αὖτ' ἐν νηυσὶν μενεαίνετε ποντοπόροισι / πῦρ ὀλοὸν βαλέειν... 'and now again you are eager to fling consuming fire on the seafaring ships'. But this would not suit the Phaeacians' freedom from war, unless it is seen as a remnant of a rather different previous condition (see also below, on the name Rhexenor).
180 LfGrE s.v. Ἐλατρεύς (B. Mader). The name may be derived from a lost noun *ἔλατρον 'oar' (von Kamptz 1982 (1958): 28, 124).
181 An enlarging element? From ἅλς 'sea'? Or from ἅλλομαι? ('spring', 'leap'); see Beekes 2010 s.v. ὠκύς.
182 Note that the name of another Anchialos, the father of Mentes (Od. 1.180), may be similarly 'suggested by the maritime character of the Taphians' (M.L. West 2014: 148).

15.473). The surrounding names imply that Euryalos too had an analogous significance[183] ('of the broad sea' or 'traveller (of the sea) far and wide').

Amphialos is son of Πολύνηος 'of many ships' and grandson of Τέκτων 'builder' – in this context, 'ship builder' (8.114). Similarly Θόων (8.113; from θοός 'fast') may here allude to the notion of a fast ship (ναῦς θοή / νῆες θοαί, e.g. *Od.* 2.389, 4.255).

Stylistically, the Phaeacian list can be paralleled with other lists of etymologically significant names, like those of Penelope's suitors (*Od.* 22.242–3, 266–8) and the Nereids (*Il.* 18.39–49). But in some aspects the Phaeacian list is unparalleled. Not all names of Penelope's suitors or the Nereids are clear expressions of the same (or similar) ideas; the Phaeacian names are – and they are far more numerous, amounting to a total of twenty (counted up to 8.132). They are all 'nautical' names, appropriate for the Phaeacians as descendants of Poseidon and mostly seamen (6.266 ff., 7.34 ff., 108 ff., 327 ff. etc.), and allude to one or other aspect of seamanship: the ability to sail, the ships and the building of ships, and the sea itself. They can be seen as expressions of personal as well as of a civic identity.[184] More importantly, it may be felt that the names create a special link between the Phaeacians and Odysseus, who is also a seaman, whose fate is linked with the sea.

While the reason for the choice or invention of the main bulk of Phaeacian names[185] is pretty straightforward, the inspiration behind the names of the predominant Phaeacian figures seems to be more complex; of the 'royal' names, only Ναυσικάα seems to fall within the above defined semantic category. It is not clear whether she is a creation of the poet of the *Odyssey*; her central role in the episode and the problematic character of her involvement with Odysseus (Alkinoos seems too eager to marry her off to the hero, cf. 7.311 ff.), together with her etymologically mysterious name,[186] may imply that she was part of an old

---

183 Cf. *LfGrE* s.v. Εὐρύαλος (B. Mader).
184 Dougherty 2001: 114. Recent scholarship recognises an early ethnographic interest in Odysseus' adventures and his meeting with other peoples and civilisations – an attractive (if not universally accepted) theory; see also Skinner 2012 (cf. 'Introductory notes', p. 26). The *Odyssey* is certainly richer in that respect than the *Iliad*.
185 'Mit Sicherheit erfunden' according to Neumann (1991: 318); cf. M.L. West (2014: 193) – but this is hard to prove.
186 Possibly a short form of *Ναυσικάστη (cf. Μηδεσικάστη, name of a Trojan's wife in *Il.* 13.173), from καίνυμαι (cf. *Od.* 3.282), meaning 'excelling in ships'. Cf. von Kamptz 1982 (1958): 112, *Comm. on Od.* v.1: 294 (Hainsworth). But the form of the name is 'noch nicht sicher erklärt', see *LfgrE* s.v. Ναυσικάα (B. Mader).

tradition.[187] The sea-related name also suits the heroine's important function of encountering Odysseus by the sea (6.139 ff.).

The king's name, Ἀλκίνοος, has more than one possible meaning. The element -νοος might allude to Odysseus' journey home,[188] made possible by the king, who authorises and oversees the relevant preparations. This is where his most important function lies – and in the fact that he provides the audience for Odysseus' narrative of his journey so far. The name's first component could indeed imply the meaning of defending and helping the *nostos* both find poetic expression and reach its desired 'end'; ἀλκή is used in the *Odyssey* to mean 'defence, help' (e.g. 22.305).[189] As Odysseus' journey is by sea, the name would also bear some relevance to the pattern of sea-related names; Alkinoos is after all the son of Nausithoos and a grandson of Poseidon (cf. also the name Ποντόνοος). It may thus seem less appealing to connect Alkinoos with νόος in its more obvious and common Homeric sense, 'mind' or 'thought, purpose, resolve'. Ἀλκί- would then allude to 'strength' (cf. *Od*. 6.305), and the name could mean 'strongly minded' or 'intellectually strong'; or alternatively 'strong at heart, courageous', as ἀλκή can also mean 'prowess', 'courage'.[190] It is hard to connect any of these meanings with Alkinoos' characterisation, other than what is suggested by the formulaic language used for him: he is said to be δαΐφρων 'wise' (8.8, 13, 56) and θεῶν ἄπο μήδεα εἰδώς 'made wise in counsel by the gods' (e.g. 6.12). We also repeatedly hear of μένος Ἀλκινόοιο 'divine might' (7.178 / 8.2, 4, 385, 421, 423 / 13.20, 24, 49, 64), and he is called μεγαλήτωρ 'great hearted' (6.17, 196, 213, 299 / 7. 85, 93 / 8.464; note especially the references in book 7). It was perhaps left to the audience to respond to the semantic ambiguity of *noos*.

The most striking example of significant naming among the Phaeacians concerns the queen Ἀρήτη. Of the Phaeacians, she is the one who is presented as

---

187 Cf. *LfgrE* s.v. Ναυσικάᾱ (B. Mader). On her characterisation see now *HE* s.v. Nausicaa (H. Roisman).
188 See Ruijgh (1967: 371–2) and Frei (1968: 48–57), who connected -νοος in personal names with the root **nes-* (cf. νέομαι), and assumed that *noos* developed semantically from 'homecoming' to 'plans for the homecoming' and then to 'plans, thoughts, intentions'. Frei drew attention to Homeric passages where *noos* may preserve traces of its most ancient sense (*Od*. 5.23 f., cf. 1.76 f.; *Il*. 23.144 ff.). For a different view see Heubeck 1987: 227–38. Beekes (2010 s.v. νόος) notes that the connection with **nes-* is possible, 'but the semantics seem to be difficult.' Cf. the discussion of the name Nestor.
189 Cf. other personal names with Ἀλκ-: Ἀλκιμέδων (e.g. *Il*. 16.197), Ἄλκανδρος (*Il*. 5.644), Ἀλκίππη (*Od*. 4.124), Ἀλκάθοος (e.g. *Il*. 12.93); see von Kamptz 1982 (1958): 179–80.
190 Cf. ἄλκιμος, also used as proper name: *Od*. 22.235 Μέντωρ Ἀλκιμίδης. See further under 'Minor' speaking names.

most important to Odysseus' *nostos:* it is her that Nausikaa advises Odysseus to supplicate (6.303–15), and Athena confirms that his homecoming will depend on her (7.74–7). The poet apparently shows awareness of the name's appropriateness: Ἀρήτη δ' ὄνομ' ἐστὶν ἐπώνυμον (*Od.* 7.54; Athena's words).[191] The poet, however, does not go on to specify what he thinks its meaning is; it is perhaps deliberately left open to more than one interpretations, depending on different contexts and aspects of the bearer's function in the narrative.

Ἀρήτη is plainly the verbal adjective (with accent shifted in the proper name) from ἀράομαι 'pray' (frequently used in both epics, cf. ἀρή 'prayer', *Od.* 4.767, 17.496). Arete is indeed 'she who is prayed to, besought': she is the object of Odysseus' supplications; the hero is encouraged by Nausikaa to address her and not the king.[192] ἀράομαι and ἀρή are only used for prayers addressed to divine beings,[193] but perhaps this difficulty is settled at 7.71, where it is said that people 'look upon her as upon a goddess'.[194] Another context, that of Arete's birth, may imply a rather different meaning 'she who is prayed for (from the gods)',[195] at least according to the scholiast (καθὸ ἀρητῶς καὶ εὐκταίως ἐγεννήθη Sch. P–V *Od.* 7.54). This also suits the way she is viewed by her husband Alkinoos and the appreciation she receives as queen – she is said to have displayed all of the qualities that could be wished for (7.65 ff.). The name could still be relevant to Odysseus if understood as 'the object of one's wishes', and it could allude to her as Odysseus' desired source of help.[196] The masculine form Ἄρητος, name of a Trojan in the *Iliad* (17.492 ff.) and of a son of Nestor in the *Odyssey* (3.414), has been similarly interpreted.[197]

---

191 Cf. Stanford (1965: 322). On the term *eponymon* see Austin 1972: 2, n. 2 (as we have seen, it is also used for Odysseus' name, 19.409). Cf. the use of the term ἐπωνυμίη in Herodotus, which suggests a connection between name and bearer. Significantly, Herodotus claims that the poets (Homer and Hesiod) gave gods their ἐπωνυμίας 'epithets' (2.53; see further Koning 2010: 69 ff.)
192 Stanford (ibid.) gave priority to this meaning, noting that the name was 'probably coined by the poet of the *Odyssey* as apt for Odysseus' supplications to her'. But she also appears in [Hes.] *Cat.* (fr. 222 M–W), and perhaps she had a place in older tradition.
193 See *LfgrE* s.v. ἀράομαι, ἀρήμεναι (C. Calame).
194 On this point see further Skempis – Ziogas 2009: 215–22. They draw attention to formulas used of Arete (especially φίλα φρονέουσα, used for Athena), which suggest divine status; also to parallels between Arete and Athena (to whom Odysseus has prayed before his meeting with Arete, where the verb ἀράομαι is also used, 6.323), as well as between Arete and Kirke.
195 This meaning is favoured by von Kamptz 1982 (1958): 150, 240.
196 Cf. Stanford 1965: 322, *Désirée*.
197 See von Kamptz 1982 (1958): 240–1 ('erwünscht, ersehnt'), Wathelet 1988: 313; but cf. *LfGrE* s.v. Ἄρητος (D. Motzkus).

The above do not exhaust the semantic potential of ἀρή, which can also mean 'curse'. An adjective ἀρητός, 'prayed against', 'accursed' is found in the *Iliad* (17.37, 24.741; but the compound πολυάρητος, *Od.* 19.404, is ambiguous and can also mean 'the object of many prayers'[198]). A meaning 'accursed' could reflect the unhappy fate of Arete's father, who was killed by Apollo at the time of his wedding (*Od.* 7.64–5).[199] This might briefly occur to an attentive audience – but Arete's main function in the epic is relevant to Odysseus and not to her father. Another possible pun is on ἀρετή 'virtue,'[200] which would suit Arete as a woman of many virtues (cf. Athena's praise of her as a woman of νόου ... ἐσθλοῦ 'good understanding' at 7.73–4), although it does not constitute a plausible 'scientific' etymology (ἀρετή has short α).[201] Finally, an elaborate case has been made for a connection between the name and the adjective ἄρ(ρ)ητος 'unspoken', which would suit Arete's characterisation, particularly in connection with her silence immediately after Odysseus' supplication to her;[202] but potential word-plays (on forms of the verbs λέγω and φημί, e.g. εἰρήσομαι and φῂς at 7.237–9, used by Arete as she addresses Odysseus) are perhaps too subtle to be noticed by the audience.

Other names in the Phaeacian royal family (7.56 ff.) deserve a comment. The name of Alkinoos' father Ναυσίθοος respects the sea-related motif and is appropriate for someone who is literally a son of Poseidon. The name is also found in Hesiod (*Th.* 1017) for one of Odysseus' sons by Kalypso (the other son is suitably named Ναυσίνοος).[203] It is hard to tell why the king's brother, and father of Arete, 'Ρηξήνωρ, is given a name that belongs to a rather different kind. The name echoes an epithet of Achilles, 'breaking the ranks of men' (from ῥήγνυμι and ἀνήρ;

---

198 It is used (as a quasi-name) for Odysseus by Eurykleia; see above, the discussion of Odysseus' naming. The compound might be seen as a linking element between the hero and the queen, who plays such an important part in his *nostos* (cf. Skempis – Ziogas 2009: 225 n. 34).
199 Other names too are inspired from a disagreeable event relating to a parent or relative (most strikingly Odysseus); see also Peradotto 1990: 108.
200 Rank 1951: 84.
201 Differences in vowel quantity do not hinder word-play, which relies on similar (not necessarily identical) sounds; cf. O'Hara 1996: 61–2. But to assume a word-play between Arete and ἀρίστη (adjective that designates the chest to be brought for the stranger Odysseus, 8.424; thus Skempis – Ziogas 2009: 229) appears a little far-fetched.
202 Skempis – Ziogas 2009: 222–8.
203 If the two Nausithooi are to be identified, the implication is that the Phaeacians are descended from Odysseus and Kalypso, which is absurd for our *Odyssey*, but not inappropriate for Hesiod, as M.L.West (1966: 436) notes. But perhaps it is preferable to see them as 'verschiedene Weiterbildungen einer älteren Gestalt', see *LfgrE* s.v. Ναυσίθοος (B. Mader).

cf. *Il.* 6.6–7, 11.538, 15.615 and *Od.* 4.5).²⁰⁴ This sense not only breaks the pattern of ship-related names, but is also rather reminiscent of the battlefield, normally a source of inspiration for Iliadic names. It thus does not seem to relate to the Phaeacian existence at all, unless it is meant to remind of a period when, according to the poet, they dwelt near hostile neighbours before moving to Scheria (*Od.* 6.4–8).²⁰⁵ The names of the semi-mythical mother of Alkinoos, Περίβοια 'worth many oxen',²⁰⁶ and her father, Εὐρυμέδων, which joins two common elements in Homeric naming (εὐρυ-, -μέδων),²⁰⁷ (7.57–8) seem to have been stock mythological names.²⁰⁸

Non-royal Phaeacian names that are equally excluded from the sea-related pattern include the name of the singer Δημόδοκος, which is apparently explained by the accompanying phrase λαοῖσι τετιμένον (8.472, 'honoured by the people'), and the worker Πόλυβος 'rich in oxen' (8.373), apparently a stock-name, roughly synonymous with Periboia.²⁰⁹ But the pattern is followed in the name of the 'elderly hero' (γέρων ἥρως) Ἐχένηος, a figure of some importance: he advises Alkinoos on how he should treat Odysseus (7.155 ff.), and the king takes his advice; relevant action is then taken by the herald Ποντόνοος (7.182).

Evidently the poet wished to mark the Phaeacian group with names mostly relevant to their sea-related identity. But the naming of the Phaeacians retains stylistic versatility, as well as features to suit individual characters, especially the ones with important roles in the action; the group also contains some stock-names, which would probably come readily to the poet / performer's memory. The names of Alkinoos' sons (8.119) reflect nicely the blending of different naming concepts: Λαοδάμας ('subduer of peoples', a generic name for a leader, appropriate for a king's son),²¹⁰ Ἅλιος, Κλυτόνηος (seamanship-related names).

---

204 Sulzberger's suggestion (1926: 397 n.30) that the name is not from ῥήγνυμι but from an Indo-European root that also gave the Latin word *rex* seems very unlikely.
205 See also above, n. 179 on Naubolides.
206 Cf. von Kamptz 1982 (1958): 57: 'reich an Rindern'; but it is probably better to think of brideprice: 'woman whose future husband will give her father (the equivalent of) many oxen'.
207 See further below under 'Minor' speaking names.
208 Cf. *Comm. on Od.* v.1: 323 (Hainsworth).
209 See von Kamptz 1982 (1958): 90, 217.
210 On this name see also under 'Minor' speaking names. See Frame 2012 for a stimulating but hard-to-prove hypothesis that the identities of Alkinoos, Arete, Nausikaa and Laodamas are (in one way or another) associated with the Ionians of the *dodecapolis*, which Frame assumes was the setting where the Homeric epics took their present form. Frame further suggests that the etymology of Alkinoos' name should be paralleled with Nestor's (see above, on Nestor's name), and that the name Alkinoos alludes to Odysseus' *nostos* (see also above, p. 123); also that Laodamas

3.3.4 Odysseus' companions

Odysseus' travels do not involve only a succession of otherwordly beings and characters, many of whom have peculiar names, but also a number of men who are his companions until they all perish. They are rather identified as a group than as individuals,[211] but certain individual names leap to mind; they are all good Greek formations, of transparent etymology, and thus present a contrast with many other names in this chapter, including Odysseus' name itself.

As a character, Εὐρύλοχος, 'wide-ambush',[212] stands out; he is the one who takes the most part in the action: he appears by name in no less than three different episodes (Kirke, *Nekyia* and the Sirens),[213] and he is appointed as leader of one of the two bands into which Odysseus splits his men on Aiaia (10.205 ff.); his name may appear vaguely suitable to his role in the exploration of Kirke's island, though there are no relevant puns. Πολίτης is labelled as 'leader of men', and 'best and dearest of companions' (10.224–5), but only takes some initiative in the Kirke episode (10.226–8). The name, which occurs also in the *Iliad* for a son of Priam (e.g. 2.791), is reminiscent of the noun πολῖται 'citizens' (also found in both epics). The original meaning of πόλις was 'citadel, stronghold' – perhaps the name Polites referred to this.[214]

Another companion mentioned in connection with the Kirke episode, Ἐλπήνωρ, is memorable for being the youngest of the group and from falling to his death from Kirke's roof under the influence of excessive drinking (10.552–60; his ghost is met by Odysseus in the *Nekyia*, 11.51 ff.). He and his sad fate are made more memorable by his significant name, from *elpis* 'hope',[215] perhaps a deliberate bitter or ironic hint, especially if Elpenor is seen as 'a characteristic invention of the poet';[216] notably it is the only Homeric name to make use of this component. He is further described as οὔτε τι λίην / ἄλκιμος ἐν πολέμῳ

---

evokes Leodamas, 'the last Neleid king of Miletus' (who is however not mentioned before the Roman period; Frame 2012 n. 59).
211 On their function in the poem see further Saïd 1998: 226–8 and *HE* s.v. Odysseus' companions (B. Louden). On the problem of Odysseus' responsibility towards them (denied in the proem, but raised at 24.426–8 by Antinous' father) see the stimulating remarks made by S.R. West (2012: 539).
212 Thus Powell 1977: 27.
213 See Saïd (1998: 226–8) for details.
214 On the meaning of πόλις in Homer cf. Hoffmann 1956.
215 Cf. ἔλπω 'make hope' (e.g. *Od.* 2.91, 13.308) and ἔλπομαι 'hope for' (e.g. *Il.* 13.609, 15.539). See also von Kamptz 1982 (1958): 61, cf. 27, 99–100. For an association between *elpis* and early death cf. *CEG* 51 (Attic, c. 510 BC).
216 *Comm. on Od.* v.2: 74 (Heubeck).

οὔτε φρεσὶν ᾖσιν ἀρηρώς ('not over valiant in war nor sound of understanding', *Od.* 10.552–3) – a character who could hardly be seen as 'hopeful'. Perhaps the name's pun on hope (subsequently 'lost hope') also relied on Elpenor's position as the youngest of Odysseus' men.[217]

One Περιμήδης is merely a name mentioned in a couple of instances together with Eurylochos (11.23, 12.195). Finally, during the Ithacan assembly (2.19), we hear of an Ἄντιφος who died during the Cyclops episode. Perimedes, Eurylochos and Antiphos all contain components (Εὐρύ-, -λοχος, -μήδης, Ἀντι-) that are regularly used in Homeric onomastics; the poet seems to make no particular effort to justify them as intentional choices for their bearers.[218]

3.4 'Secondary' Names on Ithaca

It may be felt that some persons and events on Ithaca echo those of the island of the Phaeacians.[219] Personal names, however, express rather different concepts. In the above section Phaeacian names of secondary characters were discussed mostly in respect to their adherence to (or deviation from) a sea-related meaning. Significant naming for characters on Ithaca concerns two distinct groups of a different kind: the servants in Odysseus' household and Penelope's suitors.

3.4.1 The servants

Servants are few but have an important role in the *oikos*,[220] and their names seem to be intentional choices.[221] Names of servants who have a part in the plot attract particular attention. The most important role belongs to Εὔμαιος;

---

[217] As Reinhardt argued (1960: 104). Peradotto (1990: 107) suggested the meaning 'man of delusion', to express Elpenor's state of consciousness when he fell from Kirke's rooftop; but ἐλπίς is not synonymous with delusion.
[218] Louden (1999: 14–23) posits an analogy between Eurylochos, the suitor Eurymachos and the Phaeacian Euryalos (all three verbally attack Odysseus), which is reflected in their names (similarly also between Perimedes and the suitor Amphimedon); but the relevant episodes are too far apart for the audience to make a connection.
[219] See e.g. Higbie (1995: 134–5), who compares Penelope to Arete; cf. Doherty 1995: 80 ff.
[220] On their status see Raaflaub 1997: 638–9. Some are slaves (Thalmann [1998: 16–7, 49 ff.] concludes that they are all slaves), but the context does not always make exact status clear. Some are even treated as members of the family.
[221] By contrast, servants such as those mentioned in the *Iliad* (see the references gathered in Higbie 1995: 7), who are insignificant for the plot, remain unnamed.

he and his significant name were perhaps an invention of the poet of the *Odyssey*.²²² There are several etymological possibilities. The name is phonetically close to μαίομαι, used in *Od.* 13.367 and 14.356 with the meaning 'search out', 'seek'.²²³ This may be a cognate of μέμαα 'desire' (e.g. *Il.* 10.401, ἦ ῥά νύ τοι μεγάλων δώρων ἐπεμαίετο θυμός, 'surely on great rewards was your heart set').²²⁴ Perhaps the name evoked a meaning like 'he who set out for something (in this case: helping Odysseus) with good intentions'; the nature of the intentions is suggested by the prefix Εὔ-. If so, it must have been chosen to suit the swineherd's positive function first as caterer and protector for the unknown wanderer Odysseus, and then as Odysseus' helper in destroying the suitors.²²⁵ Another etymology sees the name as a shortened form of εὐμενής,²²⁶ built in analogy with Ἀνταῖος, Πτολεμαῖος²²⁷ – a rather far-fetched assumption, and surely εὐμενής is even further away from Εὔμαιος than μαίομαι. A third possibility²²⁸ is to connect the name with the word μαῖα 'nanny' (used for Eurykleia by Odysseus, *Od.* 19.482, 500, by Telemachos 20.129 and by Penelope, 23.11 etc.). This would suit the swineherd as a kind of father-figure for Telemachos, whom he calls φίλον τέκος 'dear child' (*Od.* 16.25; he expresses paternal love for Odysseus' son in 17–9), while Telemachos calls him ἄττα 'daddy'.²²⁹ The association of μαῖα with a male figure seems somewhat difficult, as a masculine form is not attested.²³⁰ Perhaps Eumaios' invocation of Hermes as Μαιάδος υἷι (14.435) suggests a pun on his name,²³¹ but so does μαίεσθαι, a word spoken by Eumaios himself at 14.356. An allusion to this verb seems on the whole more likely: the element Εὔ- would then make better sense, and the name would seem more rel-

---

222 See *LfgrE* s.v. Εὔμαιος (B. Mader). He is said to have become a slave in the context of a rather extraordinary story (*Od.* 15.415–84).
223 The future tense μάσσεται (γυναῖκα, 'seek a wife'), *Il.* 9.394, may belong to this verb.
224 Cf. Pi. *P.* 11.51, ὄλεθρόν τινι μαίομαι, 'set out to destroy someone'.
225 Peradotto 1990: 107; cf. von Kamptz 1982 (1958): 72; Beekes 2010 s.v. μαίομαι. Beekes also mentions Οἰνόμαος (reminiscent of lesb. μάομαι) and Μαίων as possibly attached to this verb (cf. Bechtel 1914: 220). The connection was not obvious enough for Chantraine (1999 s.v. μαίομαι).
226 Not a Homeric word, but cf. εὐμενέτῃσι 'friends' (*Od.* 6.185) and Myc. *e-u-me-ne*, unanimously read as Εὐμένης (Jorro-Adrados s.v.).
227 *Comm. on Od.* v.2: 196 (Hoekstra).
228 Demont 2003: 381–5.
229 On this rare term see further *LfgrE* s.v. ἄττα (H. Brandt).
230 A plural μαῖοι 'adoptive parents' is only found on one inscription from Paros of the imperial period (*IG* XII (5) 199).
231 Demont 2004: 383 (noting that this is the only time that Hermes is thus invoked). The name of Hermes' mother is Maia in the *Homeric hymn to Hermes*.

evant to Eumaios' main function, which is not that of a father-figure, but that of a servant determined to help his master.[232]

It is apparently no coincidence that a servant of this importance for the epic story is associated with high class origin[233] (as also the name of Eumaios' father, the rather grand Ktesios Ormenides, ruler of cities, suggests; *Od.* 15.412–4). Similar noble background must be assumed for Eurykleia, who is given both a patronymic and a papponymic,[234] and whose name evokes *kleos*.[235] Εὐρὺ κλέος was a traditional (Indo-European) concept,[236] and the name Εὐρύκλεια evokes the heroic age without carrying any pointed meaning. The name's first component too, Εὐρυ-, is a generic element, widely used in names; there are three examples in the *Odyssey* for servants' names: apart from Eurykleia, there is Alkinoos' female servant Εὐρυμέδουσα (*Od.* 7.8; she who uses her wit to carry out a wide range of functions?)[237] and Penelope's servant Εὐρυνόμη (17.495 etc.). Eurynome may appear as a duplication of Eurykleia; the latter is dominant, as she has nursed and is more closely connected with Odysseus and Telemachos, the male side of the household, while Eurynome with the female, as a servant of Penelope.[238] Eurykleia is finally strongly reminiscent of Antikleia; the names of Odysseus' mother and his nanny were perhaps intentionally similar, and one

---

232 Mühlestein's suggestion (1984b: 148–51) that Eumaios' name and character are modeled on the god of the Underworld Euboulos / Eubouleus ('of good council'), who was also a swineherd, is hardly convincing.

233 On this point see also Thalmann 1998: 75–6; cf. also Higbie 1995: 8.

234 The grandfather's name, Πεισήνωρ, 'who persuades = orders the men' (1.429, 2.347, 20.148), is an aristrocratic name. Mühlestein's speculations are unconvincing (1969: 81): he assumed the meaning 'he who is obeyed', drawing support from another Peisenor, a father of Κλεῖτος (a name relevant to *kleos*) in *Il.* 15.445 (a third Peisenor, *Od.* 2.38, is a herald); but 'persuade' and 'obey' are two different concepts, and Peis- in compound names normally derives its meaning from πείθω and not πείθομαι (cf. the Aristophanic Peisetairos, see Kanavou 2011: 105–7). The three occurrences of Peisenor imply a stock-name (as *kleos* was a stock element), arguably associated with 'heroic excellence' (Thalmann 1998: 75). The name of Eurykleia's father, Ὤψ (*ὄψ = voice?), is rather obscure. It was rather arbitrarily seen by Mühlestein as a suitable name for somebody who gives orders (but note an alternative etymology from ὄψ -οπός (ὄπωπα) 'eye', 'face' (von Kamptz 1982 [1958]: 214).

235 Thus Thalmann 1998: 75 ('she of the far-flung *kleos*').

236 Cf. M.L. West 2007a: 78 f., 407; *Od.* 3.83 (for other names with *kleos* see von Kamptz 1982 (1958): 122). Hence, as in the case of Patroklos, it is difficult to assume (with Mühlestein 1969) a connection with κλυεῖν as as 'she who is heard / obeyed' – tempting though it may be, as it would reflect her role as the spirited leader of the servants (cf. *Od.* 20.149–54, 157).

237 Or 'wide-ruling' (Thalmann 1998: 75). The name relates also to that of Nausithoos' maternal grandfather Eurymedon (M.L. West 2014: 186–7).

238 Thus Thalmann 1998: 80–1; de Jong 2001: 42–3; M.L. West 2014: 257. Note that Eurynome too is called μαῖα 'nurse' (17.499). See also below, under 'Minor' speaking names.

could be meant to reflect the other. Significantly, the slave's[239] honour and authority at least equalled and perhaps even superseded that of the wife – especially if we consider her role in Odysseus' naming and the very grand introduction of her at 1.428 ff.[240]

The group of names of faithful servants, which have positive connotations, may include Philoitios, the cowherd who – like Eumaios – remains loyal to Odysseus (21.209–11), if the name is interpreted as 'of an auspicious destiny' (from φιλ- and οἶτος 'fate').[241] On the other hand, 'bad' servants receive negative-sounding names: a brother-sister pair have the similar names Μελάνθιος and Μελανθώ, where μελαν- 'black' probably functions as a hint to their evil characters:[242] the goatherd Melanthios insults Odysseus (20.178–82) and helps the suitors fight him in book 22; Melantho, Penelope's maid, sleeps with the suitor Eurymachos and, like her brother, mocks Odysseus (e.g. 18.321–42). Penelope calls her a 'bold and shameless bitch' (19.91), and she is the only maid among those killed by Odysseus to receive a name. The father of Melanthios and Melantho is named Δολίος, a name which in contexts referring to his children's treacherous behaviour (17.212 ff., 18.320–2) was perhaps meant to pun on δόλος 'ruse'.[243]

---

239 She was purchased by Laertes for the price of twenty oxen (*Od.* 1.429–31).
240 See Thalmann 1998: 77 n.74. It has even been suggested that it is the servant's name that is reflected in that of the wife; see *LfgrE* s.v. Εὐρύκλεια (W. Beck), with bibliography. The role of introductions in increasing the importance of characters was noticed by ancient critics, as suggested by the Scholia (see Nünlist 2009: 56).
241 Thalmann 1998: 84; *Comm. on Od.* v.3: 117 (Russo). Cf. von Kamptz: 'mit freundlichem Schicksal' (1982 [1958]: 67). However, οἶτος is used in Homer in a bad sense ('unhappy fate'; LSJ); perhaps the name is from φιλέω and οἶτος, and signifies 'he who embraces his sad fate' – a meaning generically appropriate for the Homeric hero who embraces suffering and death (cf. also Menoitios, see above under 'Patroklos'). An alternative etymology, from οἰσέμεναι (φέρω), proposed by Bechtel (1917: 346) for the similar name Φιλοίτης, produces no clear meaning.
242 See also Buxton 2010: 6–7. Von Kamptz (1982 (1958): 88) saw the name as a short form of *Μελάν-θυμος (an unlikely name – the combination of μέλας and θυμός is odd). See also *LfgrE* s.v. Μελανθεύς / Μελάνθιος (M. Schmidt) and de Jong 2001: 42–3. A similar negative connotation may lurk in the use of Μελάνθιος as a name for a slaughtered Trojan in the *Iliad* (6.36).
243 There is some confusion regarding this name; it also appears in 4.735–7 as that of a servant of Penelope and keeper of her estate, and of Laertes' loyal servant in 24. The father of Melanthios and Melantho may thus be a different person. The problem of Dolios cannot be separated from the wider issues surrounding the authenticity and function of the Epilogue; see S.R.West 1988: 124–5. Despite de Jong (2001: 119), Erbse (1972: 238–40) and Thalmann (1998: 69–70 and n. 54), the name's original etymology cannot be from δοῦλος 'slave', which is from *δόελος (see Beekes 2010 s.v. δοῦλος).

3.4.2 The suitors

The naming of the suitors at *Od.* 22.242–3 and 266–8 demonstrates their superior number and thus stresses the difficulty of Odysseus' effort to annihilate them and hence the magnitude of his achievement.[244] The names of most suitors (e.g. Agelaos, Amphimedon, Amphinomos etc.) seem to be of 'typical' (or 'generic') significance,[245] but it is worth asking whether the names of the two principal suitors,[246] Antinoos and Eurymachos, might be specifically appropriate for these two characters.

Ἀντίνοος is a compound of Ἀντί and νόος, 'he who has a contrary / hostile mind'; this should describe his position as an enemy of Odysseus.[247] He may also be seen more generally as an 'enemy of discernment':[248] Antinoos indeed apparently refused or was unable to think and act according to common sense and justice; he is said to owe a debt of gratitude to Odysseus (16.417–33), thus his behaviour is particularly misjudged,[249] and leads to his destruction. Alternatively, -νόος (as in Alkinoos, Pontonoos) may allude to νέομαι 'return' and νόστος, 'homecoming'; the name could then mean 'being and / or acting against the homecoming'. This suits a character whose primary preoccupation is to prevent the return of Odysseus (and also of Telemachos, whom he tries to prevent from going to Pylos, and then plots to kill him before he sets foot on Ithaca, cf. 4.663–72). The double potential of *noos* leaves its interpretation open to the audience; but either way the name sounds appropriate, and was perhaps a deliberate choice for a character who is hostile to the purposes of the poem's hero. Antinoos' characterisation may be further also reflected in the name of his father, Εὐπείθης, if taken to mean 'persuasive' and allude to the suitor's skills in rhetoric and persuasion[250] (cf. e.g. 2.84–128, where he addresses the Ithacan assembly; his suggestions are regularly met with approval, e.g. 4.660–73; 18.42–50).

---

244 As Higbie notes (1995: 7).
245 Von Kamptz 1982 (1958): 36. Of the 108 suitors, some 15 are named (M.L. West 2014: 56). Amphinomos stands out as the only suitor with a good character, whom Odysseus calls πεπνυμένος (*Od.* 18.125).
246 They are called ἀρχοὶ μνηστήρων 'leaders of the suitors', *Od.* 4.629 = 21.187.
247 See Louden 1999: 18–20, 36–40.
248 Peradotto 1990: 107.
249 Note also that he is unfair to the beggar Odysseus, whom he insults, although the beggar greets him in a friendly way (17.415 ff.).
250 Thus Louden ibid.; cf. Mühlestein 1971: 46–7; M.L. West 2014: 304. But εὐπειθής (not a Homeric adjective) can also have a passive meaning: 'easily persuaded', 'obedient'; cf. von Kamptz 1982 (1958): 76.

The name of the second best of the suitors, Εὐρύμαχος (4.628 f.), may also have a meaning that corresponds (albeit rather vaguely) to his role in the poem:²⁵¹ 'of many fighting plans', in a broad sense as 'endeavours'. Indeed Eurymachos is active in more ways than the official chief, Antinoos: he devises machinations and murderous plans (4.669 ff.), he uses both actions and words (e.g. his discourse with Telemachos at 1.399 ff.) and employs a bullying manner (2.177 ff.) and even treachery in order to save himself (he blames Antinoos to Odysseus, 22.44 ff.). He appears at times as Odysseus' most powerful opponent.²⁵² *Eury-* is, as we have seen, a common name component; and it cannot be ignored that the element –μαχος is usually found in heroic names alluding to war and battle: Ἀντίμαχος, Ἀμφίμαχος, Ἱππόμαχος, Πρόμαχος, Ἀνδρομάχη, to name a few examples from the *Iliad*; Telemachos and Eurymachos – which does not occur in the *Iliad* – are the only such names in the *Odyssey*, and we have seen that Telemachos has a traditional war-related significance. However, a broader, almost metaphorical use of –μαχος is not impossible.²⁵³ Perhaps the sense of fighting in Eurymachos' name contains an ironic hint, as the suitor's 'fighting' has nothing to do with the noble field of heroic battle but is spent on unlawful, immoral and self-denigrating purposes.

---

251 Despite von Kamptz (1982 (1958): 72) who saw the name as 'vielleicht sinnlose (?) Nachbildung von Eurymedon etc.' He is the son of Polybos, a generic heroic name (used for five different people in the epics; see also above, under 'Some Phaeacian names').
252 See *LfgrE* s.v. Εὐρύμαχος (W. Beck). Note that Eurymachos is at one point considered as the best possible match for Penelope by her father and brothers, for surpassing the other suitors in his presents (*Od.* 15.16–23).
253 μάχομαι was used to mean 'struggle', 'make an effort to do' in later literature, e.g. Arist. *HA* 552a23.

4 'Minor' speaking names

We have seen that the effect of 'speaking' names of main heroes depends to a great extent on the heroes' characterisation, as well as on the narrow and the broader narrative contexts. On the other hand, 'minor' names usually 'arise out of a simple association of ideas in the singer's mind'.[1] The audience's attention to such 'minor', 'right' names was frequently attracted by intentional linguistic affinities between the name and the immediate context. The names in question are usually generic: they suggest an idea, capacity or concept, which is not specific to one individual character but applies to a group of figures that share similar characteristics (for example, names of warrior heroes evoking war and fight are frequent in the *Iliad*; the names of the Phaeacians in the *Odyssey* share a sea-related significance). Names of lesser characters involved in basic aspects of the plot of the epics were mentioned in previous chapters (especially the *Odyssey* chapter); the present chapter looks at some additional significantly named characters, at selected word-plays with names and at further concepts frequently suggested – and shared – by such 'minor' names. Occasionally one name is used for more than one characters in the same epic or across the epics,[2] but retains its semantic power: as we have already seen, etymologies of epic stock-names may be activated by contexts and often suggest more than one nuances of meaning; hence a strict semantic categorisation is difficult to achieve. Still, the examination of a sample from the vast field of names of 'minor' figures implies some possible semantic groups.

Most of the Homeric (primarily the Iliadic) heroes are ἄριστοι and ἄνακτες, with connections to the royal households of Greece and Troy. This status has inspired names such as Κοίρανος ('ruler', 'commander';[3] *Il.* 5.677; cf. 17.611), Κρείων ('ruler', 'prince';[4] *Il.* 9.84, cf. *Od.* 11.269), Δμήτωρ ('subduer', 'conqueror';[5]

---

[1] Cf. Kirk 1990: 57–8. On the difficult question whether such names constitute Homeric inventions or stem from an older poetic tradition see Hoekstra 1981: 56–66; also above p. 4. The ancient critics clearly considered many names (especially of minor characters) as invented by Homer (see Nünlist 2009: 243–4, with references).
[2] Homonymies attracted significant attention from ancient scholars, who commented on them extensively (see Nünlist [2009: 240–1] for references); it is unlikely that they would have bothered ancient audiences.
[3] From a noun κοίρανος (e.g. *Il.* 2.204); on its etymology see Beekes 2010 s.v.
[4] From κρείων (-οντος), 'an inherited word from Indo-European poetic language' (Beekes 2010 s.v.). It has several attestations in Homer (e.g. *Il.* 1.130).

Od. 17.443), Πρύτανις ('chief';[6] *Il.* 5.678), Πάλμυς (*Il.* 13.792),[7] Μέδων ('ruler';[8] *Il.* 2.727), which reflect 'des dignités royales ou des vertus aristocratiques'.[9] The centrality of the concept of glory in the epic justifies the numerous compound names with κλέος (discussed earlier in connection with the name of Patroklos). Other names emphasise the heroes' role as guardians and protectors of their people: Φύλακος ('watcher'; *Il.* 6.35, cf. *Od.* 15.231),[10] Ἀμύντωρ (name of the father of Phoinix; *Il.* 9.448, 10.266),[11] Ἀστύνοος (*Il.* 5.144, 15.455)[12].

While most heroic names are conceived as praise for their bearers and their virtues, some are rather unglamorous in sense, such as those that express the warriors' moves and actions during flight from battle. For example, some of the fleeing Trojans in *Il.* 5.38–82 have names that may reflect their motion while fleeing: Ὀδίος (39, from ὁδός 'way'),[13] Πήδαιος (69, from πηδάω 'leap', 'spring', cf. *Il.* 21.269);[14] the name of Skamandrios' father Στροφίος (49) may have emerged from the idea of being hit from behind while on the run, as στρεφθέντι (40) suggests. This group of names can further serve as a good example of the complex character that onomastic inspiration can have. The name Σκαμάνδριος (49) alludes to the river Skamandros (which was just mentioned in 36), while the father's name too, Στροφίος, may seem to suit a river-related context, in referring to the movement of a river, possibly to its swirling (cf. *Il.* 21.125 f., 16.792).[15] Personal names were not uncommonly derived from rivers

---

5 Relevant Homeric vocabulary: δαμάω / δάμνημι 'to subdue' (e.g. *Il.* 1.61), δμῆσις 'taming' (of horses) (*Il.* 17.476).
6 See Beekes 2010 s.v. πρύτανις: the word 'probably belongs to the Anatolian-Aegean stratum of social designations' (together with βασιλεύς, ἄναξ, τύραννος).
7 The name means 'king' in Lydian, as in Hipponax (e.g. fr. 3W, 38W). See also Janko 1992: 143.
8 From substantive participle μέδων, e.g. *Il.* 2.79: ἡγήτορες ἠδὲ μέδοντες.
9 Thus Sulzberger 1926: 398.
10 From φυλακός (*Il.* 24.566).
11 See above, on Phoinix.
12 Cf. von Kamptz 1982 (1958): 75: 'wer den Sinn auf die Stadt gerichtet hat, auf (das Wohl der) Stadt bedacht ist.'
13 Also spelt as Ὀδίος in the ms tradition; M.L. West prints a rough breathing (which certainly helps the pun). He is mentioned in the 'Trojan catalogue' as the leader of the Halizones (2.856), together with Ἐπίστροφος – the semantic harmony between the two names can hardly be a coincidence (even if Epistrophos may also be related to seamanship: the name appears also at 2.517–8 for a leader of the Phocians, there with a brother Schedios and an ancestor Naubolos; cf. Mühlestein 1969: 74).
14 There is a toponym Πήδαιον (*Il.* 13.172); but the context encourages the pun on πηδάω.
15 Thus Mühlestein 1969: 75. The name was interpreted by Sch. bT 5.49 as suitable for a hunter on the grounds that hunters tend to spend time at rivers and woods. But Kirk (1990: 59) has rightly noticed that there is no hint on the relevance of the rivers, while mountains and their

and river-gods.[16] The name of another fleeing Trojan, Φαῖστος (43), has different associations: as the name of Idomeneus' opponent, it may reflect the hero's connection with Crete through the city of Phaistos (mentioned in *Il.* 2.648 and *Od.* 3.296), which rivalled Idomeneus' own city Knossos. Perhaps Phaistos was connected with φάος 'light' (cf. Pl. *Cra.* 407c on the etymology of Hephaistos[17]); σκότος (47) could then appear as a deliberate contrast, with an ironic hint at the fate of Phaistos, 'the man of light', who was eventually taken by the darkness (death).[18] Phaistos is the son of Βῶρος, which can appropriately mean 'eye'.[19]

Word-plays with names (what Sulzberger[20] called 'amusettes philologiques') confirm semantic intentionality and allow a relatively clearer (if not a perfect) grasp of the semantic concepts involved. Examples include the following:

Πρόθοος θοός 'swift Prothoos' (*Il.* 2.758): Prothoos is mentioned in the *Catalogue of ships* as the leader of the Magnetes. The name is clearly significant, probably 'he who dashes forward' (cf. the use of the verb προθέω, e.g. *Il.* 22.459, *Od.* 11.515).[21] Prothoos does not receive another mention in the *Iliad*, and later sources only report his death after the fall of Troy.[22] The name is apparently used here for the sake of a pun on θοός 'swift'. The adjective expresses a generic heroic characteristic: it is commonly used of warriors in the *Iliad*

---

forests are mentioned in 1.52. (For Skamandrios as the name of Hektor's son see above, 'The "Greek" Trojans.').

16 Cf. the name of the hero Σιμοείσιος, so named because his mother bore her child next to the river Σιμόεις (*Il.* 4.474–7). The practice continued in historical times, see Parker 2000: 53 ff.; Thonemann 2006: 33 ff.; list of river-inspired names in Bechtel 1917: 555–6.
17 ΕΡΜ. Τί δὲ δὴ τὸν Ἥφαιστον, πῇ λέγεις; / ΣΩ. Ἦ τὸν γενναῖον τὸν "φάεος ἵστορα" ἐρωτᾷς; ... Οὐκοῦν οὗτος μὲν παντὶ δῆλος "Φαῖστος" ὤν, τὸ / ἦτα προσελκυσάμενος; [HERM.] 'And how do you explain Hephaistos? [SOCR.] You ask about "the noble master of light"? ... Hephaistos is Phaistos, with the eta added by attraction; anyone could see that, I should think.' (transl. Fowler).
18 Interestingly, an Aphrodite σκοτία was said to be celebrated in Phaistos, the 'city of light'. Cf. *EM* 543, 48 s.v. Κυθέρεια. Mühlestein 1969: 75.
19 Cf. Pape-Benseler and Hsch. s.v. βῶροι· ὀφθαλμοί. This is also the name of the mortal father of Spercheios' son Menesthios, about whom it is said that he married Menesthios' mother ἀναφανδόν 'visibly', 'before all eyes' (*Il.* 16.177–8).
20 1926: 384. On word-plays and significant names see further Edwards 1987: 120–3.
21 See von Kamptz 1982 (1958): 73–4. Cf. Latacz 2003: 226.
22 Tz. *ad Lyc.* 899, 902, citing Apollod. (6.15a). Nothing more is known of his father Τενθρηδών (756) and his unusual name; the word is mentioned as a feminine noun in Arist. *HA* 6.29a31, meaning 'oak-apple wasp' (cf. Dsc. 5.109; Sch. Nic. *Al.* 547a-b). Prothoos is the name of two more figures in later sources, related to Kalydon: a son of Agrios and nephew of Oineus, i.e. Meleagros' cousin (Apollod. 1.77–9) and a son of Thestios and a participant in the hunt for the Kalydonian boar (Paus. 8.45.6).

(cf. 2.542, 5.462, 536, 571 etc.) and seems to have been a generic element in names of heroes, cf. Ἱππόθοος (2.840 etc.), Ἀλκάθοος (12.93 etc.), Ἀρηΐθοος (7.8 etc.), and from the *Odyssey* Βοηθοΐδης (4.31 etc., from Βοήθοος), Ναυσίθοος (6.7 etc.);[23] cf. also, from the *Iliad*, Προθόων (14.515), Θόων (5.152), Θοώτης (12.342–3).

ὑπὸ Κυλλήνης ὄρος αἰπύ / Αἰπύτιον παρὰ τύμβον 'beneath the steep mountain of Cyllene, / beside the tomb of Aipytos' (*Il.* 2.603–4): this is another example from the *Catalogue*. There is an obvious pun between αἰπύ and the name of the Arkadian hero Αἴπυτος.[24] ὄρος αἰπύ was formulaic (cf. 2.829 and *Od.* 3.287, 4.514), which may suggest that the use of the name in this context was triggered by the adjective. αἰπύς 'high and steep' is used mostly of mountains and cities (especially Troy, cf. *Od.* 3.485 etc.), but it also had a figurative meaning 'difficult, hard' and was used in both epics of ὄλεθρος (*Il.* 6.57, 10.371 etc., *Od.* 1.11, 37 etc.), of φόνος and of the turmoil of war (*Il.* 21.651). This meaning would suit a warrior's name, and perhaps a secondary such allusion was intended.

...Πολύκτωρ. Ἀφνειὸς μὲν ὅ γ᾽ ἐστι '[my father is] Polyktor. He is rich in substance' (*Il.* 24.397–8). This is part of the god Hermes' false self-introduction to Priam, where he pretends to be a Myrmidon, the son of a Polyktor. The god's intention is to help Priam cross into the Greek camp and reach Achilles safely; his self-introduction by a false name is a manifestation of the trickery traditionally associated with him. Πολύκτωρ is clearly meant to suggest a rich man,[25] but the etymology of the name is elusive. –κτωρ could be related to an original *-κτήτωρ or to κτέαρ 'possession', in which case the name suggested the 'possessor'.[26] If associated with a root κτερ– 'to give, to spend' (cf. κτέρεα 'funeral gifts' and κτέρας 'gift';[27] *Il.* 10.216, 24.235), then the name would mean 'he who spends much or offers gifts'.[28] Both meanings would suit ἀφνειός, which clearly alludes to the meaning of the proper name. Polyktor may also be meant to reflect one of the god's best known functions as a 'giver of good things' (cf. *Il.* 14.491, *Od.* 8.335, 15.319–20).[29] In that case, a touch of irony may also have been felt in the name,[30] resulting from Priam's not knowing that he is facing a god and the god's playing with this ignorance. Polyktor may further allude to the greed which is a feature of the god's characterisation elsewhere; notably in the *Iliad* he is paired with a

---

23 For more examples (including women's names in –θοη) see von Kamptz 1982 (1958): 74.
24 Cf. Kirk 1985: 217.
25 Cf. Latacz 2009b: 144–5.
26 Cf. Russo (1992: 27) who translates 'much possessing'.
27 'Possession' according to LSJ.
28 Thus von Kamptz 1982 (1958): 69, Chantraine 1999 s.v. κτέρας (uncertain etym.).
29 Cf. Richardson 1993: 314.
30 On the irony of the scene see Richardson 1993: 309 ff.

lover and a son that bear names of similar significance to Polyktor (16.179–86).[31] The name recurs in the *Odyssey* (17.207, identified by the Scholia there as one of the founders of Kephallenia and Ithaca, and in 18.299 and 22.243 as the patronymic of one of the suitors),[32] and ἀφνειός is also used of other heroes (cf. *Il.* 5.9 ff.). Still, the semantic closeness between name and adjective suggests that they were placed together here intentionally.[33]

Ἠνιοπῆα, / ἵππων ἡνί' ἔχοντα '… Eniopeus / as he was holding the reins' (*Il.* 8.120–1): this is a pun on a charioteer's name, which echoes ἡνία 'reins' and ἔπω (for the use of the verb to mean 'to be about, busy oneself with' cf. *Il.* 6.321).[34] Apart from the different aspiration, the similarity of sound is quite striking and would certainly be noticed. The phrase ἡνί' ἔχοντα recurs at 16.379, but the name is not mentioned elsewhere.[35] However, the fact that his name is mentioned together with a patronymic (Θηβαίου Ἠνιοπῆα) bestows this briefly mentioned figure – a charioteer of Hektor – with additional importance.[36] It is noteworthy that this man is replaced by the also significantly named Ἰφιτίδης Ἀρχεπτόλεμος (Archeptolemos, son of Iphitos[37]; 8.128, 8.312–3), appropriately characterised as θρασύς. His replacement, Kebriones (8.318–9 – a step-brother of Hektor), is perhaps also a name with associations of power and strength, as we may infer from its use in Aristophanes (*Birds* 553) together with the name of the giant Porphyrion.[38] Homeric charioteers often carry significant names – some are discussed later in this chapter.

---

31 Polymele 'of many flocks' and Eudoros 'of many gifts.' Cf. Vergados 2011: 99 (and 98 on Hermes' greed).
32 Von Kamptz 1982 (1958): 36–7 saw it as a 'typical' heroic name. (He used the term 'typische Namen', following Kretschmer 1917: 124 f.) See also Russo 1992: 27.
33 Cf. the (probably deliberate) combinations: Ἀρχεπτόλεμον θρασύν *Il.* 8.128; Ἀντιμάχοιο δαΐφρονος *Il.* 11.123, 138.
34 Cf. von Kamptz 1982 (1958): 27, 71. See also Perpillou 1973: 208.
35 The similar (but irrelevant) Ἦνοπις (*Il.* 14.444) probably meant 'brilliant' (from ἤνοψ 'gleaming', mostl used of bronze, cf. *Il.* 16.408 etc.; see Janko 1992: 217). This man's son is called Σάτνιος, from the name of the river near which he was born, cf. Σιμοείσιος (4.474), Σκαμάνδριος (5.49).
36 Cf. Higbie 1995: 8.
37 On this name, from the old instrumental dative ἶφι 'with power', see further von Kamptz 1982 (1958): 201–2.
38 Note however that the exact nature of this Kebriones is uncertain, see further Dunbar 1995: 375. On the charioteer see Burgess 2001: 71 with n. 82. On the name's etymology (perhaps from a river name Kebros) see von Kamptz 1982 (1958): 293.

Βριάρεων... / ὃ γὰρ αὖτε βίην οὗ πατρὸς ἀμείνων (*Il.* 1.403–4): the giant notably has two names: Βριάρεως is his divine name (also found in Hes. *Th.* 149),[39] while men call him Αἰγαίων; this is another example of the different languages of gods and men.[40] βριαρός means 'strong' (cf. *Il.* 16.413, 19.381), which makes the name appropriate for a giant, and it evidently puns on βίη. The pun is made explicit by the parenthetic statement of 404: '(he is named so) for being stronger than his father'.[41]

Βαθυκλῆα... / ὅς... / ὄλβῳ τε πλούτῳ τε μετέπρεπε Μυρμιδόνεσσιν 'Bathykles... who... for wealth and substance was preeminent among the Myrmidons' (*Il.* 16.594–6): the phrase may be formulaic (cf. 16.194 Μαιμαλίδης, ὃς πᾶσι μετέπρεπε Μυρμιδόνεσσιν). Similarly ὄλβῳ τε πλούτῳ recurs at 24.536 (of Peleus) and in the *Odyssey* (14.206).[42] However, Βαθυκλῆα and μετέπρεπε are semantically related, and βαθύς is a word that can be associated with πλοῦτος;[43] perhaps there are no less than two simultaneous hints at the meaning of the proper name.[44]

Πρωτεσίλαος (*Il.* 2.698) is a 'speaking' name, as is clearly suggested by νηὸς ἀποθρώσκοντα πολὺ πρώτιστον Ἀχαιῶν (2.702). Protesilaos was the first hero to land at Troy and the first to be killed. It has been argued that this notion of 'first' has its roots in Indo-European poetry, and in a poetic expression of the meaning 'to slay or be slain first'.[45] The theme is elsewhere connected with a hero's slaying of a beast (cf. Pi. *I.* 6.48, of Herakles: ... θηρός, ὃν πάμπρωτον ἀέθλων κτεῖνά ποτ' ἐν Νεμέᾳ 'from the beast that I once killed in Nemea as the very first of my labors'), which (with a shift of roles) could apply to Protesilaos as a victim. The onomastic play might additionally reflect a general interest (inherent in human nature) in the 'first' doer of a striking act or the 'first' deed.

An attentive audience may notice evocative etymologies even when word-plays are absent:

---

39 Hesiod (*Th.* 617, 734) provides the alternative form Ὀβριάρεως (ὀ is an old prepositional prefix); see further M.L.West 1966: 210.
40 Cf. above, on the river name Skamandros (under 'The "Greek" Trojans').
41 Rank (1951: 84) calls this example an 'etymologisierende Namensdeutung'. There seems to be no ground for Kirk's view (1985: 94–5) that the name does not have this meaning, and that the parenthetic statement βίη οὗ πατρὸς ἀμείνων refers to the whole context.
42 See further Janko 1992: 389.
43 Cf. the adjective βαθύπλουτος (B. 3.82; A. *Supp.* 554).
44 Interestingly, Βαθυκλέης is the only name with βαθύς in early Greek epic poetry. Κλέος βαθύ is first found in Pi. *O.* 7.53, cf. βαθύδοξοι (*P.* 1.66). See *LfgrE* s.v. Βαθυκλέης (R.Führer).
45 Watkins 1995: 507, in comparison with *Beowulf* (2077–9), where the warrior Hondscio is the first to be slain by Grendel. Cf. V. *Aen.* 1.1: qui primus ab oris...

Ἀγκαῖος (Il. 23.635): this is the wrestler who is beaten by Nestor. The name must be related to ἄγκεα 'valley', 'gorge', ἀγκών 'elbow', ἄγκυλον 'curved', 'bent', and most of all to ἀγκάς 'in the arms'. It thus appears to be relevant to wrestling.[46] ἀγκὰς δ' ἀλλήλων λαβέτην ('led hold each of the other in close grip', 23.711) seems to encourage this etymology – the phrase, however, is part of the account of a different wrestling match and thus cannot allude to Ankaios.

The name Στέντωρ (Il. 5.785) has been thought to match the bearer's distinctively loud voice,[47] which is emphasised in the context (785–6: Στέντορι ... μεγαλήτορι χαλκεοφώνῳ, / ὃς τόσον αὐδήσασχ' ὅσον ἄλλοι πεντήκοντα 'Stentor ... of the brazen voice, whose voice is as great as that of fifty other men'[48]). στένω usually means 'to groan', 'to sigh' (e.g. Il. 24.776), but also 'roar' at one instance (of the sea; Il. 23.230). The fact that Stentor became a proverbial figure (κῆρυξ ... Στεντόρειος, Arist. Pol. 4.1326b) was at least partly due to his name.

The name of the Trojan seer Μέροψ (Il. 11.329–30) has been connected with the root *mer-, also assumed in μέρμερος 'baneful', 'evil' (as in the expression μέρμερα ἔργα 'grim deeds', e.g. Il. 8.453),[49] and in μέροπες, epithet of ἄνθρωποι ('mortal men'? e.g. Il. 18.288, 20.217). Perhaps the name was suggestive of ominous divination: Merops, 'who was above all men skilled in prophecying', attempted to prevent his sons from taking part in the war, but they did and were eventually killed (Il. 11.329–34). However, other interpretations of *meropes* assume different meanings for *mer-.[50] Merops is the name of the autochthonous hero of Kos, whose inhabitants were called *meropes* ('autochthonous'?)[51] Another possible meaning is 'bright-faced'; this is perhaps the meaning of the name Μερόπη, which thus seems appropriate for a daughter of the Sun and one of the Pleiads (Apollod. 1.85; 3.110; Hyg. Fab. 192.5). A Hesychian gloss (μέρα·

---

46 Cf. Scholia (which also give an explanation for his ethnic name: ἴσως δὲ καὶ παρὰ τὰς πλευρὰς Πλευρώνιος) and Eust. 1321.11 (on Il. 23.635). See von Kamptz 1982 (1958): 26.
47 Von Kamptz 1982 (1958): 253 f., Kirk 1990: 139–40.
48 Note than l. 786 was rejected by Didymus διὰ τὴν ὑπερβολήν.
49 Cf. also Mermeros, name of a hero (Od. 1.259), the father of Ilos, skilled in making poison.
50 See J. Russo's overview of the possibilities in HE s.v. *meropes*.
51 h.Ap. 42 – a possible totemic name for a pre-Greek tribe, according to LfgrE s.v. Μέροπες (W. Beck). μέροψ is also the name of a bird that buries its eggs in the earth (Chantraine 1999 s.v. μέροπες). Note that μέροπες is reminiscent of other groups of names of heroes, birds and tribes: δρύοψ, δρύοπες· ἄεροψ, ἄεροπες. Chantraine (ibid.) noted that their formation may suggest foreign (Thracian or Phrygian) origin; notably the seer's two sons are Trojan allies leading troops from Phrygia (Il. 2.831). See also LfgrE s.v. Μέροπες, Μέρο(ψ) (W. Beck); Nagy 1990: 198. Other possible explanations of *mer-* in von Kamptz 1982 (1958): 328.

ὄμματα 'eyes') might make Μέροψ sound an appropriate name for somebody gifted with 'second sight'.⁵²

Merops is not the only religious man to be assigned a potentially significant name. Helenos was briefly discussed earlier (in connection with Helen), while the names of the priestess Θεανώ (wife of the Trojan Antenor, *Il.* 6.300)⁵³ and the seer Theoklymenos (*Od.* 15.225–57)⁵⁴ express appropriate divine connections. The genealogical details provided for the latter two suggest a high social status.⁵⁵

Another group of characters whose naming evokes a generic concept is that of heralds. Numerous heralds have names which reflect their function.⁵⁶ For example, the heralds of Agamemnon and Odysseus are both called Εὐρυβάτης (Agamemnon's: *Il.* 1.320; Odysseus': 2.184, perhaps 9.170,⁵⁷ and *Od.* 19.247), a name alluding to the need for covering long distances in order to deliver and receive messages.⁵⁸ Another example is Ὀδίος (9.170), partner of Eurybates in the embassy to Achilles, whose name may also allude to the travelling done by heralds.⁵⁹ Another 'generic' herald name is Ταλθύβιος, which evoked the Talthybiadai, the family or guild of heralds in Sparta perhaps from pre-Homeric times.⁶⁰ Both Talthybios and Eurybates are described as ὀτρηρὼ θεράποντε (*Il.* 1.321), 'busy helpers', who go on various errands, which could imply that they cover long distances. There are more mentions of Talthybios in the *Iliad* than of Eurybates, but the latter is given the important role of accompanying the embassy to Achilles (9.170), perhaps because he can be nicely partnered with the also significantly

---

52 Thus Carnoy 1956: 121 (rather fanciful).
53 See also Latacz 2008: 103 (she may have had a presence in pre-Homeric tradition as a priestess of Athena).
54 On this name see below. It is perhaps no coincidence that *mer-* and *klymenos* names mix in later literature: Merope, daughter of Okeanos, the mother of Phaethon by Klymenos (Hyg. *Fab.* 154); and Merops, king of the Aithiopians, was married to Klymene (Str. 1.2.27).
55 See Higbie 1995: 8–9. Higbie notes that the poet provides no information of family or origin for the two most prominent mythical sheers, Teiresias and Kalchas (except for the ethnic 'Theban' for Teiresias at *Od.* 10.492–3); this is certainly explained by the audience's familiarity with these two characters, and is not to be seen as an indicator of status.
56 Cf. von Kamptz 1982 (1958): 26.
57 See Kirk 1985: 134 and Hainsworth 1993: 83; cf. M.L. West 2011a: 219.
58 Kirk 1985: 134 suggested the meaning 'broad ranger', cf. 'der Weitausschreitende' (*LfgrE* s.v. Εὐρυβάτης [B.Mader]; Latacz 2000b: 120 and 2003: 62).
59 See Hainsworth 1993: 83. Cf. Hodios, epithet of Hermes: 'god of the road', 'who protects the journey'. The name was mentioned earlier in this chapter for the leader of the Halizones who is killed at flight (*Il.* 5.39); the different capacities of bearers arguably inspire different nuances of meaning.
60 Cf. Kirk 1985: 85.

named Odios.⁶¹ Another appropriately named herald is Θοώτης (*Il.* 12.342), a name that denotes rapidity, a highly desirable characteristic in a herald; the name's etymology is noticed by the Scholia.⁶²

In addition to the heralds, the epics feature a number of significantly named charioteers. Names in the two groups share similarities. Two charioteers are called Εὐρυμέδων (Agamemnon's in *Il.* 4.228 and Nestor's in *Il.* 8.114, cf. 11.620), a similar compound to Eurybates. There is also Αὐτομέδων (*Il.* 24.574), Achilles' charioteer (and the name of a herald in *Od.* 4.675). The other charioteer at *Il.* 24.574 is called Ἄλκιμος – a parallel name for Ἀλκιμέδων.⁶³ μέδων means 'ruling' (see above), but as a component in a charioteer's name it may allude to 'driving' (Latin *rego* had a similar development in the reverse direction).⁶⁴ Μέδων is also the name of a herald in the *Odyssey*, who renders service to Odysseus' family, when he warns Penelope of the suitors' intent to harm Telemachos (4.677–715); he further tries to discourage the suitors' relatives from revenge (24.439–50). His name is on both occasions accompanied by the formula πεπνυμένα εἰδώς 'wise of heart' (4.696; 24.442).

μέδων has a versatile use in Homeric names, and it functions as a link with yet another group of significantly named individuals. As noted earlier, the name of Εὐρυμέδουσα (*Od.* 7.8), Alkinoos' female servant, sounds appropriate for somebody who skillfully carries out a broad range of duties. Εὐρυ- was perhaps felt to be an appropriate component in servants' names, judging by examples such as Εὐρύκλεια (*Od. passim*), Εὐρυνόμη (*Od.* 17.495 etc.); perhaps one of these functioned as the model for the choice or creation of the others.⁶⁵ Another popular component for servants' names is ἱππο-: Ἀλκίππη (*Od.* 4.124), Ἱπποδάμεια (*Od.* 18.182).

Another type of siginificant naming of 'minor' heroes brings together names of people who belong to the same family, especially fathers and sons. The mention of a famous patronymic is enough to allude to stories and exploits associated with the heroic father, and to underline the significance of a hero's genealogical

---

61 The appropriately significant name might imply that Eurybates is an invention of the poet of the *Iliad*; but the description of Eurybates in personal detail in the *Odyssey* is suggestive of an old character (see also Kirk 1985: 134).
62 Sch. to *Il.* 12.342 and 343: ἀπὸ τοῦ θέειν or ταχύνειν (a synonym of θέω 'run'). On the function of Homeric heralds, a point of difference between the *Iliad* and the *Odyssey*, see also Higbie 1995: 9.
63 Alkimos and Alkimedon are the same man, cf. M.L. West 2011a: 338.
64 Thus Hainsworth 1993: 291.
65 Von Kamptz 1982 (1958): 37. Note that the masculine form of Eurynome, Eurynomos, occurs as the name of one of the suitors (*Od.* 22.242).

past (thus e.g. Diomedes, son of Tydeus, the famous attacker of Thebes),[66] but the poetic interplay between different generations often acquires also an etymological dimension – a strong indication of poetic invention.[67] There are numerous examples, such as the commonly mentioned and straightforward Φήμιος Τερπιάδης ('Singer, son of Pleasure-Man'), the name of the *aoidos* at Odysseus' palace on Ithaca (*Od.* 22.330–1; he is called πολύφημος).[68] There are also more complex onomastic plays, such as the one that evolves around Antenor and his sons (eleven in the *Iliad*, seven of whom die). Three are called Λαόδοκος (*Il.* 4.87), Ἰφιδάμας ('mighty subduer';[69] *Il.* 11.221), and Λαοδάμας ('subduer of peoples'; *Il.* 15.517). The poem also mentions the grandfather's name, Λαομέδων (*Il.* 15.419–21, 525–43). Λαοδάμαντα / ἡγεμόνα πρυλέων (*Il.* 15.516–7) must be a pun on the name's meaning.[70] Ἀντήνωρ is commonly seen as a compound of ἀντί and ἀνήρ, with the meaning 'he who stands up against men' or 'worth (many) men'.[71] This would be an appropriate meaning for a generic heroic name, but Ἀντήνωρ may have a more special kind of appropriateness, encouraged by his strong presence in the epic tradition (he is the host of Odysseus and Menelaos in the *Cypria*, cf. *Il.* 3.207, 11.138–42).[72] Perhaps it is felt that 'he stands up against' Paris (7.347 ff., esp.357) when he proposes the return of Helen. The patronymic Ἀντηνορίδης may reflect the fight between Antenor's sons (although they are never victorious) and their Achaean opponents; when Iphidamas and Koon face Agamemnon (11.219 ff.), there is perhaps a pun between ἀντίον – Ἀντηνορίδης.[73] Λαόδοκος, too, appears to be an old name.[74] It can mean 'receive / stand up to the enemy in battle' (cf. *Il.* 5.238,

---

66 Cf. Higbie 1995: 10.
67 Cf. Higbie 1995: 12.
68 See also above, on the name of the Cyclops Polyphemos. The other Odyssean singer, Demodokos (at Phaeacia) is also appropriately named (see above, under 'Some Phaeacian names'), but lacks a patronymic.
69 On the name's first component see Chantraine 1999 s.v. 1 ἴς.
70 Janko (1992: 284–5) assumed that Laodamas only received the title 'leader of the infantry' (which is unique) 'to put him on a par with the Greek victims listed either side, since the poet could give his unit no geographical name'. The name, which has a generic sound, is used also for the eldest son of the Phaeacian king in the *Odyssey* (8.119, 130 etc.).
71 See *LfgrE* s.v. Ἀντήνωρ (H.-J. Newiger), cf. von Kamptz 1982 (1958): 56.
72 See Kirk 1985: 294. His name is found in Mycenaean, see Jorro-Adrados 1985 s.v. *a-ta-no*. Mühlestein (1969: 76–9) assumed a pre-Homeric epic, where Antenor's role as a host was primary and the name was understood to mean 'he who receives men'. This would demand that the name be derived from ἄντομαι ('meet, encounter', which however is not quite the same as 'receive'), but this does not seem likely in view of names such as Antikleia, Antinoos.
73 Thus Mühlestein 1969: 77 ff.
74 Already Mycenaean, PY Ea 802 *ra-wo-do-ko*.

τόνδε δ' ἐγὼν ἐπιόντα δεδέξομαι ὀξέϊ δουρί 'I will receive this man's approach with my sharp spear')[75] and may reflect a particular use of military chariots in Homer, where the charioteer stands behind the line of battle, so that he can take the fighter on the chariot in the case he is on retreat;[76] Antilochos' charioteer is called Laodokos (17.699).[77] The name of the Trojan Ἀστύνοος (Polydamas' charioteer, 15.455) may well have a relevant sense and denote the charioteer's function to bring the fighters safe back to the city.[78]

Naming motives that influence the naming of members of the same family often focus on the connection between father and son (or daughter). In a number of examples, the name's significance relates to the bearer's father. Such names emphasise qualities of the father, but can cause the named offsprings to fade in importance, as they are seen through their names as extensions of their fathers. Names that evoke a capacity of a prominent father are likely to have been invented or chosen specially for that purpose. Some of them belong to mythical and divine figures, which may suggest a very old onomastic habit; cf. the names of the Sun's daughters Λαμπετίη, Φαέθουσα (Od. 12.132) and son Φαέθων,[79] and the names of Nereus' daughters (Il. 18.39–49, cf. Hes. Th. 240–69) that correspond to Hesiod's description of him in Th. 233–6.[80] Similarly the name of Proteus' daughter Εἰδοθέη (Od. 4.366, cf. Scholia[81]) alludes to her father's prophetic power.

Among names that belong to the older generation of heroes, the name of Herakles' son Τληπόλεμος (Il. 2.657 ff.) could well characterise the father, as does the name of Odysseus' son Telemachos (both fathers spend time fighting far away). Another appropriately named son of a major hero is Εὐρυσάκης, son of Aias, whose name is clearly inspired by his father's characteristically large shield (εὐρὺ ... σάκος at Il. 11.527 leaves little doubt as to the name's meaning; cf. 17.132 and the description of the shield at 7.219–24). The *Iliad* mentions

---

75 Von Kamptz 1982 (1958): 73.
76 See further van Wees 1994: 9, 137.
77 Elsewhere the name Laodokos is associated with the idea of receiving and hosting (Mühlestein ibid.). It is the name under which Athena appears to Pandaros (91), to whom (s)he speaks as a kind host(ess).
78 See also above, pp. 123, 132, on the semantic possibilities of –*noos*.
79 Euripides wrote a play about him. φαέθων is found in Homer as an epithet of the Sun (ἠέλιος φαέθων, Il. 11.735, Od. 5.479, 11.16, 19.441, 22.388) and as the name of one of the two horses of Eos 'Dawn' (Od. 23.246; the other horse too, Λάμπων, is appropriately named).
80 See Edwards (1991: 147–50) for a detailed explanation of the names.
81 ἀπὸ τῆς εἰδήσεως καὶ ἐπιστήμης τοῦ πατρὸς τὸ ὄνομα. It is noted there that also Aeschylus in his *Proteus* names her so, while Zenodotus knows her as Eurynome.

the name of a son of Jason called Εὔνηος (7.468, 23.747), which must refer to the good ship Argo.[82] We have seen the connection between the names Agamemnon, Menelaos and Atreus. The names of Agamemnon's daughters, Χρυσόθεμις, Λαοδίκη, Ἰφιάνασσα (Il. 9.145, 287), from θέμις, δίκη 'justice' and ἀνάσσειν 'to rule', were perhaps invented here to reflect qualities of their father and Mycenae[83] – the three seem to have otherwise no presence in mythology. The components *themis* and *dike* in two of the names may sound like a hint at Agamemnon's resolution to restore justice: the names are mentioned by Agamemnon in the context of his promise to make amends for Achilles' unfair treatment early in the poem, by offering him gifts and whichever one of his daughters as his bride (9.114–61); but the generic appropriateness of the name Λαοδίκη for a king's daughter is visible in its use for another such daughter, Priam's (Il. 3.124, 6.252). The names of three of Nestor's sons express aspects of the father's character and function: Ἐχέφρων 'sensible', 'prudent',[84] Θρασυμήδης 'daring in thought or plan',[85] Πεισίστρατος 'army leader'[86] (Od. 3.413–5; Nestor had seven sons altogether). We have seen that the name of Menelaos' son Μεγαπένθης (Od. 4.11) reflects Menelaos' great grief (πένθος) at Helen's desertion,[87] and that the eldest son of the Phaeacian king is appropriately called Λαοδάμας (Od. 8.119 etc.).

Some 'minor' characters have patronymics that are synonymous with their own names; both members of each pair may have been chosen or invented together. Examples of this kind include Νοήμων 'intelligent' (the man from whom Athena orders a ship for Telemachos' trip), son of Φρόνιος 'prudent' (Od. 2.386; cf. Scholium πεποίηκεν πλάστα ὀνόματα).[88] This combination of names marks Noemon as a sensible man. Πρόφρων at 2.387 (he promised Athe-

---

[82] Kirk 1990: 291 is surely wrong in his interpretation of the name as 'apt for a despatcher of ships to Troy'. On Eurysakes see also above, p. 38.
[83] Cf. Sulzberger 1926: 391; on Chrysothemis and Laodike as related to the notion of justice, arguably an important concern in the *Iliad*, see Bouvier (2002: 292–3). The tradition about the names of Agamemnon's daughters is very problematic, see Hainsworth 1993: 77. Agamemnon's mythologically significant daughters are Iphimede and Electra (the only two mentioned in [Hes.] *Cat.* fr. 23 M–W).
[84] From adj. ἐχέφρων, e.g. *Od.* 13.332.
[85] An adjective θρασυμήδης occurs in Pindar (*P.* 4.143); see also above, p. 49.
[86] The name might alternatively refer to Nestor's eloquence and wise counsel (cf. *Il.* 1.248–9; see also M.L. West 2014: 90). Peisistratos is not in the list of Nestor's sons in the Hesiodic *Catalogue* (fr. 35 M–W) and was possibly invented by the *Odyssey* poet. One of Peisistratos' brothers is called Στρατίος (*Od.* 3.413).
[87] Von Kamptz 1982 (1958): 32, cf. Alden 2000: 55, n.22. See also above, p. 91.
[88] Cf. adjective νοήμων (e.g. *Od.* 2.282) and noun φρόνις (ἡ) (e.g. *Od.* 3.244).

na the ship 'with a ready heart') may be intended as a pun. He reappears at 4.630 ff., where he is contrasted with the suitors; he shows his wit in noticing that Mentor seems to have been present at two places at once (654–6).[89] There is also the captain of Menelaos' ship on his way home from Troy, Φρόντις Ὀνητορίδης (*Od.* 3.282),[90] an appropriate name and patronymic combination for somebody who is entrusted with the care of the ship's course; and Odysseus' self-introduction to his father (*Od.* 24.304–6), as υἱὸς Ἀφείδαντος Πολυπημονίδαο (which was discussed in detail under 'Names from the *Odyssey*').

Μέντωρ (*Od. passim*), son of Ἄλκιμος (*Od.* 22.235), appears first (2.224–41) as a comrade of Odysseus, who was left in charge of his household when Odysseus went to Troy; his identity is then assumed by the goddess Athena who in the guise of Mentor acts as Telemachos' advisor during his journey to Pylos. The name and patronymic are a good combination of heroic names: Alkimos was mentioned above as the name of a charioteer, and Mentor is etymologically relevant to Menelaos. We have seen that the exact meaning of the root *men-* is rather hard to determine. However, Mentor's role in the *Odyssey* may encourage a semantic connection between the name and μέμονα 'to have in mind' or μιμνήσκω 'to remember / remind' (or even μάντις 'seer'). Perhaps the name meant 'advisor',[91] which is suitable both for Mentor's original appearance (when he delivers an admonishing speech to the Ithacans) and for Athena's guise. The same meaning must be true also for Μέντης, a previous false identity assumed by Athena, under which she encourages and advises Telemachos in book 1 (104–324). 'Mentes' (an old friend of Odysseus, leader of the Taphians) condemns the suitors' behaviour and suggests to Telemachos that he should travel in order to seek news of his father. The similarity between the two names is probably intentional: Mentes and Mentor are both trustworthy friends of Odysseus in their proper persons, and as Athena's guises they both approach Telemachos and perform similar roles.[92]

---

[89] Cf. *Comm. on Od.* v.1: 154 (S.R. West); M.L. West 2014: 160. Νοήμων also occurs in *Il.* 5.678 (one of a number of Lycians slaughtered by Odysseus) and 23.612 (a comrade of Nestor's son Antilochos), but there is no other Φρόνιος.

[90] The noun φροντίς 'thought, care' first occurs in Pindar (*N.* 10.22), but it is clearly relevant to the Homeric φρόνις 'wisdom' (*Od.* 3.244). There is also a female Φρόντις (*Il.* 17.40). Ὀνήτωρ means 'beneficial' (cf. ὄνησις 'benefit', *Od.* 21.402); see also *Comm. on Od.* v.1: 154 (S.R. West).

[91] Cf. *HE* s.v. Mentor (J. Heath); Nagy 1990: 113 ('the reminder'). The likely association with the notion of 'mind' may extend from Mentor to the father's name, Alkimos, if ἀλκή is taken to refer to the power of the mind (cf. Alkinoos).

[92] Thus *Comm.on Od.* v.1: 89 (S.R. West), cf. *LfgrE* s.v. Μέντης (B. Mader).

To return to the *Iliad*, Agamemnon's praise of Tydeus' valour (*Il.* 4.394–8), part of his effort to rouse Diomedes, contains two significant name-patronymic pairs, for the leaders of the Kadmeans who once ambushed Tydeus. The names Πολυφόντης 'killer of many', for one of the leaders, and Αὐτόφονος,[93] his father (395), are obviously put together for their murderous sense (φόνος 'murder'). The other leader is named Μαίων Αἱμονίδης (394). Μαίων is perhaps relevant to μαίομαι 'to seek', 'to explore'; the name should then mean 'he who reaches for, pursues'.[94] αἵμων only occurs at *Il.* 5.49, in the sequence αἵμονα θήρης: 'he who hunts or seizes', or 'skilled (in chase)'.[95] As a personal name it is also found in a list of names of Pylian commanders (4.295–6), and again for the grandfather of the Myrmidon Alkimedon (17.467), which may suggest that it was otherwise used as a stock-name without particular significance.[96] However, the alliterative effect of the two names, as well as the clearly significant pair Autophonos – Polyphontes in the next line (395), indicate strongly that Μαίων Αἱμονίδης was a deliberate combination;[97] both pairs seem intended to enhance Tydeus' praise, by stressing the abilities of his opponents.

In a father-daughter pair, Ἑκαμήδη daughter of Ἀρσίνοος (*Il.* 11.624, 626), the second elements of the names (*-mede* and *–noos*) could be understood as synonymous, both evoking mental ability. We hear in the next line (627) that Hekamede was selected as a prize for Nestor, because he outdid all Achaeans in wisdom (a special prize indeed, given her presumably noble origins: her father is given the heroic epithet μεγαλήτωρ).[98] One cannot help thinking that she was deemed particularly suitable for Nestor thanks to her name and patronymic, that echoed a basic feature of the honoured warrior. The name Ἑκαμήδη is further similar to (and was perhaps modeled on) that of Ἀγαμήδη 'very intelligent', whose knowledge of 'all drugs' suggests sorcery, and who is mentioned in Nestor's narrative of exploits of his youth (*Il.* 11.740–1; he killed her husband Moulios).[99] Heka-

---

[93] Here probably 'killer (by his own hand)', cf. αὐτουργός 'who works with his own hands'. On other uses and senses of Autophonos see von Kamptz 1982 (1958): 71.
[94] Kirk 1985: 371. See also above, p. 129.
[95] Ancient lexicography connected αἵμων with δαίμων / δαήμων (*EM* s.v. αἵμων). A connection with αἱμύλος 'cunning' is not accepted by Chantraine (1999 s.v. αἵμων). A meaning 'bloody in the chase' (in view of E. *Hec.* 90 λύκου αἵμονι χαλᾷ 'a wolf's bloody jaws') is not unlikely (despite Kirk 1990: 59). A hellenistic funerary epigram for a Ἱππαίμων Αἵμονος, described as a hunter (*AP* 7.304; Page 1981: 80–2), provides a striking parallel.
[96] See Kirk 1985: 371.
[97] Von Kamptz (1982 (1958): 26) translated: '*cupidus*, son of *rapax*'.
[98] See Higbie 1995: 113.
[99] See Wilamowitz 1916: 199; Schadewaldt 1938: 59; Cantieni 1942: 82. Hainsworth (1993: 291) speculated that the name came from heroic tales of Achilles' raids (cf. *Il.* 11.624–6).

mede performs functions which indicate excellent domestic skills, but are also reminiscent of magic: she prepares a *kykeon*, a restorative cocktail (*Il.* 11.624, 638–41; cf. Kirke's in *Od.* 10, hers a poisonous one), and later cleans a wound (14.6).[100]

A variation of the naming motive exemplified so far in this section, is found in names of fathers and sons that refer to a profession (in traditional societies it was customary for sons to follow in their fathers' professions[101]). The best known example of this kind is from the *Iliad* (5.59–62): Μηριόνης δὲ Φέρεκλον ἐνήρατο, Τέκτονος υἱόν / Ἁρμονίδεω, ὃς χερσὶν ἐπίστατο δαίδαλα πάντα / τεύχειν, …/ ὃς καὶ Ἀλεξάνδρῳ τεκτήνατο νῆας ἐΐσας… 'And Meriones slew Phereklos, son of Tekton, Harmon's son, whose hands were skilled in fashioning all manner of elaborate work … He it was who had also built for Alexander the shapely ships.' It must be noted that Tekton might be spelt with either a small or a capital initial (either as a noun[102] or as a proper name): τέκτονος or Τέκτονος?, i.e. the son of the carpenter, Joiner, or the son of Tekton (Carpenter), Joiner. If τέκτονος is read as a personal name,[103] then the onomastic point would cover three generations. A personal name is clearly encouraged by *Od.* 8.114: Ἀμφίαλός θ', υἱὸς Πολυνήου Τεκτονίδαο.[104]

The seer Melampous 'black foot' (*Od.* 15.225–56) does not have a chance name, judging by the adjective ἀνιπτόποδες 'with unwashed feet' (*Il.* 16.235) which is used for the diviners of the temple of Zeus at Dodone; perhaps both name and adjective reflect an ancient taboo,[105] though other explanations are

---

100 Mühlestein (1969: 70–1; cf. 1984a: 324–5) saw -μήδη as a generic element in names of 'clever women', cf. Μήδεια (see also above under 'Diomedes'); this however does not preclude a context-specific significance. He went on to suggest other, more complicated and less plausible explanations for the names of father and daughter: that the pair alluded to Apollo, Ἑκαμήδη being reminiscent of ἑκάεργος, an epithet of Apollo ('die sich um den Apollon Hekaergos Kümmernde'), and Arsinoos of Ἀρσινόη, by whom Apollo had Asklepios (Paus. 4.3.2); or that the name had Messenian connections (because of the nymph Arsinoe of Messene, Paus. 4.31.6), which would be suitable for a maid of the Pylian Nestor. But the name Arsinoe is indeed appropriately explained as a compound of ἄρδειν 'to water', and νοά 'spring'; and Hekamede's first component Ἑκα- must mean 'from far away', as in ἑκάεργος (see Beekes 2010 s.v. ἑκάεργος).
101 Cf. Eust. 1108.36 (on *Il.* 17.323–4) and on *Od.* 2.22.
102 A noun τέκτων occurs e.g. at *Il.* 4.110, 6.315.
103 Thus the majority of editors, W. Leaf (London 1900), C. Hentze (Teubner 1940), P. Mazon (Belles Lettres 1946), M.L. West (Teubner 1998), vs only D.B. Monro and T.W. Allen (OCT 1920).
104 In the list of Phaeacian names (see above).
105 See further Janko 1992: 349–50; cf. Buxton 2010: 9–10 and n. 45 (with bibliography). Melampous is an important figure in Greek heroic tradition; a poem entitled *Melampodia* is ascribed to Hesiod.

not lacking: according to a fragment of the historian Dieuchidas (*FGrH* 485 F 9), Melampous' mother protected her baby from the sun by placing him in the shade, except his feet that were accidentally left in the sunshine and got tanned (μελανθῆναι). We hear from Herodotus (2.49) that he brought divination to Greece from Egypt; Egyptians are later called μελάμποδες (Apollod. 2.1.4).[106] Many names in Melampous' family may be relevant to divination: Ἀντιφάτης[107] and Μάντιος (μάντις 'seer'), sons of Melampous (*Od.* 15.242); Ἀμφιάρηος,[108] grandson of Antiphates (244) and Θεοκλύμενος 'he who hears divine things',[109] grandson of Mantios (256). Another example involving divination is that of the Trojan Πολύιδος 'much-knowing' (mentioned only as he is slain by Diomedes, *Il.* 5.148–9), who has the same name as the Korinthian seer mentioned later in the poem (13.663, 666 f.); he is appropriately paired with a father introduced as a ὀνειροπόλος 'dream interpreter'.[110]

Περίφας the herald (*Il.* 17.323–4) is significantly named (from φημί, with the intensifying περί-), and he is further called Ἠπυτίδης the son of Hepytos (from ἠπύω 'to call out, shout', cf. *Il.* 7.384 ἠπύτα κήρυξ 'loud-voiced herald'). The longer name Περιφήτης (15.638–40), for the son of a herald called Κοπρεύς, reflects the capacity of the father, while the father's name, reminiscent of Augeas' dung (κόπρος), is apparently inspired from his connection with Heraklean mythology ('[Kopreus] had been used to go as messenger from king Eurystheus to the mighty Herakles', 15.639–40).[111]

The names of the priest Δάρης (*Il.* 5.9) and his sons Φηγεύς and Ἰδαῖος (*Il.* 5.11) sound significant; there is no further mention of these characters, and they may well be inventions of the poet of the *Iliad*. Dares is a name of Phrygian origin;[112] it is known to Aelian (*VH* 11.2) as the name of a Phrygian composer of a

---

106 See also Buxton (ibid.: 10), who rightly concludes that 'the blackness in the name of Melampous cannot be pinned down to just one meaning.'
107 The name is usually derived from θείνω 'kill' (e.g. *LfGrE* s.v. Ἀντιφάτης [M. Imhof]), but in this context a pun on φημί / φάτις might be heard, perhaps alluding to a seer's function of responding to requests for prophecy, or of speaking in the name of god (cf. Wathelet 1989: 36).
108 The name is perhaps etymologically related to ἱερός 'holy'; von Kamptz 1982 (1958): 101–2; *LfGrE* s.v. Ἀμφιάρηος (Th. Rüsing). Cf. Ion. ἀρχιέρεως (Hdt. 2.142); the name is most likely attested in Mycenaean (see Jorro-Adrados 1985 s.v. *a-pi-ja-re-wo*).
109 Heraclit. *All.* 75.2: Θεοκλύμενος ... ὁ τὰ θεῖα κλύων.
110 See Kirk 1990: 73.
111 Cf. Edwards 1991: 93–4.
112 See von Kamptz 1982 (1958): 338 f., who suggested that the name is a cognate of the Thracian Δαρίκιος (*LGPN* IV) and Δαρεῖος, glossed in Hesychius as: ὑπὸ Περσῶν ὁ φρόνιμος, ὑπὸ δὲ Φρυγῶν ἕκτωρ. This was taken by Kretschmer (1896: 184) to suggest that the meaning of the

pre-Homeric *Iliad*. But Dares may have obtained an appropriate Greek meaning in the Homeric context thanks to its phonetic similarity to δέρω 'to skin, flay', which might suggest a name suitable for a priest, whose duties included the skinning of sacrificial animals.¹¹³ As for the sons' names, Phegeus alludes to the tree-name φηγός 'wild oak' (frequently found in the *Iliad*), and Idaios to Ἴδη, a mount in the Troad;¹¹⁴ ἴδη literally means 'wooded hill', and it is used in Herodotus (1.110) as a common noun in that sense. Both sons' names may therefore allude to wood – perhaps more specifically to wood-cutting, a practice mentioned in Homer (as in the expedition to fetch wood for Patroklos' funeral pyre, *Il.* 23.115–22; notably the wood to be cut is from δρῦς 'oak', used in the *Odyssey* – and elsewhere – in the place of φηγός).¹¹⁵

The above examples, which combine a diversity of meanings with the predictability of generic concepts, encourage the view that the poet worked within divisions of a large stock of names, in order to choose (and perhaps occasionally invent) appropriate names for the lesser characters of the epics. Significant naming momentarily increases the importance of these characters and contributes to a web of associations, which sometimes reach further than the names' immediate context.

---

name in Phrygian was connected with the root **dher-* 'to support, to possess', but this loses relevance in a Greek context.
113 Thus *EM*: Παρὰ τὸ δείρω καὶ ἐκδέρω γίνεται δέρης, καὶ τροπῇ, Δάρης. Εἰκὸς γὰρ, ὡς ἱερεὺς, ἔσχε καὶ τὸ ὄνομα παρὰ τὸ ἐκδέρειν τὰ θύη. Cf. the Mycenaean priests (names or titles) *o-wi-de-ta* (PY Un 718.2), *ai-ki-de-ta*. But see Jorro-Adrados (1985: 58): the second component could be –δέτας (from δέω) and not –δέρτας, which may allude to binding the sheep, not skinning them.
114 Idaios is also the name of a herald (*Il.* 3.248 etc.); cf. Latacz 2009a: 96: the name, derived from Zeus' mountain Ida, may express the god's protection of his heraldic status. This is much likelier than the etymology proposed by the Scholia at 7.278 (πεπνυμένα μήδεα εἰδώς ... δεῖ δὲ συνετὸν εἶναι τὸν κήρυκα). See also above, the discussion of Idomeneus' name.
115 See *DGE* s.v. δρῦς (B.2). Mühlestein (1969: 67–9) regarded the names as an allusion to the father's profession. However, a connection between wood and priesthood (on the basis that wood is burned for the sacrificial fire) is far-fetched (and is not followed by Kirk 1990: 54).

5 Afterword

There can be no doubt that the epic poet could exercise less inventiveness in the choice of characters and names than was allowed to other genres. While some minor heroes may well have carried invented names, main characters in Homer are traditional figures, as opposed, for example, to the protagonists of Aristophanes' comedy, who are mostly the poet's own creations. Still, this book has argued that even traditional names are exploited for their significance, although the age of (and our familiarity with) some Homeric names, along with their etymological obscurities, may blur our perception of their meanings. Some Homeric names are historical names, but because of their age[1] they are, as linguistic items, significantly 'darker' than the onomastic stock of the classical period. This study did not aim to reach definite conclusions about 'correct' etymologies; it demonstrates instead that obscure names can have meaning(s) that become alive in specific contexts. These meanings are often subtle and implicit, though there is no lack of word-plays, and they are occasionally suggested to us by ancient (folk-)etymological attempts, which are potentially revealing as to the imagination and assumptions of ancient audiences.

The two epics have yielded onomastic examples of a different kind. Aside from those names that are of course common to both, personal names from the *Iliad* mostly have a heroic background, while in the *Odyssey* they reflect the greater variety of contexts active in this poem and the convergence of myth and folktale. Naming reflects the much greater prominence and versatility of female characters in the *Odyssey*, where traditional 'heroic' women (such as Penelope) coexist with mysterious semi-divine witches such as Kalypso and Kirke. Female names in both epics draw on a large pool of semantic associations: some reflect the concepts and concerns of the male hero's world (e. g. Andromache), while others may find their justification in the areas of religion and folklore (Helen, Penelope).

Evidently the demands of the epic genre have affected the choice and invention of names. Some naming motives found in later literature and in historical onomastics (such as naming for physical traits) are virtually absent from Homer. Most Homeric personal names have meanings that fall within the sphere of heroic status and express social primacy and excellence in the battlefield. Notably, not every relevant notion is represented; while names with κλέος are frequent, τιμή (a term used in Homer with the sense of 'status', 'honour', 'recogni-

---

[1] Cf. M.L. West (2011a: 41), who notes that some must be as old as the second millennium BC.

tion')² is not found in Homeric onomastics, despite its immense importance for both the Iliadic and the Odyssean plot: the deprivation of *timē* is the reason behind Achilles' *mēnis* and ultimately his *achos* (see e.g. *Il.* 1.510), while Odysseus' return entails reparation for the damage done by the suitors to his honour, and to the honour of his family and to his household (cf. *Od.* 22.57), while he was absent. The fact that *timē* is one of the commonest name components in the classical period[3] can be seen as a characteristic example of the well-known change and fluctuation that defines name formation.

Several names discussed in this book suggest that Homeric etymologies might allow for semantic fluidity: the interpretation of name components that have several semantic possibilities may vary depending on the context and the characterisation of their bearers. This has led to motley explanations of compounds such as those starting with *Anti-* and those ending in *–noos* (Alkinoos, Antinoos, Pontonoos). *Anti-* is of course found in compound adjectives with the meanings 'contrary to' and (less frequently) 'equal to'; the interpretation of other components is rather more speculative, but we have seen that poetic etymology is no fixed concept, and when clear word-plays are absent, it is up to the audience to choose among different possible meanings. The recurrence of certain name components has further suggested groupings of characters who share similar traits and functions: e.g. servants whose names start with *Eury-*, and pairs such as Hekamede and Agamede. We have seen that even though explanations of names with the same component are not always identical, shared name components invariably create links between characters.

Names can be felt to match a basic feature of Homeric characterisation: Homeric characters are often defined primarily by public or external status, or by martial capabilities; they have one or two particular qualities or functions that stand out and are often detectable in their names. This is true mostly for minor figures, but also for main heroes, who may not lack individual feelings, but are mainly defined through, and arguably named for, status and function (e.g. Agamemnon = king). This is not to deny that heroes, even minor ones, are often granted individuality and at times also psychological complexity;[4] but we might say that as a rule, whatever subtle psychological hints are present in Homeric poetry, they do not find expression in name-giving.

However, two heroes are exempt from this rule: Achilles and Odysseus – the central heroes of the two epics; the poet creates links between their names[5] and

---

2 See *HE* s.v. *timē* (D. Cairns) for a concise definition, and further Yamagata 1994: 121–38.
3 A search in the *LGPN* database yields more than 500 different names.
4 On Homeric characterisation, a complex issue, see e.g. Griffin 1980: 50–80; Zanker 1994.
5 Metrically very similar, see Higbie 1995: 52.

their emotions.⁶ Names in Homer may signal emotion by providing a means of addressing individuals and by stressing identities at important moments,⁷ but the names of the two protagonists are further exploited for the 'emotional' etymological echoes they produce.⁸ Notably the emotions of Achilles and Odysseus that find expression in their names, can appear just as relevant to generic status, as to individualised character and experience: Achilles' feelings are relevant to his status as hero *par excellence* (the embodiment of ultimate valour but also of the grief and sorrow that often accompany *kleos*), while Odysseus' feelings are those of the 'wanderer hero', encompassing heroic elements from the Iliadic background as well as other features that are relevant to a tale of homecoming. Although Achilles is traditionally regarded as the 'superior' hero of the two,⁹ this superiority finds no reflection in the semantics of the names; in fact, both names hint at the psychologically negative aspect of each character's heroism. More specifically, we have seen that both Achilles and Odysseus experience pain and suffering.¹⁰ Achilles' suffering in the *Iliad* is mostly spiritual and emotional, while Odysseus' is also physical (he is maltreated by Poseidon, the beings he meets during his adventures and finally the suitors). Both heroes experience anger, and this emotion finds an echo in both names (for Achilles it is 'angry grief', for Odysseus it is his reaction to the anger of others against him, and his own anger at the unjust treatment he receives, e.g. by the suitors, but also by many of the beings he meets during his travels). While both names may seem to reflect a broader psychological state, each name's etymological meaning leans towards one or more particular aspects of this state: for Achilles it is the notion of pain, while for Odysseus it is pain and hatred. These notions are in their turn associated with a central element in each hero's characterisation:

---

6 We have seen that the names of Agamemnon and Menelaos may contain a hint at emotions, if *menos* (as 'fury') is read into them, but this association is obscure. The etymological play on the name Aias in tragedy relies on an 'emotional' sense.

7 As Higbie notes (1995: 9–10), pointing out the practice of recalling warriors' names and patronymics at a time of crisis (*Il.* 10.67–9).

8 Terms of emotion are notably used in the formation of historical personal names – a point of intersection between literary and historical onomastics; see further Kanavou 2013.

9 Famously, Achilles was a role model for Alexander the Great. Posterity does not seem to have idolised Odysseus in a similar manner. Plato's subversive comparison of the two types of heroism in *Hippias Minor* (cf. also *Protagoras*) takes as its assumption that Achilles was the superior hero in ordinary thought (see also Hobbs 2000: 193 ff.).

10 Cf. Cook 2009: 113 n. 8, 114. Note the over-emotional image of Achilles painted by Plato (*R*. 388a-b; see also above pp. 31–2). The two heroes embody different notions of heroism (Cook ibid.: 116): Achilles is the traditional epic hero, while Odysseus assimilates traditional heroism and the character of a 'trickster' (see also above, the discussion of Odysseus' name).

Achilles' pain is inextricably linked with the causes, results and manifestations of his *mēnis*; the suffering and hatred that surrounds Odysseus is largely a by-product of the works of his *mētis*. Unlike Achilles, Odysseus also receives other appellations (Outis, his false self-introductions on Ithaca), which reflect a greater fluidity of character, possibly relevant to this hero's alleged folktale origins. The emotional state suggested by each hero's name is bound to last after the end of the epics: at the end of the *Iliad*, Achilles has not yet met his destiny, for which his mother already grieves (*Il.* 24.84–6: ... ἣ δ' ἐνὶ μέσσης / κλαῖε μόρον οὗ παιδὸς ἀμύμονος, ὅς οἱ ἔμελλεν / φθείσεσθ' ἐν Τροίῃ ἐριβώλακι, τηλόθι πάτρης 'and she in the middle [of other sea goddesses] was weeping for the fate of her incomparable son, who was to perish in the deep-soiled land of Troy, far from his native land'); and even after his long-awaited return, Odysseus has more adventures and more pain ahead, as he warns his wife (*Od.* 23.248–50: ... ἀλλ' ἔτ' ὄπισθεν ἀμέτρητος πόνος ἔσται, / πολλὸς καὶ χαλεπός, τὸν ἐμὲ χρὴ πάντα τελέσσαι 'but still hereafter there is to be measureless toil, long and hard, which I must fulfill to the end').[11] It is finally no coincidence that both these heroes, who bear especially telling names, are also laden with a meta-poetic function: they both sing of heroes (Achilles: *Il.* 9.185–9; Odysseus sings of himself!).

To bestow a name equals to bestow importance, even a momentary one – the fact that adherents to particular status groups, such as servants, often remain nameless implies their insignificance. However, we have seen that servants with a part in the plot receive names. The noble background of such named servants as *Odyssey*'s Eumaios and Eurykleia (who both also receive a father's and grandfather's name) confirms the social importance attached to naming.[12] Other social groups deemed worthy of names and patronymics (often significant pairs) are the charioteers, heralds, and religious men.[13] The case of Thersites is particularly revealing in terms of the significance attached to naming: he is the protagonist in a memorable episode (*Il.* 2.244–69: he displays offensive behaviour and is maltreated by Odysseus as a result), and receives a name (Θερσίτης, from θέρσος / θάρσος 'audacity')[14] in this connection (while insignificant Achaean warriors often do not receive names). However, he is not given a patronymic or other genealogical attributes; according to the ancient Scholia,[15] the

---

11 See further Schein (1997: 354–5) and Silk (2004: 43–4) on the implications of the endings of the *Iliad* and the *Odyssey* respectively; both foreshadow events regarding the future of the two major heroes that fall outside the narrative time of the respective poems.
12 As Higbie argues (1995: 7–8).
13 See above, under 'Minor' speaking names. Cf. Higbie 1995: 8–9.
14 On the name see further Chantraine 1963a.
15 Sch. bT *Il.* 2.212b ex. (with Nünlist 2009: 52).

poet may have consciously opted to include only the information that was pertinent to the current scene, i.e. about Thersites' character and physique – but the lack of patronymic may also imply his low status in Homeric society.[16]

Homer was an endless source of influence for all ancient literature,[17] and literary naming was not exempt from this influence. Connections between epic and tragic naming have been mentioned as part of the discussion of numerous epic names that also occur in tragedy. Allusions to Homeric onomastics in later literature (tragedy and comedy[18] are both good examples) are significant for Homeric reception. It is further noteworthy that the naming of some socially insignificant characters in Homer seems to foreshadow comic usage. This is true for the already mentioned Thersites (a quasi-comic figure with a name that reflects the silly behaviour which earns him a beating),[19] and more strikingly for *Odyssey*'s Arnaios – Ἶρος – Ἄϊρος: Iros is an explicit nickname of comic sound, for the beggar Arnaios who is used to running errands, like the goddess Iris (18.5–6), and who becomes Airos (Un-Iros, 18.73, a 'Nobody'?[20]) when he unwisely shows animosity to the disguised Odysseus.

Discussion of all names in this book, like in every study of Homeric names, began with etymology – its results, its complexities and impossibilities. It should end with the realisation that no Homeric name, even of the most obscure kind, is to be dismissed as meaningless. Further studies in Homeric names will no doubt continue to uncover hidden (or not immediately obvious) connections between names, characters and poetic inspiration.

---

16 See also Higbie (1995: 11), who notes that low status is further underlined by Thersites' poor looks (*Il.* 2.216).
17 For a concise presentation of this influence see Hunter 2004: 235–53. Cf. the famous saying that Athenaeus (8.39.16–18 = 347e) ascribed to Aeschylus.
18 Aristophanes must have been aware of epic naming (and perhaps even played with it a little, as his comic use of such names as Pheidippos and Orsilochos may suggest); the connection between the names of fathers and sons, which in Homer is a serious reflection of a real-life tradition, is treated jokingly by the comic poet. See also Kanavou 2011: 19.
19 On the comic nature of the Thersites episode see Rosen 2007: 72 ff.
20 The sense of this name is not altogether clear, but the privative alpha probably implies the man's potential extinction by a stronger opponent, Odysseus (Higbie 1995: 15, Thalmann 1998: 107; for a different suggestion see Nagy 1979: 229–30). On the comic character of this episode see Thalmann ibid.: 103.

6 Appendix.
Homeric Personal Names as Historical Names: Preliminary Remarks

Many[1] Homeric personal names entered the pool of real-life onomastics and were used for historical people. This is true, for example, for numerous compound names that adhere to formation patterns known to historical onomastics, such as the various –*machos* and –*lochos* compounds. The use of Homeric names for real, historical people attracts curiosity, as it might allow inferences about the way different Homeric heroes were perceived in historical times. This is not a topic that has received much attention, and the following pages are not intended as an exhaustive treatment of it; they contain some initial thoughts on the use of the names of some of the epics' prominent characters as historical names. We are naturally more curious about names of main or important characters – these are far more likely to have retained an epic flavour than names belonging to minor figures, which in later times were probably used with reference to qualities suggested by etymological meanings and not to particular epic characters.

Perceptions of Homeric heroes as reflected in the afterlife of their names may also depend on geographical and chronological settings: a Homeric name may have been popular in a certain region, but not in another, and during a particular period; it is therefore necessary to start with the relevant data collected by *LGPN*. The following tables present an overview of historical attestations of names discussed in this book's chapters on the *Iliad* and the *Odyssey* (not every name discussed there is included here, only a selection of names of the most important characters); columns in each table comprise data from the *LGPN* database (the distribution in volumes is followed here so as to give a more systematic idea of the geographical regions involved):

The following observations emerge:
1) There is a marked difference in the historical career of the names of the epics' two principal heroes, Achilles and Odysseus. The name Achilles is fairly well attested (140 examples, widespread). Odysseus only has a single

---

[1] Not all: as noted in the Introduction, a significant proportion of Homeric proper names are *hapax legomena*; see also Edwards 1991: 53. But note also that often when Homeric names are historically unattested, their components do occur in historical onomastics; e.g. there is no historical Pontonoos (name of one of *Odyssey*'s Phaeacians), but –*noos* is a regular name component. For an early list of heroic names (not just Homeric) used as personal names, see Bechtel 1917: 571 ff.

TABLE[a)] 1: *Iliad*

Name	Vol.I – The Aegean Islands/ Cyprus/ Cyrenaica	Vol.IIA – Attica	Vol.IIIA – The Peloponnese/ Western Greece/ Sicily and Magna Graecia	Vol.IIIB – Central Greece/ From the Megarid to Thessaly	Vol.IV – Macedonia/ Thrace/ Scythia Minor/S. Russia	Vol.VA – Coastal Asia Minor: Pontos to Ionia	Vol.VB – Coastal Asia Minor: Caria to Cilicia
Ἀχιλ(λ)εύς	15 (hell.-imp.)	22 (from 6B)	11 (from 5B)	4 (hell.-imp.)	38 (from 4B)	25 (hell.-imp.)	25 (hell.-imp.)
Αἴας[b)]	1 (Thasos imp.)	1 (c.307BC)	0	1 (Naupaktos c.261BC)	0	2 (Mysia 2B; Bithynia imp.)	1 (Cilicia 3A)
Νέστωρ	7 (from 4B)	12 (from 5B)	26 (from 4B)	2 (imp.)	7 (hell.-imp.)	19 (hell.-imp.)	22 (hell.-imp.)
Ἰδομενεύς	9 (hell.-imp.)	3 (from 5B)	0	0	0	11 (hell.-imp.)	1 (Caria 1A)
Μηριόνης	0	0	0	2 (4B,[c)] imp.)	1 (imp.)	0	0
Πάτροκλος	0	4 (imp.)	1 (2B)	1 (imp.)	2 (3B, 3A)	3 (2B-3A)	3 (2B-3A)
(Πατροκλέας)	0	0	1 (5B)	8 (hell.-imp.)	0	0	0
Ἑλένη	6 (imp.)	6 (imp.)	15 (imp.-byz.)	7 (hell.-imp.-byz.)	9 (imp.)	15 (imp.-byz.)	25 (imp.-byz.)
(Ἑλένα)	3 (hell.-imp.)	0	2 (hell.-imp.)	2 (hell.-imp.)	0	0	0

Name	Vol.I – The Aegean Islands/ Cyprus/ Cyrenaica	Vol.IIA – Attica	Vol.IIIA – The Peloponnese/ Western Greece/ Sicily and Magna Graecia	Vol.IIIB – Central Greece/ From the Megarid to Thessaly	Vol.IV – Macedonia/ Thrace/ Scythia Minor/S. Russia	Vol.VA – Coastal Asia Minor: Pontos to Ionia	Vol.VB – Coastal Asia Minor: Caria to Cilicia
Ἀγαμέμνων	0	0	2 (Korinth 6B, her.;[d] hell.)	0	0	2 (Aiolis her.; Mysia imp.)	5 (hell.-imp.)
Μενέλαος	30 (hell.-imp.)	16 (hell.-imp.)[e]	17 (hell.-imp.)	10 (hell.-imp.)	43 (from 5B)	49 (hell.-imp.)	49 (hell.-imp.)
(Μενέλ(λ)ας)	1 (3B)	0	0	0	1 (2A)	1 (imp.)	0
Διομήδης	19 (hell.-imp.)	18 (from 6B[f])	19 (from 5B)	12 (hell.-imp.)	21 (imp.[g])	65 (hell.-imp.-byz.)	72 (4B-imp.)
Πρίαμος	0	2 (2A)	2 (imp.)	0	2	1 (Mysia 2 – 1B)	4 (hell.-imp.)
Ἑκάβη	0	0	0	0	0	0	0
Ἕκτωρ	1 (Chios her.)	1 (c.500BC)	3 (Epiros 4 – 2B)	0	4 (4B-imp.)	1 (Lydia 1B)	1 (Caria imp.)
Ἀστυάναξ /	7 (5/4 – 1B)	4 (?5 – 4B)	2 (3B, her.)	0	2 (4B, 2A)	9 (4 – 1B)	2 (Caria 504 BC, 4B)
Σκαμάνδριος	0	6 (6B-1A)	0	0	0	6 (?6B-3/2B)	0
Ἀνδρομάχη	0	0	0	2 (Thessaly 1B?, 3A)	0	1 (Mysia 2 – 1B?)	0

Name	Vol.I – The Aegean Islands/ Cyprus/ Cyrenaica	Vol.IIA – Attica	Vol.IIIA – The Peloponnese/ Western Greece/ Sicily and Magna Graecia	Vol.IIIB – Central Greece/ From the Megarid to Thessaly	Vol.IV – Macedonia/ Thrace/ Scythia Minor/S. Russia	Vol.VA – Coastal Asia Minor: Pontos to Ionia	Vol.VB – Coastal Asia Minor: Caria to Cilicia
(Ἀνδρομάχα)	0	0	2 (4B; byz.)	1 (3A?)	1 (3B)	0	0
Πάρις[b]	5 (imp.)	1 (3–2B)	24 (imp.)	3 (hell.-imp.)	6 (hell.-imp.)	2 (?3B; 1A)	1 (Lycia imp.)
Αἰνείας	10 (hell.-imp.)	10 (2B – 2A)	3 (5–3B)	0	6 (hell.-imp.)	12 (hell.-imp.)	32 (hell.-imp.)
(Αἰνέας)	35 (from 4B)	11 (from 6B)	20 (from 5B)	19 (from 5B)	0	11 (from 4B)	36 (hell.-imp.)

[a] In the Tables, B and A are used with centuries, B=BC and A=AD; her.=heroic.
[b] Note also two Αἴτας, one from Olympia (5B, *LGPN* IIIA) and one from Pamphylia (?2B, *LGPN* VB); but the former is certainly the Homeric Aias, see now Siewert-Taeuber 2013: 155–6 (no. 112).
[c] From Pherai; a Μηριόνη, daughter of a Πατροκλῆς is also attested there for the hellenistic or imperial period.
[d] Vase inscription – but it may be a dedication to the Homeric hero.
[e] A few undated attestations are unlikely to be earlier.
[f] But the person depicted and named on a 6th c. BC Attic vase is the hero himself.
[g] With the exception of one doubtful example from 5/4B ([Διο]μήδης? [Εὐ]μήδης?)
[h] A name used in Homer in alternation with Alexandros – there is hardly a need to stress the popularity of that name, especially from the hellenistic period onwards.

TABLE 2: *Odyssey*

Name	Vol.I – The Aegean Islands/ Cyprus/ Cyrenaica	Vol.IIA – Attica	Vol.IIIA – The Peloponnese/ Western Greece/ Sicily and Magna Graecia	Vol.IIIB – Central Greece/ From the Megarid to Thessaly	Vol.IV – Macedonia/Thrace/ Scythia Minor/S. Russia	Vol.VA – Coastal Asia Minor: Pontos to Ionia	Vol.VB – Coastal Asia Minor: Caria to Cilicia
Ὀδυσσεύς	0	0	1 (Italy imp.)	0	0	0	0
Λαέρτης	0	0	0	0	0	1 (Lydia imp.)	1 (Caria hell.)
(Λαέρτας)	4 (Kos hell.)	0	0	0	0	0	0
Ἀντίκλεια	0	2 (4B, 3–2B)	0	1 (Thebes 4B)	0	0	0
Τηλέμαχος	20 (from 5B)	15 (from 4B)	14 (from 6B)	9 (from 6/5B)	2 (4B; 1–2A)	7 (4B-imp.)	24 (4B-imp.)
Πηνελόπη	0	0	0	0	0	0	0
Καλυψώ	0	0	0	0	0	0	0
Κίρκη	0	0	0	0	0	0	0
Πολύφημος	0	1 (5B)	0	0	6 (hell.-imp.)	1 (Aiolis 4–3B)	6 (Caria 3–2B)
(Πολύφαμος)	0	0	1 (Korinth 6B, her.)	0	0	0	0
Ναυσικάα	0	0	1 (Sikyon 2A)	0	0	0	0

Homeric Personal Names as Historical Names — 161

Name	Vol.I – The Aegean Islands/ Cyprus/ Cyrenaica	Vol.IIA – Attica	Vol.IIIA – The Peloponnese/ Western Greece/ Sicily and Magna Graecia	Vol.IIIB – Central Greece/ From the Megarid to Thessaly	Vol.IV – Macedonia/Thrace/ Scythia Minor/S. Russia	Vol.VA – Coastal Asia Minor: Pontos to Ionia	Vol.VB – Coastal Asia Minor: Caria to Cilicia
Ἀλκίνοος	1 (Crete ?2B)	0	2 (4B)	4 (hell.)	0	2 (Ionia, Lydia 2–3A)	1 (Caria 1B)
(Ἀλκίνους)	2 (hell.)	1 (1B)	2 (4–3B)	0	1 (Thrace 3B)	4 (3–2B)	1 (Caria 2A)
Ἀρήτη	0	2 (4B, ?3B)	0	0	2 (4–3B)	2 (Ionia 4/3B; Mysia 2–3A)	1 (Lycia 3A)
(Ἀρήτα)	0	0	0	0	1 (Thrace 3-4A)	0	0
Εὔμαιος	0	1	2	5	0	2	1 (Caria 2B)
Εὐρύκλεια	0	(1B)	2 (2B, imp.)	(Naupaktos 2B)	0	1 (imp.)	0
Ἀντίνοος	2 (3–2B)	0	2 (4–3B)	0	0	1 (210AD)	0
Ἀντίνοος	2 (3–2B)	2 (5B, 2B)	1 (Epiros 2B)	2 (?4B, 3B)	2 (imp.)	2 (Pontos 4B; Bithynia 2A)	0
(Ἀντίνους)	0	6 (4–3B, ca 200AD)	7 (3–2B)	0	0	3 (Ionia 4B, 2–3A)	0

Name	Vol.I – The Aegean Islands/ Cyprus/ Cyrenaica	Vol.IIA – Attica	Vol.IIIA – The Peloponnese/ Western Greece/ Sicily and Magna Graecia	Vol.IIIB – Central Greece/ From the Megarid to Thessaly	Vol.IV – Macedonia/Thrace/ Scythia Minor/S. Russia	Vol.VA – Coastal Asia Minor: Pontos to Ionia	Vol.VB – Coastal Asia Minor: Caria to Cilicia
Εὐρύμαχος	4 (from 5B)	5 (5 – 1B)[a]	2 (6 – 5B)[b]	14 (from 6/5B)	1 (3 – 2B)	1 (400BC)	0

[a] An early attestation of Eurymachos (around 510 BC) is on a vase depicting Aias and Hektor fighting – a fictitious person?
[b] 6B: a heroic name, attested on a Korinthian vase.

attestation in *LGPN* (from Nola, Italy, of the imperial period: the name is in the Latin form *Odysseus*);[2] a further three, also imperial, are found in Kyrenaika and in Asia Minor.[3] Clearly Achilles' name appealed more to name-givers than Odysseus'; the two heroes were differently received by posterity. Achilles is further known to have been the object of a hero cult, which must have contributed to the name's popularity; in particular, the frequency of attestations of the name in South Russia in the imperial period (there are about twenty-five examples) must be relevant to the presence of a cult of Achilles in the Pontic region, more specifically at Λευκὴ νῆσος.[4] The contrast in the popularity of the two names may also be a consequence of the heroes' epic image: Achilles' traditional heroic virtue was probably deemed more attractive than Odysseus' adventures and his association with the suffering of a long *nostos*. Moreover, later Greeks clearly held Achilles' heroism in greater esteem than Odysseus'; Odysseus' basic feature, his cunning, was not always regarded as estimable.[5] The popularity of Achilles' name confirms his status as a role model.

2) Among other main heroes' names listed in *LGPN*, Agamemnon, with nine attestations, and Aias, with six,[6] are the rarest. The name Aias seems to have been used for its literary associations on one occasion: in *SEG* 6, 318 a deceased young boy of that name is compared to the Homeric hero; but neither this name nor Agamemnon ever became popular. It is fair to wonder whether this may have something to do with the fact that they were both troubled heroes, associated with unhappiness and misfortune, as clearly suggested by their depiction in tragedy.[7] Their names are followed in rarity by that of Patroklos (fourteen examples, plus nine of the form Patrokleas)[8] – anoth-

---

2 The bearer was a member of a 'burial club' (*collegium funeraticium*), and possibly a slave; see Simonelli 1972: 396. Note also a doubtful Ὀλυσσείδας ([Π]ολυσσείδας? Ὀδυσσείδας?) from Thebes of the 5th c. BC (*LGPN* IIIB).
3 *SEG* 26, 1843 (Kyrenaika); *SEG* 17, 599 (Pamphylia – not in *LGPN* VB) and *SEG* 46, 1660–1 (Phrygia). Here – and for other Anatolian instances of Homeric names – I am indebted to Peter Thonemann for sharing the draft of his forthcoming article on heroic onomastics in Roman Anatolia.
4 See also above, the discussion of Achilles' name.
5 Cf. e.g. his willingness to deceive Philoktetes, presented as ignoble in Sophocles' homonymous tragedy. See also above, pp. 95, 153.
6 We may add one further occurrence from Roman Phrygia, not in *LGPN* (*SEG* 6, 318; 2nd-3rd c.AD).
7 Sophocles' Aias is afflicted by madness; Agamemnon's numerous failings (already felt in the *Iliad* and elaborated in tragedy) are listed by Holway 2012: 93–4.
8 Note that the similar name Πατροκλῆς is markedly more common (76 attestations, *LGPN*).

er name that did not evoke a story with a particularly happy ending. Idomeneus, with 24 occurrences (from Athens, the Aegean islands and Asia Minor), is equally common, while the name of his companion, Meriones (a peculiar formation by historical standards), is scarcely attested. Nestor, Diomedes, Menelaos and Telemachos occur frequently enough; we might think that the treatment of these heroes in the epic and surrounding myths allowed their names to carry associations of a more positive kind.

3) As far as the date of the attestations is concerned, there is a very wide span, but not an equal distribution among historical periods. Early attestations are infrequent, though not entirely absent: Achilles has a couple of attestations from the sixth and fifth centuries (*LGPN* IIA); Agamemnon occurs as the name of a king of Kyme in Aiolis.[9] The name Diomedes numbers a few classical attestations, but has a marked concentration in Asia Minor of the hellenistic period. Menelaos' earliest attestations are from Macedonia of the fifth century BC: a son of Alexander I and brother of Perdikkas II, and a son of Amyntas III;[10] these uses may have been laden with heroic associations. The earliest occurrence of Aias is on an ephebic inscription from Athens, dating from the end of the fourth century BC. Telemachos occurs as a heroic name, for a great-grandfather of Theron, who founded a dominion in Sicily.[11] Another early attestation of the name (sixth century) is for an Olympic victor from Pharsalos, a son of Aknonios (*LGPN* IIIB). On the whole, however, the largest proportion of attestations date from the hellenistic and imperial periods.

4) It seems that names of Trojan heroes were employed in name-giving on equal terms as names of Greek heroes.[12] Among names of main Trojan heroes, one of the oldest attestations is that of Hektor, for an early (perhaps mythical) king of Chios.[13] Astyanax, the name of Hektor's son, was perhaps also used as a heroic name, for an Arkadian hero, but the evidence is

---

[9] *LGPN* VA; Poll. 9.83; *FGrH* 499 F 7. He is said to be the father of Demodike or Hermodike (who married Midas). M.L. West (2011a: 217–8) suggests that the name of one of the daughters of the Homeric Agamemnon, Laodike, may reflect Demodike.
[10] *RE* (3), (4) (Geyer).
[11] *LGPN* IIIA; *FGrH* 568 F 2; Sch. Pi. *O.* 3.38 (son of Samos, father of Emmenidas and Xenodikos); see also *RE* (2) (H. Lamer).
[12] Cf. Wathelet (1989: 33–4). Of course most 'Trojan' names are normal Greek formations, see also above under 'The "Greek" Trojans'.
[13] *LGPN* I; *FGrH* 392 F *1 (Ion of Chios), Paus. 7.4.8–10; see further Hornblower 2003: 53–4. Another early attestation of the name is from around 500 BC on an Attic vase for a *kalos*. Hektor has a total of 11 examples in *LGPN*; we may add a hellenistic occurrence from Gordion (*SEG* 37, 1149; Thonemann 2013: 21).

scant.¹⁴ Attestations of the boy's alternative name, Skamandrios, are divided between the Troad (the region of the river Skamandros¹⁵) and Attica; the use of this name at Athens has been thought to reflect renewed Athenian interest in the Troad after Sigeion was captured by Peisistratos.¹⁶ The earliest attestation of the name Aineias is for a Peloponnesian from Stymphalos mentioned in Xenophon *Anabasis* 4.7.13 (401 BC; but the form Aineas is already archaic). Paris, on the whole an unusual name, is disproportionately highly represented in *LGPN* IIIA; but most of the attestations are from Pompeii, and clearly do not refer to the Trojan hero,¹⁷ but to a popular actor called Paris, who lived at the time of Nero, and whose fame may have made the name fashionable.¹⁸

5) Names of the epics' female characters never became popular choices for real-life women. There is not a single attestation of Penelope. This may appear strange in view of her depiction as a virtuous woman; but perhaps a long wait for an absent husband was not an allusion that parents would want to include in the name of a young daughter.¹⁹ Helen's characterisation in epic and myth clearly did not suggest her name as particularly auspicious either: attestations of the name are few and mostly date from the imperial period. Neither Eurykleia nor Antikleia became popular names; they figure among a large number of female names in –*kleia* with occasional or scarce attestations.²⁰ Of names of Trojan women, Hekabe is entirely absent; apart from its rather undesirable associations, the name would have sounded as a rather odd formation. Unsurprisingly perhaps, the name Andromache was unpopular, despite the fact that –*mache* was not uncommon as a second component in feminine names.²¹

---

14 Only Paus. 8.38.5 (he reports that he saw the base of a statue bearing an inscription that named Astyanax, of the *genos* of Arkas). See also *LIMC* s.v. Astyanax II (M.-L. Bernhard).
15 The river name occurs as a personal name (*LGPN*) and has also produced a number of – admittedly rare – compound names, on which see Thonemann 2006: 33–4.
16 One Skamandrios was archon in 510/9 BC; see Cadoux 1948: 113.
17 The historical career of the hero's other name, Alexandros (more than 2000 examples in *LGPN*), hardly needs commenting.
18 It apparently belonged to more than one actors, which suggests that it came to be used as an artistic pseudonym; see *RE* s.v. Paris (2)-(6) (E. Wüst).
19 Note though that Penelope as the incorporation of female virtue features frequently on epitaphs of hellenistic and imperial women, who are praised by the comparison; see Mactoux 1975: 167–8.
20 Exceptions include Aristokleia, Agathokleia, Eukleia, Herakleia, which are common.
21 -*mache* names seem to have been distinctly Athenian; Aristomache, Lysimache, Nikomache were characteristic examples.

6) Kalypso and Kirke are entirely absent from historical nomenclature. Both these names presumably had negative connotations, that emerged from the witch-like nature of their bearers,[22] and the danger they presented to Odysseus' *nostos*. Polyphemos, the name of the defeated monster, has a scant presence, and its few attestations may be rather related to Polyphemos the Argonaut.[23] The names of the principal Phaeacian characters are not very frequent either, though Alkinoos was clearly more common than Arete. Nausikaa, a name that does not fall into name formation patterns of the historical period, only has a single attestation.

7) Of the names of the two main suitors, Eurymachos, a good Greek name, is unsurprisingly the commonest. The lesser popularity of Antinoos[24] may be related to its ambiguous sense; Eumaios too may have sounded too obscure to be used in name-giving, though it is not entirely unattested.

The motives for the preference for certain epic names and avoidance of others are not easy to trace and leave ground for much speculation – this difficulty is not to be separated from the broader problem of determining the reasons behind the choice of this or that name in Greek name-giving.[25] It is possible, however, to establish a link between use of names and perceptions of Homeric heroes,[26] and assume that names of heroes who were associated with negative or unpleasant experiences were avoided, just like certain divine names were;[27] after all, Homeric heroes were deemed to have higher than human status.[28] A purely aesthetic factor might also be at play: some Homeric names would

---

[22] Note that the name of Medea, a sorceress and Kirke's niece in several versions of myth, is also hardly attested (Μήδεια, single attestation, 4th c. BC, *LGPN* IIA).

[23] Founder of the city of Kios (A.R. 1.321–2). Early sources for him include Euphorion fr. 74 Lightfoot and Sokrates of Argos (*FGrH* 310 F 18); see further Hunter 1993: 38–41. On the form Polyphamos as the possible name of a couple of (otherwise unknown) heroic figures depicted on Korinthian vases, see *LIMC* s.v. Polyphamos I and (?) II (O. Touchefeu-Meynier).

[24] One famous bearer was the Bithynian Greek youth who was favoured by emperor Hadrian (*LGPN* VA no. 1).

[25] See e.g. Fraser 2000: 149–50. The reason behind the use of names of negative or absurd (to us) etymological meaning often remains a mystery; on such names see now Curbera 2013.

[26] Wathelet (1989: 33–4) assumed that the use of names of Trojan characters in real-life Greek onomastics is partly due to fact that these characters had 'côtés sympathiques'.

[27] Notably names of deities of the Underworld, see further Parker 2000: 54–5.

[28] Some heroic names have even produced 'theophoric' names, of the type commonly associated with divine names (e.g. Aiantodoros, Achillodoros; see Parker 2000: 56).

have sounded odd,²⁹ as they do not comply with patterns of name formation that were standardised in later times.

Homeric epic names, which are generally not very common in the classical period, seem to rise in popularity in later times.³⁰ Many heroic names were used as slave names in the Roman period.³¹ Some were also used as gladiators' 'names' (perhaps stage-names).³² With rarely attested Homeric names it is hard to raise the topic of geographical concentration, though in some cases such a concentration is obvious enough (Achilles, Diomedes, Menelaos). It has been noticed that names from Thessalian mythology and the Achaean substratum were frequently used as names for real people in the Thessalian region Atrax;³³ this may have been part of local identity construction. There apparently were Ithacan families in the fourth century BC that claimed descent from Telemachos, Eumaios and Philoitios (Plutarch, *Greek Questions* 14 = *Mor.* 294d = Arist. fr. 507 Rose).³⁴ This may have prompted the re-use of certain Homeric names. LGPN has not yet covered inland Asia Minor (to be covered in the next volume, VC, currently under preparation); but studies already indicate that some Homeric names were popular in that area in the hellenistic and imperial periods.³⁵ The use of heroic Greek names in Anatolia is an aspect of the well-known process of cultural hellenisation of that area; the use of each name may hide individual motives that need to be explored, but Homeric echoes should express cultural identity – an identity in which both name-givers and name-recipients would almost certainly take pride.

Instances of recourse to Homeric material might indeed be seen as a way of raising the status of the present (people and deeds of the heroic age were considered superior to the present). This is certainly true in the cases of heroes of the archaic period (Agamemnon, Hektor, Astyanax, Telemachos) who were named after Homeric heroes. Even though there is no consistent attitude to Homeric names (some were clearly avoided), there can be no doubt that the intentions / realities surrounding certain heroes have in some cases turned their names into 'model' names for future use.³⁶ This attitude to names persists in modern

---

29 Despite Morpurgo Davies (2000: 36) who questions phonological and morphological considerations as a reason for avoiding certain name forms (e.g. names in *-eus*).
30 Cf. Morpurgo Davies 2000: 36 n. 46.
31 See Solin 1996: 322–59. Notable exceptions are: Agamemnon, Aias and Odysseus.
32 The Thasian Aias is a gladiator, as are the two Odysseuses from Asia Minor.
33 See Decourt – Tziafalias 2007.
34 See also M.L. West 2014: 88.
35 See Ma 2007: 103–7 on the use of the name Nestor in Roman Lykaonia.
36 Cf. Masson (1990–2001 vol.3: 227) on the name Achilles: 'un Ἀχιλλεύς devait être un nouvel Achille'.

societies (one 'can make a name for oneself', and certain names undoubtedly gain specific associations) – even the rationalistic modern world has retained a subconscious awareness of the power of names.³⁷

---

37 Debus (2002) has gathered relevant writings and quotations from linguists and literary authors, and Freud on the psychological influence of one's name. To mention only one modern (and still Greek-related!) example, the spelling of the so well known in English literature name 'Brontë' was first adopted by Patrick Brontë for its psychological effect, because it echoed the Greek word for thunder, βροντή; this spelling was felt more appropriate than the original 'Brunty', which sounded plebeian; see Barker 1994: 6.

7 Bibliography

Note: Names of periodicals are abbreviated as in *L'Année Philologique*.

Ademollo, F., 2011. *The Cratylus of Plato: a commentary*. Cambridge / New York.
Alden, M., 2000. *Homer beside himself. Para-narratives in the Iliad*. Oxford.
Allen, J., 2005. 'The Stoics on the origin of language and the foundations of etymology.' In: D. Frede – B. Inwood (eds.), *Language and learning: philosophy of language in the hellenistic age*: 14–35. Cambridge.
Ameis, K.F. – Hentze, C., 1868–1932. *Homers Ilias*. Leipzig. (Repr. Amsterdam 1965).
Andersen, Ø., 1978. *Die Diomedesgestalt in der Ilias*. Oslo / Bergen / Tromsoe.
Andersen, Ø. – Haug, D.T.T. (eds.), 2012. *Relative chronology in early Greek epic poetry*. Cambridge.
Anderson, J.M., 2007. *The grammar of names*. Oxford.
Anttila, R., 2000. *Greek and Indo-European etymology in action: Proto-Indo-European *aĝ-*. Amsterdam / Philadelphia.
Austin, N., 1972. 'Name magic in the *Odyssey*.' *CSCA* 5: 1–19 (= In: Doherty [ed.]: 91–110).
—, 1975. *Archery at the dark of the moon: poetic problems in Homer's Odyssey*. Berkeley / Los Angeles.
—, 1994. *Helen of Troy and her shameless phantom*. Ithaca, New York.
Bakker, E.J., 2002. 'Polyphemos.' *ColbyQ* 38: 135–50.
Bannert, H., 1988. *Formen des Wiederholens bei Homer: Beispiele für eine Poetik des Epos* (= Wiener Studien, Beiheft 13). Wien.
Barck, C., 1971. 'Menelaos bei Homer.' *WS* 84: 5–28.
Barker, J., 1994. *The Brontës*. London.
Barnes, J. 1982. *The presocratic philosophers*. Cambridge.
Barney, R., 2001. *Names and nature in Plato's Cratylus*. New York / London.
Barthes, R., 1989. *The rustle of language* (Transl. by R. Howard). Oxford.
Barton, A., 1990. *The names of comedy*. Oxford.
Bartoněk, A., 1995. 'Mycenaean common nouns in the disguise of proper names.' In: Deger-Jalkotzy – Hiller – Panagl (eds.), (Vol. 1): 121–30.
Baxter, T.M.S., 1992. *The Cratylus: Plato's critique of naming*. Leiden.
Bechtel, F., 1902. *Die Attischen Frauennamen nach ihrem Systeme dargestellt*. Göttingen.
—, 1914. *Lexilogus zu Homer: Etymologia und Stammbildung homerischer Wörter*. Halle. (Repr. Hildesheim 1964).
—, 1917. *Die historischen Personennamen des Griechischen bis zur Kaiserzeit*. Halle.
—, 1921–4. *Die Griechischen Dialekte* (3 Vols.). Berlin.
Beekes, R., 2010. *Etymological dictionary of Greek* (2 Vols.). Leiden.
Bell, J.M. – O'Cleirigh, P. – Barrell, R., 2000. *An introduction to Greek mythology: story, symbols and culture (based on the lectures of John M.Bell)*. Lewiston / Queenston / Lampeter.
Bennet, J., 2014. 'Linear B and Homer.' In: Duhoux – Morpurgo Davies (eds.), (Vol.3): 187–233.
Benveniste, E., 1948. *Noms d'agent et noms d'action en Indo-Européen*. Paris.
Bernabé, A. (ed.), 2004. *Poetae Epici Graeci* (Pars 2, fasc. 1). Leipzig / Munich.

Bers, V. et al. (eds.), 2012. *Donum natalicium digitaliter confectum Gregorio Nagy septuagenario a discipulis collegis familiaribus oblatum. A virtual birthday gift presented to Gregory Nagy on turning seventy by his students, colleages, and friends* (http://chs.harvard.edu/).
Beye, C.R., 1964. 'Homeric battle narrative and catalogues.' *HSCP* 68: 345–73.
Biebuyck, D.P., 1987. 'Names in Nyanga society and in Nyanga tales.' In: J.M. Foley (ed.), *Comparative research on oral traditions: a Memorial for Milman Parry*: 47–71. Ohio.
Blomfield, C.J., 1826. *Aeschyli Agamemnon* (3rd ed.). London.
Blondell, R., 2013. *Helen of Troy: beauty, myth, devastation*. Oxford.
Blount, B.G., 2009. 'Anthropological linguistics.' In: G. Senft et al. (eds.), *Culture and language use*: 29–40. Amsterdam / Philadelphia.
Blumenthal, A. von, 1930. 'Ägäisches.' *IF* 48: 50.
Bonanno, M.G., 1980. 'Nomi e soprannomi Archilochei.' *MH* 37: 65–88.
Bosshardt, E., 1942. *Die Nomina auf –ευς*. Zürich.
Bouvier, D., 2002. *Le sceptre et la lyre: l'Iliade ou les héros de la mémoire*. Grenoble.
Bowie, E.L., 1995. 'Names and a gem: aspects of allusion in Heliodorus' *Aethiopica*.' In: D. Innes, H. Hine and C.B.R. Pelling (eds.), *Ethics and rhetoric: classical essays for Donald Russell on his seventy-fifth birthday*: 269–80. Oxford.
Bowra, C.M., 1930. *Tradition and design in the Iliad*. Oxford.
Braswell, B.K., 1988. *A commentary on the fourth Pythian ode of Pindar*. Berlin / New York.
Braund, S. – Most, G.W. (eds.), 2003. *Ancient anger: perspectives from Homer to Galen* (Yale Classical Studies Vol. XXXII). Cambridge.
Brilliant, R., 1995. 'Kirke's men: swine and sweethearts.' In: Cohen (ed.): 165–74.
Broadbent, M., 1968. *Studies in Greek genealogy*. Leiden.
Brommer, F., 1983a. *Odysseus. Die Taten und Leiden des Helden in Antiker Kunst und Literatur*. Darmstadt.
—, 1983b. 'Zur Schreibweise des Namens Odysseus.' *ZvS* 96: 88–92.
Bryce, T., 1998. *The kingdom of the Hittites*. Oxford.
Buitron-Oliver, D. & Cohen, B., 1995. 'Between Skylla and Penelope: female characters of the *Odyssey* in archaic and classical Greek art.' In: Cohen (ed.): 29–58.
Burgess, J.S., 2001. *The tradition of the Trojan war in Homer and the epic cycle*. Baltimore.
—, 2011. *The death and afterlife of Achilles*. Baltimore.
Burkert, W., 1985. *Greek Religion* (Transl. by J. Raffan). Cambridge Mass.
—, 2004. *Babylon, Memphis, Persepolis: eastern contexts of Greek culture*. Cambridge Mass. / London.
Buxton, R., 2010. 'The significance (or insignificance) of blackness in mythological names.' In: M. Christopoulos et al. (eds.), *Light and darkness in ancient Greek myth and religion*. Plymouth: 3–13.
Cadoux, T.J., 1948. 'The Athenian archons from Kreon to Hypsichides.' *JHS* 68: 70–123.
Cairns, D.L. (ed.), 2001. *Oxford readings in Homer's Iliad*. Oxford.
—, 2003. 'Ethics, ethology, terminology: Iliadic anger and the cross-cultural study of emotion.' In: Braund – Most (eds.): 11–49.
Camera, C., 1971. 'Digamma nel greco miceneo.' *SMEA* 13: 123–35.
Cantieni, R., 1942. *Die Nestorerzählung im 11. Gesang der Ilias*. Zürich.
Carnoy, A., 1956. 'Notes d' onomastique mythologique grecque.' *BN* 7: 117–22.
—, 1957. *Dictionnaire étymologique de la mythologie gréco-romaine*. Paris.
Carpenter, R., 1946. *Folk tale, fiction, and saga in the Homeric epics*. Berkeley.

Carter, J.B., 1995. 'Ancestor cult and the occasion of Homeric performance.' In: J.B. Carter – S.P. Morris (eds.), *The ages of Homer: a tribute to Emily Townsend Vermeule*: 285–312. Austin.
Casevitz, M., 1991. 'Sur l'étymologie des quelques noms propres.' *RPh* (3e Serie) 65: 83–88.
—, 1992. 'Remarques sur la forme, la place et la fonction des noms propres chez Homère.' In: *Sens et pouvoir de la nomination dans les cultures hellénique et romaine* (textes recueillis et presentés par Gély Suzanne), Tome II: *Le nom et la métamorphose*: 7–23. Montpellier.
Chadwick, J. – Baumbach, L., 1963. 'The Mycenaean Greek vocabulary.' *Glotta* 4: 157–271.
Chandler, H.W., 1881. *A practical introduction to Greek accentuation* (2nd ed.). Oxford.
Chantraine, P., 1963a. 'A propos de Thersite.' *AC* 32: 18–27.
—, 1963b. 'Notes d'étymologie grecque.' *RPh* 37: 12–22.
—, 1986. *Grammaire Homérique, tome II: syntaxe* (6th ed.). Paris.
—, 1999. *Dictionnaire étymologique de la langue grecque* (new ed., with Supplement). Paris.
Chickering, H.D., Jr., 1977. *Beowulf: a dual-language edition*. New York.
Clader, L.L., 1976. *Helen: the evolution from divine to heroic in Greek epic tradition* (= Mnemosyne Suppl. 42). Leiden.
Clarke, M., 2004. 'Manhood and heroism.' In: Fowler (ed.): 74–90.
Clay, J.S., 1983. *The wrath of Athena: gods and men in the Odyssey*. Princeton.
Clayton, B., 2004. *A Penelopean poetics: reweaving the feminine in Homer's Odyssey*. Lanham.
Cohen, B. (ed.), 1995. *The distaff side: representing the female in Homer's Odyssey*. Oxford.
Cook, E., 2009. 'Active and passive heroics in the *Odyssey*.' In: Doherty (ed.): 111–34 (= *CW* 93 [1999] 149–67).
Crane, G., 1988. *Calypso: backgrounds and conventions of the Odyssey*. Frankfurt on the Mein.
Cunliffe, R.J., 1931. *Homeric proper and place names* (A Supplement to 'A Lexicon of the Homeric Dialect'). London / Glasgow.
Curbera, J., 2013. 'Simple names in Ionia.' In: R. Parker (ed.), *Personal names in Anatolia* (= Proceedings of the British Academy 191): 107–43. Oxford / New York.
Currie, B., 2012. 'The *Iliad*, *Gilgamesh* and neoanalysis.' In: F. Montanari et al. (eds.): 543–80.
Curtius, E.R., 1948. *Europäische Literatur und lateinisches Mittelalter*. Bern.
Curtius, G., 1858. *Grundzüge der Griechischen Etymologie*. Leipzig.
Danek, G., 1998. *Epos und Zitat: Studien zu den Quellen der Odyssee*. Wien.
Darcy, L., 1985. 'The name of Circe and the Portolans of archaic Greece.' *LEC* 53.2: 185–91.
Davies, M., 1989. *The epic cycle*. Bristol.
—, 2009. 'Folk-tale vestiges in the second half of the Odyssey.' *Prometheus* 35: 1–10.
Debus, F., 2002. *Namen in literarischen Werken: (Er-)Findung – Form – Funktion*. Mainz / Stuttgart.
Decourt, J.-C. – Tziafalias, A., 2007. 'Mythological and heroic names in the onomastics of Atrax (Thessaly).' In: E. Matthews (ed.), *Old and new worlds in Greek onomastics* (= Proceedings of the British Academy 148): 9–20. Oxford / New York.
Deger-Jalkotzy, S. – Hiller, S. – Panagl, O. (eds.), 1995. *Floreant studia Mycenaea: Akten des X. internationalen mykenologischen Colloquiums in Salzburg vom 1.–5. Mai 1995* (2 Vols.). Wien.

Del Bello, D., 2007. *Forgotten paths: etymology and the allegorical mindset.* Washington D.C.
Demont, P., 2003. 'Le nom d'Eumée dans l'Odyssée.' *REG* 116: 377–85.
De Simone, C., 1978. 'Nochmals zur Namen Ἑλένη.' *Glotta* 56: 40–2.
Dickinson, O.T.P.K., 1994. *The Aegean Bronze Age.* Cambridge.
—, 2006. *The Aegean from Bronze Age to Iron Age: continuity and change between the twelfth and eighth centuries BC.* London/New York.
Dimock, G. E., 1956. 'The name of Odysseus.' *The Hudson Review* 9: 52–70.
Dindorf, G. (ed.), 1855. *Scholia Graeca in Homeri Odysseam* (2 Vols.). Oxford.
Dodds, E.R., 1960. *Euripides' Bacchae* (2nd ed.). Oxford.
Doherty, L.E., 1995. *Siren songs: gender, audiences and narrators in the Odyssey.* Michigan.
— (ed.), 2009. *Oxford readings in classical studies: Homer's Odyssey.* Oxford.
Dornseiff, F., 1956. *Antike und alter Orient: Interpretationen.* Leipzig.
Dougherty, C., 2001. *The raft of Odysseus: the ethnographic imagination of Homer's Odyssey.* Oxford / New York.
Dowden, K., 1992. *The uses of Greek mythology.* London.
—, 2004. 'The epic tradition in Greece.' In: Fowler (ed.): 188–205.
Dubois, L., 2000. 'Hippolytos and Lysippos: remarks on some compounds in Ἱππο-, -ιππος.' In: Hornblower – Matthews (eds.): 41–52.
Duhoux, Y. – Morpurgo Davies, A. (eds.) 2008, 2011, 2014. *A companion to Linear B: Mycenaean Greek texts and their world* (3 Vols). Louvain-La-Neuve / Walpole, MA.
Dunbar, H., 1962. *A complete concordance to the Odyssey of Homer* (rev. B. Marzullo). Hildesheim.
Dunbar, N., 1995. *Aristophanes: Birds.* Oxford.
Durante, M., 1967. 'Νείλεως e Νηλεύς.' *SMEA* 21: 33–46.
Dyer, R.R., 1964. 'The use of καλύπτω in Homer.' *Glotta* 42: 29–38.
Eco, U., 1976. *A theory of semiotics.* Bloomington.
Edgeworth, R.J., 1983. 'Terms for 'brown' in ancient Greek.' *Glotta* 61: 31–40.
Edmunds, L., 2007. 'Helen's divine origins.' *ElectronAnt* 10.2: 1–45.
Edwards, A., 1985. *Achilles in the Odyssey: ideologies of heroism in the Homeric epic.* Königstein.
Edwards, M.W., 1987. *Homer, poet of the Iliad.* Baltimore / London.
—, 1991. *The Iliad: a commentary,* V: books 17–20. Cambridge.
Eisler, R., 1951. *Man into wolf: an anthropological interpretation of sadism, masochism, and lycanthropy.* London.
Elmer, D.F., 2013. *The poetics of consent: collective decision making in the Iliad.* Baltimore.
Erbse, H. (ed.), 1969–88. *Scholia Graeca in Homeri Iliadem* (7 Vols.). Berlin.
—, 1972. *Beiträge zum Verständnis der Odyssee.* Berlin.
Farnell, L.R., 1921. *Greek hero cults and ideas of immortality.* Oxford.
Farron, S., 1978. 'The character of Hektor in the *Iliad*.' *AClass* 21: 39–57.
—, 1979. 'The portrayal of women in the *Iliad*.' *AClass* 22: 15–31.
Fenik, B., 1974. *Studies in the Odyssey.* Wiesbaden.
Fick, A., 1905. *Vorgriechische Ortsnamen als Quelle für die Vorgeschichte Griechenlands.* Göttingen.
—, 1911. 'Äoler und Achäer.' *ZvS* 44: 1–11.
Fick, A. – Bechtel, F., 1894. *Die Griechischen Personennamen nach ihrer Bildung erklärt und systematisch geordnet.* Göttingen.
Finglass, P.J. 2011. *Sophocles: Ajax.* Cambridge.

Finkelberg, M., 2005. *Greeks and pre-Greeks: Aegean prehistory and Greek heroic tradition.* Cambridge.
Finley, M.I., 1957. 'Homer and Mycenae: property and tenure.' *Historia* 6: 133–59.
—, 1970. *Early Greece: the bronze and archaic ages.* New York.
—, 1977. *The world of Odysseus* (2nd ed.). London.
Finnegan, R., 1970. *Oral literature in Africa.* Oxford.
—, 1977. *Oral poetry: its nature, significance and social context.* Cambridge.
Foley, H.J., 1995. 'Penelope as moral agent.' In: Cohen (ed.): 93–115.
Foley, J.M., 1990. *Traditional oral epic: the Odyssey, Beowulf, and and the Serbo-Croatian Return Song.* Berkeley.
—, 1997. 'Oral tradition and its implications.' In: Morris – Powell (eds.): 146–73.
—, 2004. 'Epic as genre.' In: Fowler (ed.): 171–87.
Fordyce, C.J., 1932/3. 'Puns on names in Greek.' *CJ* 28: 44–6, 290.
Forrer, E., 1924. 'Vorhomerische Griechen in den Keilschrifttexten von Boghazköi.' *MDOG* 63: 1–22.
—, 1926. *Forschungen I.* Berlin.
Fowler, R. (ed.), 2004. *The Cambridge companion to Homer.* Cambridge.
—, 2004. 'The Homeric question.' In: Fowler (ed.): 220–32.
Frame, D., 1978. *The myth of return in early Greek epic.* New Haven / London.
—, 2009. *Hippota Nestor* (Hellenic Studies 34). Cambridge Mass. / Washington D.C.
—, 2012. 'New light on the Homeric question: the Phaeacians unmasked.' In: V. Bers et al. (eds.)
Fraser, P.M., 2000. 'Ethnics as personal names.' In: Hornblower – Matthews (eds.): 149–57.
Frazer, J.G., 1922. *The golden bough: a study in magic and religion.* Kent.
Frei, P., 1968. 'Zur Etymologie von griech. voῦς.' In: *Lemmata: Donum natalicium Guilelmo Ehlers sexagenario a sodalibus Thesauri linguae Latinae oblatum.* Munich: 48–57.
Friis Johansen, K., 1961. *Ajas und Hektor: ein vorhomerisches Lied?* Copenhagen.
Frisk, H., 1960–72. *Griechisches etymologisches Wörterbuch* (3 Vols.). Heidelberg.
Gallavotti, C., 1949. 'Archilocho.' *PP* 4: 130–53.
Gambarara, D., 1984. *Alle fonti della filosofia del linguaggio: ‹lingua› e ‹nomi› nella cultura greca arcaica.* Rome.
Gancarski, J. (ed.), 2002. *Między Mykenami a Baltykiem: kultura Otomani-Füzesabony = Between Mycenae and the Baltic Sea.* Krosno / Warsow.
García Ramón, J.L., 2011. 'Mycenaean onomastics.' In: Duhoux – Morpurgo Davies (eds.), (Vol.2): 213–51.
George, A.R., 2003. *The Babylonian Gilgamesh epic: introduction, critical edition and cuneiform texts* (Vol. 1). Oxford.
Georgiev, V., 1966. 'Mycénien et Homérique: le problème du digamma.' In: L.R. Palmer – J. Chadwick (eds.), *Proceedings of the Cambridge colloquium in Mycenaean studies:* 104–24. Cambridge.
Gera, D.L., 2003. *Ancient Greek ideas on speech, language, and civilization.* Oxford / New York.
Germain, G., 1954. *Genèse de l'Odyssée: le fantastique et le sacré.* Paris.
Goebel, A., 1878–80. *Lexilogus zu Homer und den Homeriden* (2 Vols.). Berlin. (Repr. Amsterdam 1967).
Goldhill, S., 1991. *The poet's voice.* Cambridge.
Gomme, A.W., 1954. *The Greek attitude to poetry and history.* Berkeley / Los Angeles.

Gow, A.S.F., 1952. *Theocritus* (ed. with a translation and commentary) (2 Vols.). Cambridge.
Gray, D.H.F., 1958. 'Mycenaean names in Homer.' *JHS* 78: 43–8.
Graziosi, B., 2002. *Inventing Homer: the early reception of epic.* Cambridge.
Greco, A., 2002. 'Aiace Telamonio e Teucro: le tecniche di combattimento nella Grecia Micenea dell'età delle tombe a fossa.' In: F. Montanari – P. Ascheri (eds.), *Omero tremila anni dopo: atti del congresso di Genova 6–8 Luglio 2000:* 561–78. Rome.
Grethlein, J., 2006. *Das Geschichtsbild der Ilias. Eine Untersuchung aus phänomenologischer und narratologischer Perspektive.* Göttingen.
—, 2010. 'From "imperishable glory" to history: the *Iliad* and the Trojan war.' In: D. Konstan – K.A. Raaflaub (eds.), *Epic and history:* 122–44. Malden, MA / Oxford / Chichester.
Griffin, J., 1980. *Homer on life and death.* Oxford.
—, 1995. *Homer, Iliad Book ix.* Oxford.
Grossardt, P., 2001. *Die Erzählung von Meleagros: zur literarischen Entwicklung der Kalydonischen Kultlegende.* Leiden. (= *Mnemosyne* Suppl. 215).
—, 2009. *Achilleus, Coriolan und ihre Weggefährten: ein Plädoyer für eine Behandlung des Achilleus-Zorns aus Sicht der vergleichenden Epenforschung.* Tübingen.
Gruppe, O., 1906. *Griechische Mythologie und Religionsgeschichte.* Munich.
Güntert, H., 1919. *Kalypso: bedeutungsgeschichtliche Untersuchungen auf dem Gebiet der indogermanischen Sprachen.* Halle.
Güterbock, H.G., 1984. 'Hittites and Akhaeans: a new look.' *PAPhS* 128: 114–22.
—, 1986. 'Troy in Hittite texts? Wilusa, Ahhiyawa, and Hittite history.' In: M.J. Mellink (ed.), *Troy and the Trojan War:* 33–44. Bryn Mawr.
Hahn, E.A., 1969. *Naming-constructions in some Indo-european languages.* London / Michigan.
Hainsworth, B., 1993. *The Iliad: a commentary,* III: books 9–12. Cambridge.
Hansen, W., 2002. *Ariadne's thread: a guide to international tales found in classical literature.* Ithaca, New York.
Hanson, A.E., 2003. '‹Your mother nursed you with bile›: anger in babies and small children.' In: Braund – Most (eds.): 185–207.
Hartmann, I.J., 2002. '‹What name? What parentage?› The classification of Greek names and the Elean corpus.' In: *Oxford University Working Papers in Linguistics, Philology & Phonetics* 7: 55–81.
Henderson, J., 1975. *The maculate muse: obscene language in Attic comedy.* New Haven / London.
Heubeck, A., 1961. *Praegreca: sprachliche Untersuchungen zum vorgriechisch – indogermanischen Substrat.* Erlangen.
—, 1965. '*ke-ra-so:* Untersuchungen zu einem mykenischen Personennamen.' *Kadmos* 4: 138–45.
—, 1968. 'Ἀγαμέμνων.' In: *Studien zur Sprachwissenschaft und Kulturkunde. Gedenkschrift für W. Brandenstein:* 357–61. Innsbruck.
—, 1974. *Die Homerische Frage.* Darmstadt.
—, 1987. 'Zu den griech. Verbalwurzeln *nes- und *neu-.' *Minos* 20/22: 227–38.
Higbie, C., 1995. *Heroes' names, Homeric identities.* New York / London.
Hijmans, B.J., 1976. 'Archers in the *Iliad.*' In: *Festoen (Festschrift A.N. Zadoks-Josephus Jitta):* 343–52. Groningen.
Hobbs, A., 2000. *Plato and the hero: courage, manliness and the impersonal good.* Cambridge.

Hoekstra, A., 1981. *Epic verse before Homer: three studies.* Amsterdam / Oxford / New York.
Hoffmann, W., 1956. 'Die polis bei Homer.' In: H. Erbse (ed.), *Festschrift Bruno Snell: zum 60. Geburtstag am 18. Juni 1956 von Freunden und Schülern überreicht*: 153–65. Munich.
Hohendahl-Zoetelief, I.M., 1980. *Manners in the Homeric epic.* Leiden. (= Mnemosyne Suppl. 63).
Holland, G.B., 1993. 'The name of Achilles: a revised etymology.' *Glotta* 71:17–27.
Hölscher, U., 1989. *Die Odysee: Epos zwischen Märchen und Roman.* Munich.
Holway, R., 2012. *Becoming Achilles: child-sacrifice, war, and misrule in the Iliad and beyond.* Lanham MD / Plymouth.
Hommel, H., 1980. *Der Gott Achilleus.* Heidelberg.
Hooker, J.T., 1980a. *Linear B: an introduction.* Bristol.
—, 1980b. 'The meaning of ἔκλυον at ζ 185.' *ZvS* 94: 140–6.
—, 1988. 'The cults of Achilles.' *RhM* 131: 1–7.
Hornblower, S., 2003. 'Panionios of Chios and Hermotimos of Pedasa (Hdt. 8.104–6).' In: P. Derow – R. Parker (eds.), *Herodotus and his world*: 37–57. Oxford.
Hornblower, S. – Matthews, E. (eds.), 2000. *Greek personal names: their value as evidence* (= Proceedings of the British Academy 104). Oxford / New York.
Howald, E., 1920/4. 'Meleager und Achill.' *RhM* 73: 402–425.
—, 1947. 'Aineias.' *MH* 4: 69–73.
Hunter, R., 1993. *The Argonautica of Apollonius.* Cambridge.
—, 2004. 'Homer and Greek literature.' In: Fowler (ed.): 235–53.
Hutchinson, G., 1985. *Aeschylus: Septem contra Thebas.* Oxford.
Immerwahr, H. R., 1990. *Attic script: a survey.* Oxford.
Janko, R., 1982. *Homer, Hesiod and the hymns.* Cambridge.
—, 1984. 'H. von Kamptz, *Homerische Personennamen*.' (Review). *CR* NS 34: 305–6.
—, 1992. *The Iliad: a commentary,* IV: *books 13–16.* Cambridge.
—, 2012. 'πρωτόν τε καὶ ὕστατον αἰὲν ἀείδειν: Relative chronology and the literary history of the early Greek epos.' In: Ø. Andersen – D.T.T. Haug (eds.): 20–43.
Jensen, M.S., 2011. *Writing Homer: a study based on results from modern fieldwork.* Copenhangen.
Jespersen, O., 1924. *The philosophy of grammar.* London.
Jones, F., 1996. *Nominum ratio: aspects of the use of personal names in Greek and Latin.* Liverpool.
de Jong, I.J.F., 1987. 'Paris / Alexandros in the *Iliad*.' *Mnemosyne* 40: 124–8.
—, 1993. 'Studies in Homeric denomination.' *Mnemosyne* 46: 289–306.
—, 2001. *A narratological commentary on the Odyssey.* Cambridge.
Jorro, F.A. – Adrados, F.R., 1985. *Diccionario Micénico.* Madrid.
Kahn, C.H., 1979. *The art and thought of Heraclitus: an edition of the fragments with translation and commentary.* Cambridge.
Kakridis, J.T., 1949. *Homeric researches.* Lund.
Kalinka, E., 1943. *Agamemnon in der Ilias.* Wien.
von Kamptz, H., 1982 (1958). *Homerische Personennamen: sprachwissenschaftliche und historische Klassifikation.* Göttingen.
Kanavou, N., 2011. *Aristophanes' comedy of names: a study of speaking names in Aristophanes.* Berlin / New York.

—, 2013. 'Negative emotions and Greek names.' In: A. Chaniotis – P. Ducrey (eds.), *Emotions in Greece and Rome: texts, images, material culture*. Stuttgart: 167–89.
Katz, M.A., 1991. *Penelope's renown: meaning and indeterminacy in the Odyssey*. Princeton.
Kim, L., 2010. *Homer between history and fiction in imperial Greek literature*. Cambridge.
Kindstrand, J.F. (ed.), 1990. *[Plutarchus] De Homero*. Leipzig.
Kirigin, B. – Čače, S., 1998. 'Archaeological evidence for the cult of Diomedes in the Adriatic.' *Hesperia* 9: 63–110.
Kirk, G.S., 1964a. *The Homeric poems as history*. Cambridge.
— (ed.), 1964b. *The language and background of Homer*. Cambridge.
—, 1976. *Homer and the oral tradition*. Cambridge.
—, 1985. *The Iliad: a commentary*, I: *books 1–4*. Cambridge.
—, 1990. *The Iliad: a commentary*, II: *books 5–8*. Cambridge.
Kirk, G.S. – Raven, G.E., 1957. *The presocratic philosophers: a critical history with a selection of texts*. Cambridge.
Kirkwood, G.M., 1974. *Early Greek monody*. New York / London.
Köhnken, A., 2009. 'Odysseus' scar: an essay on Homeric epic narrative technique.' In: Doherty (ed.): 44–61 (transl. of 'Die Narbe des Odysseus', *A&A* 22 [1976] 101–14, repr. in: J. Latacz (ed.), 1991. *Homer: die Dichtung und ihre Deutung*. Darmstadt: 491–514 [with 'Nachtrag 1990']).
Koning, H.H., 2010. *Hesiod: the other poet. Ancient reception of a cultural icon*. Leiden / Boston.
Konstan, D., 2006. *The emotions of the ancient Greeks: studies in Aristotle and Greek literature*. Toronto.
Kraus, M., 1987. *Name und Sache: ein Problem im frühgriechischen Denken*. Amsterdam.
Kretschmer, P., 1894. *Die griechischen Vaseninschriften ihrer Sprache nach untersucht*. Gütersloh.
—, 1896. *Einleitung in die Geschichte der griechischen Sprache*. Göttingen.
—, 1913. 'Mythische Namen 1.' *Glotta* 4: 305–9.
—, 1917. 'Mythische Namen 5.' *Glotta* 8: 121–9.
—, 1924. 'Alakšanduš, König von Viluša.' *Glotta* 13: 205–13.
—, 1940. 'Die vorgriechischen Sprach- und Volksschichten.' *Glotta* 28: 231–78.
—, 1951. 'Die ältesten Sprachschichten auf Kreta.' *Glotta* 31: 1–20.
Kullmann, W., 1960. *Die Quellen der Ilias*. Wiesbaden.
—, 1992. *Homerische Motive*. Stuttgart.
Kwapisz, J., 2013. *The Greek figure poems* (Hellenistica Groningana 19). Leuven / Paris / Walpole, MA.
Lamberton, R., 1997. 'Homer in antiquity.' In: Morris – Powell (eds.): 33–54.
Laroche, E., 1970/2. 'Linguistique asianique.' *Minos* 11: 112–35.
Larson, J., 1995. *Greek heroine cults*. Madison.
Latacz, J., 1996. *Homer: his art and his world* (Transl. by J.P. Holoka). Michigan.
— (ed.), 2000a. *HomersIlias: Gesamtkommentar, Prolegomena*. Munich / Leipzig.
— (ed.), 2000b. *Homers Ilias: Gesamtkommentar* (Band I – 1. Gesang). Munich / Leipzig.
— (ed.), 2003. *Homers Ilias: Gesamtkommentar* (Band II – 2. Gesang). Munich / Leipzig.
—, 2004. *Troy and Homer: towards a solution of an old mystery* (Transl. by K.Windle and R. Ireland). Oxford. (= *Troia und Homer*. Munich / Berlin 2001).
— (ed.), 2008. *Homers Ilias: Gesamtkommentar* (Band IV – 6. Gesang). Munich / Leipzig.
— (ed.), 2009a. *HomersIlias: Gesamtkommentar* (Band III – 3. Gesang). Munich / Leipzig.

—— (ed.), 2009b. *Homers Ilias: Gesamtkommentar* (Band VIII – 24. Gesang). Munich / Leipzig.
Lateiner, D., 2004. 'The *Iliad*: an unpredictable classic.' In: Fowler (ed.): 11–30.
Lazzeroni, R., 1957. 'Lingua degli Dei e lingua degli uomini.' *Ann. Scuola Norm. Sup. Pisa* 26: 1–25 (= T. Bolelli – S. Sani (eds.), 1997. *Scritti scelti di Romano Lazzeroni*: 209–35. Pisa).
Lejeune, M., 1963. 'Noms propres de boeufs à Cnossos.' *REG* 76: 1–9.
Lévi-Strauss, C., 1966. *The savage mind*. London.
——, 1976. *Tristes tropiques* (Transl. by John and Doreen Weightman). Harmondsworth. (First published: Paris 1955).
Levin, S.B., 1997. 'Greek conceptions of naming: three forms of appropriateness in Plato and the literary tradition.' *CPh* 92: 46–57.
Lightfoot, J.L. (ed.), 2009. *Hellenistic collection: Philitas, Alexander of Aetolia, Hermesianax, Euphorion, Parthenius*. Cambridge Mass. (Loeb).
Linde, P., 1924. 'Homerische Selbsterläuterungen.' *Glotta* 13: 223–4.
Liović, Z., 2012. 'Aspects of poetic etymology of personal names in Homer.' In: S. Wojciech – S. Schaffner (eds.), *Greek and Latin from an Indo-European perspective (Proceedings of the conference held at the Comenius University Bratislava, July 8th-10th 2010)*: 65–80. Munich.
Lloyd-Jones, H., 1982. *Aeschylus: Oresteia*. London.
Lloyd, M., 1989. 'Paris / Alexandros in Homer and Euripides.' *Mnemosyne* 42: 76–9.
Louden, B., 1999. *The Odyssey: structure, narration, and meaning*. Baltimore / London.
——, 2011. *Homer's Odyssey and the Near East*. Cambridge.
Luckenbill, D.D., 1911. 'A possible occurrence of the name Alexander in the Boghaz-keui tablets.' *CPh* 6: 85–6.
Lyons, J., 1981. *Language and linguistics: an introduction*. Cambridge.
Ma, J., 2007. 'The worlds of Nestor the poet.' In: S. Swain – S. Harrison – J. Elsner (eds.), *Severan culture*: 83–113. Oxford.
Maas, P., 1973. 'Ährenlese.' *Kleine Schriften*: 181–92 (ed. W.Buchwald). Munich.
Macleod, C.W. (ed.), 1982. *Homer: Iliad, book XXIV*. Cambridge.
Mactoux, M.-M., 1975. *Pénélope: légende et mythe*. Paris.
Maguire, L., 2009. *Helen of Troy: from Homer to Hollywood*. Oxford.
Makkay, J., 2003. *Origins of the proto-Greeks and proto-Anatolians from a common perspective*. Budapest.
Maronitis, D.N., 1973. Ἀναζήτηση καὶ νόστος τοῦ Ὀδυσσέα: ἡ διαλεκτικὴ τῆς Ὀδύσσειας. Ἀθήνα.
Marót, K., 1960. 'Odysseus – Ulixes.' *Acta Antiqua* 8: 1–6.
——, 1961. 'Autolykos.' In: V.I. Georgiev – J. Irmscher (eds.), *Minoica und Homer: eine Aufsatzsammlung*: 24–30. Berlin.
Martin, R., 1989. *The language of heroes: speech and performance in the Iliad*. Ithaca, New York.
——, 2005. 'Epic as genre.' In: J.M. Foley (ed.), *A companion to ancient epic*: 9–19. Malden, MA / Oxford / Chichester.
Masson, O., 1990–2001. *Onomastica Graeca Selecta* (C. Dobias – L. Dubois (eds.), 3 Vols.). Nanterre.
Mastronarde, D.J., 1994. *Euripides' Phoenissae*. Cambridge.
Maul, S.M., 2014. *Das Gilgamesh-epos* (6th ed.). Munich.

McCartney, E.S., 1918/9. 'Puns and plays on proper names.' *CJ* 14: 343–58.
McKay, K.J., 1974. 'Alcman Fr. 107 Page.' *Mnemosyne* 27: 413–4.
Meier-Brügger, M., 1983. 'H. von Kamptz, *Homerische Personennamen*.' (Review). *BN* NF 18: 341–2.
—, 1992. *Griechische Sprachwissenschaft* (Bd. 2). Berlin.
—, 2010. *Indogermanische Sprachwissenschaft* (9th ed.). Berlin / NewYork.
Meister, K., 1921. *Die homerische Kunstsprache*. Leipzig.
Meuli, K., 1921. *Odyssee und Argonautika: Untersuchungen zur griechischen Sagengeschichte und zum Epos*. Berlin.
Mill, J. S., 1973/4. *A system of logic, ratiocinative and inductive: being a connected view of the principles of evidence and the methods of scientific investigation*. (J.M. Robson (ed.), Vol. 7 of the collected works. 1st ed.: London 1843). Toronto / London.
Mondi, R., 1983. 'The Homeric Cyclopes: folktale, tradition and theme.' *TAPA* 113: 17–38.
Monro, D.B., 1901. *Homer's Odyssey: books XIII-XIV*. Oxford.
Montanari, F. et al. (eds.), 2012. *Homeric contexts: neoanalysis and the interpretation of oral poetry*. Berlin / New York.
Morales, M.S. – Mariscal, G.L, 2003. 'The relationship between Achilles and Patroclus according to Chariton of Aphrodisias.' *CQ* NS 53: 292–5.
Morpurgo Davies, A., 1995. 'The morphology of personal names in Mycenaean and Greek: some observations.' In: Deger-Jalkotzy – Hiller – Panagl (eds.), (Vol.2): 389–405.
—, 2000. 'Greek personal names and linguistic continuity.' In: Hornblower – Matthews (eds.): 15–39.
Morris, I. – Powell, B. (eds.), 1997. *A new companion to Homer*. Leiden (= *Mnemosyne* Suppl. 163).
Most, G.W., 2003. 'Anger and pity in Homer's *Iliad*.' In: Braund – Most (eds.): 50–75.
Muellner, L., 1996. *The anger of Achilles: mēnis in Greek epic*. Ithaca, New York.
Mühlestein, H., 1965. 'Namen von Neleiden auf den Pylostäfelchen.' *MH* 22: 155–65.
—, 1967. 'Le nom des deux Ajax.' *SMEA* 18: 41–52.
—, 1969. 'Redende Personennamen bei Homer.' *SMEA* 9: 67–94.
—, 1971. 'Sieben Personennamen aus der Odyssee.' *Zant* 21: 45–8.
—, 1972. 'Euphorbos und der Tod des Patroklos.' *SMEA* 15: 79–90.
—, 1981. 'Der homerische Phoinix und sein Name.' *ZAnt* 31: 85–91.
—, 1984a. 'Nestors Magd, sein jüngster Sohn und der letzte Bearbeiter der homerischen Epen.' *SMEA* 25: 323–35.
—, 1984b. 'Der göttliche Sauhirt und die Namen.' *A&A* 30: 146–53.
—, 1987. *Homerische Namenstudien*. Frankfurt am Mein.
Mühll Von der, P., 1930. *Der grosse Aias*. Basel.
Murnaghan, S., 1986. 'Penelope's *Agnoia*: knowledge, power, and gender in the *Odyssey*.' *Helios* NS 13: 103–15 (= In: Doherty [ed.]: 231–46).
Nagy, G., 1979. *The best of the Achaeans*. Baltimore / London.
—, 1990. *Greek mythology and poetics*. Ithaca, New York.
—, 1992. 'Homeric questions.' *TAPA* 122: 17–60.
—, 1994. 'The name of Achilles: question of etymology and ‹folk-etymology›.' *ICS* 19: 3–9.
—, 1996a. *Homeric questions*. Austin-Texas.
—, 1996b. *Poetry as performance: Homer and beyond*. Cambridge.
—, 2004. *Homer's text and language*. Urbana.
—, 2010. *Homer the preclassic*. Berkeley / Los Angeles.

Nappi, M.P., 2002. 'Note sull' uso di Αἴαντε nell' *Iliade.*' *RCCM* 44 (n.2): 211–35.
Neumann, G., 1991. 'Die homerischen Personennamen: ihre Position im Rahmen der Entwicklung des griechischen Namenschatzes.' In: J. Latacz (ed.), *Zweihundert Jahre Homerforschung: Rückblick und Ausblick*: 311–28. Stuttgart.
Niemeier, W.-D., 2012. 'Griechenland und Kleinasien in der späten Bronzezeit. Der historische Hintergrund der Homerischen epen.' In: M. Meier-Brügger (ed.), *Homer, gedeutet durch ein großes Lexikon (Akten des Hamburger Kolloquiums vom 6. -8. Oktober 2010 zum Abschluss des Lexikons des frühgriechischen Epos)*. Berlin / Boston: 141–80.
Nikolaev, A., 2007. 'The name of Achilles.' In: C. George et al. (eds.), *Greek and Latin from an Indo-European perspective (PCPS* Suppl. Vol. 32): 162–73.
Nilsson, M.P., 1932. *The Mycenaean origin of Greek mythology*. Berkeley.
Nünlist, R., 2009. *The ancient critic at work: terms and concepts of literary criticism in Greek scholia*. Cambridge.
O'Hara, J.J., 1996. *True names: Vergil and the Alexandrian tradition of etymological wordplay*. Michigan.
Olschansky, H., 1996. *Volksetymologie*. Tübingen.
Ong, W.J., 1982. *Orality and literacy: the technologizing of the word*. London.
—, 1986. *Hopkins, the self and God*. Toronto.
Page, D.L., 1955. *The Homeric Odyssey: the Mary Flexner Lectures delivered at Bryn Mawr College, Pennsylvania*. Oxford.
—, 1959. *History and the Homeric Iliad*. Berkeley / Los Angeles.
—, 1973. *Folktales in Homer's Odyssey*. Cambridge Mass.
—, 1981. *Further Greek epigrams* (rev. R.D. Dawe – J. Diggle). Cambridge.
Palmer, L.R., 1956. 'Notes on the Personnel of the o-ka Tablets.' *Eranos* 54: 1–13.
—, 1963. *The interpretation of Mycenaean Greek texts*. Oxford.
—, 1979. *A Mycenaean 'Akhilleid'?* Innsbruck.
—, 1980. *The Greek language*. London / Boston.
Pape, W. – Benseler, G.E., 1911. *Wörterbuch der griechischen Eigennamen* (2 Vols.) (3rd ed.). Braunschweig.
Parker, R., 2000. 'Theophoric names and the history of Greek religion.' In: Hornblower – Matthews (eds.): 53–79.
—, 2011. *On Greek religion*. Ithaca, New York.
Paschalis, M., 1997. *Virgil's Aeneid: semantic relations and proper names*. Oxford.
Pellizer, E., 2006. 'Présentation du dictionnaire de la mythologie grecque *on line.*' *Kernos* 19: 245–8.
Peradotto, J., 1969. 'Cledonomancy in the Oresteia.' *AJPh* 90: 1–21.
—, 1990. *Man in the middle voice: name and narration in the Odyssey*. Princeton.
Peraki-Kyriakidou, H., 2002. 'Aspects of ancient etymologizing.' *CQ* NS 52: 478–93.
Perpillou, J.L., 1973. *Les substantifs Grecs en –eus*. Paris.
Pestalozzi, H., 1945. *Die Achilleis as Quelle der Ilias*. Zurich.
Pfeiffer, R., 1949. *Callimachus Vol. 1: Fragmenta*. Oxford.
Philippson, P., 1947. 'Die vorhomerische und die homerische Gestalt des Odysseus.' *MH* 4: 8–22.
Pokorny, J., 1959–69. *Indogermanisches etymologisches Wörterbuch* (2 Vols.). Bern / Munich.
Pontani, F., 2007. *Scholia Graeca in Odysseam: I. Scholia ad libros α–β*. Rome.
Powell, B.B., 1977. *Composition by theme in the Odyssey*. Meisenheim am Glan.

Prendergast, G.L., 1962. *A complete concordance to the Iliad of Homer* (rev. B. Marzullo). Hildesheim.
Pucci, P., 1987. *Odysseus polytropos: intertextual readings of the Odyssey and the Iliad.* Ithaca, New York.
—, 1998. *The song of the sirens: essays on Homer.* New York and Oxford.
Puhvel, J., 1987. *Comparative mythology.* Baltimore.
Quincey, J.H., 1963. 'Etymologica.' *RhM* 106: 142–8.
Raaflaub, K.A., 1997. 'Homeric society.' In: Morris – Powell (eds.): 624–48.
Radin, P., 1956. *The trickster.* New York.
Rank, L.Ph., 1951. *Etymologiseering en verwandte verschijnselen bij Homerus.* Assen.
Rankin, H.D., 1977. *Archilochus of Paros.* New Jersey.
—, 1978. 'The new Archilochus and some Archilochean questions.' *QUCC* 28: 7–27.
Reece, S., 2009. *Homer's winged words: the evolution of early Greek epic diction in the light of oral theory.* Leiden.
Reinhardt, K., 1960. *Tradition und Geist.* Göttingen.
—, 1961. *Die Ilias und ihr Dichter.* Göttingen.
Richardson, N.J., 1974. *The Homeric hymn to Demeter.* Oxford.
—, 1993. *The Iliad: a commentary,* VI: *books 21–24.* Cambridge.
Richardson, R.B., 1896. 'Inscriptions from the Argive Heraeum.' *American Journal of Archaeology and of the History of the Fine Arts* 11: 42–48.
Risch, E., 1947. 'Namensdeutungen und Worterklärungen bei den ältesten griechischen Dichtern.' In: *Eumusia. Festgabe für Ernst Howald zum 60. Geburtstag.* Erlenbach / Zürich.
—, 1974. *Wortbildung der homerischen Sprache* (2nd ed.). Berlin.
—, 1987. 'Die ältesten Zeugnisse für κλέος ἄφθιτον.' *ZvS* 100: 3–11.
Roscher, W.H. (ed.), 1884–1890. *Ausführliches Lexikon der griechischen und römischen Mythologie.* Band I: *A–H.* Leipzig.
Rosen, R.M., 2007. *Making mockery: the poetics of ancient satire.* Oxford.
Rotstein, A., 2010. *The idea of iambos.* Oxford.
Rousseau, P., 2012. 'Le nom de Diomède.' In: V. Bers et al. (eds.)
Ruijgh, C.J., 1967. *Études sur la grammaire et le vocabulaire du grec mycénien.* Amsterdam.
—, 1995. 'D' Homère aux origines proto-mycéniennes de la tradition epique.' In: J.-P. Crielaard (ed.), *Homeric questions: essays in philology, ancient history and archaeology.* Amsterdam: 1–96.
—, 2011. 'Mycenaean and Homeric language.' In: Duhoux – Morpurgo Davies (eds.), (Vol.2): 253–98.
Rutherford, R.B., 1986. 'The philosophy of the *Odyssey*.' *JHS* 106: 145–62 (= In: Doherty [ed.]: 155–86, with Afterword [187–8]).
—, 2001. 'From the *Iliad* to the *Odyssey*.' In: Cairns (ed.): 117–46 (= *BICS* 38 [1991–3] 47–54. Repr. with minor revisions).
Saïd, S., 1998. *Homère et l'Odyssée.* Paris (= *Homer and the Odyssey,* transl. by R. Webb, Oxford / New York 2011).
Salvadore, M., 1987. *Il nome, la persona: saggio sull' etimologia antica.* Genoa.
Schachermeyr, F., 1986. *Mykene und das Hethiterreich.* Wien.
Schadewaldt, W., 1965. *Von Homers Welt und Werk: Aufsätze und Auslegungen zur homerischen Frage* (4th ed.). Stuttgart.
—, 1966. *Iliasstudien* (3rd ed.). Darmstadt.

Schein, S.L., 1970. 'Odysseus and Polyphemos in the *Odyssey.*' *GRBS* 2: 73–83.
—, 1995. 'Female representations and interpreting the *Odyssey*'. In: Cohen (ed.): 17–27.
— (ed.), 1996. *Reading the Odyssey: selected interpretive essays.* Princeton.
—, 1997. 'The *Iliad:* structure and interpretation.' In: Morris – Powell (eds.): 345–59.
Schmitt, R., 1967. *Dichtung und Dichtersprache in indogermanischer Zeit.* Wiesbaden.
— (ed.), 1977. *Etymologie* (Wege der Forschung 373). Darmstadt.
Schofield, M., 2001. '*Euboulia* in the *Iliad.*' In: Cairns (ed.): 220–59 (= *CQ* NS 36 [1986] 6–31, repr. with minor revisions).
Schulze, W., 1892. *Quaestiones epicae.* Gütersloh.
—, 1933. *Kleine Schriften.* Göttingen.
Scodel, R., 2002. *Listening to Homer: tradition, narrative, and audience.* Ann Arbor.
Seaford, R., 1994. *Reciprocity and ritual: Homer and tragedy in the developing city-state.* Oxford.
Sedley, D., 2003. *Plato's Cratylus.* Cambridge.
Segal, C., 1994. *Singers, heroes and gods in the Odyssey.* Ithaca, New York.
Sergent, B., 2002. 'Les Phéaciens avant l'*Odyssée.*' In: A. Hurst – F. Letoublon (eds.), *La mythologie et l' Odyssée: hommage à Gabriel Germain*: 199–222. Geneva.
Siewert, P. – Taeuber, H., 2013. *Neue Inschriften von Olympia: die ab 1896 veröffentlichten Texte (= Tyche* Sonderband 7). Wien.
Silk, M., 2004. 'The *Odyssey* and its explorations.' In: Fowler (ed.): 31–44.
Simonelli, P.J., 1972. 'Nuovi ritrovamenti di inscrizioni in Nola.' *AAP* 21: 385–408.
Skempis, M. – Ziogas, I., 2009. 'Arete's words: etymology, *Ehoie*-poetry and gendered narrative in the *Odyssey.*' In: J. Grethlein – A. Rengakos (eds.), *Narratology and interpretation: the content of narrative form in ancient literature*: 213–40. Berlin / New York.
Skinner, J.E., 2012. *The invention of Greek ethnography: from Homer to Herodotus.* Oxford / New York.
Skutsch, O., 1987. 'Helen, her name and nature.' *JHS* 107: 188–93.
Snodgrass, A.M., 1967. *Arms and armour of the Greeks.* Ithaca, New York.
—, 1974. 'An historical Homeric society?' *JHS* 94: 114–25.
—, 1998. *Homer and the artists: text and picture in early Greek art.* Cambridge.
—, 2000. *The Dark Age of Greece* (2nd ed.). Edinburgh.
Solin, F., 1996. *Die stadtrömischen Sklavennamen: ein Namenbuch. II.Teil: Griechische Namen.* Stuttgart.
Solmsen, F., 1901. *Untersuchungen zur griechischen Laut- und Verslehre.* Strassburg.
—, 1909a. *Beiträge zur griechischen Wortforschung I.* Strassburg.
—, 1909b. 'Odysseus und Penelope.' *ZvS* 42: 207–33.
Sommer, F., 1932. *Die Ahhijavā-Urkunden.* Munich.
—, 1937. 'Ahhijava und kein Ende?' *IF* 55: 169–297.
—, 1948. *Zur Geschichte der griechischen Nominalkomposita.* Munich.
Stanford, W.B., 1939. *Ambiguity in Greek literature.* Oxford.
—, 1952. 'The Homeric etymology of the name Odysseus.' *CPh* 47: 219–213.
—, 1965. *The Odyssey of Homer* (corrected 2nd ed.). London / New York.
Starke, F., 1997. 'Troia im Kontext des historisch-politischen und sprachlichen Umfeldes Kleinasiens im 2. Jahrtausend.' *Studia Troica* 7: 447–87.
Stefanelli, R., 2008. 'ἄχος, ἄχνυμαι: etimologia e dintorni.' *Quaderni del Dipartimento di Linguistica – Universita de Firenze* 18: 121–32.

—, 2010. 'Νόος ovvero la "via" del pensiero.' *Glotta* 85: 217–63.
Stoevesandt, M., 2000. 'Zum Figurenbestand der *Ilias:* Menschen.' In: Latacz (ed.) 2000a: 133–44.
Stray, C., 1998. *Classics transformed: schools, universities, and society in England, 1830–1960.* Oxford.
Sulzberger, M., 1926. 'ONOMA ΕΠΩΝΥΜΟΝ: les noms propres chez Homère et dans la mythologie grecque.' *REG* 39: 383–447.
Suter, A., 1984. *Paris / Alexandros: a study in Homeric techniques of characterization* (doctoral thesis). Princeton.
—, 1991a. 'Language of gods and language of men: the case of *Paris /Alexandros*'. *Lexis* 7–8: 13–25.
—, 1991b. 'Δύσπαρι, εἶδος ἄριστε...'. *QUCC* 68 (NS 39): 7–30.
Swain, S.C.R., 1988. 'A note on *Iliad* 9.524–99: the story of Meleager.' *CQ* NS 38: 271–6.
Szemerényi, O.J.L., 1956/7. 'The Greek nouns in –εύς.' In: H. Kronasser (ed.), *Μνήμης χάριν: Gedenkschrift Paul Kretschmer* (Vol.2): 159–81. Wien.
—, 1996. *Introduction to Indo-European linguistics* (Transl. by D. and I. Jones). Oxford. (= *Einführung in die vergleichende Sprachwissenschaft* (4th ed.). Darmstadt 1990).
Taplin, O., 1990. 'Agamemnon's role in the *Iliad*.' In: C. Pelling (ed.), *Characterization and individuality in Greek literature:* 60–82. Oxford.
Thalmann, W.G., 1984. *Conventions of form and thought in early Greek epic poetry.* Baltimore / London.
—, 1998. *The swineherd and the bow: representations of class in the Odyssey.* Ithaca, New York.
Thomas, R., 1992. *Literacy and orality in ancient Greece.* Cambridge.
Thonemann, P., 2006. 'Neilomandros: a contribution to the history of Greek personal names.' *Chiron* 36: 11–43.
—, 2013. 'Phrygia: an anarchist history, 950 BC – AD 100.' In: P. Thonemann (ed.), *Roman Phrygia: culture and society:* 1–40. Cambridge.
—, forthcoming. 'Heroic onomastics in Roman Anatolia.' *Historia.*
Tichy, E., 1990. 'J.Untermann, Einführung in die Sprache Homers.' (Review). *Kratylos* 35: 130–3.
Tsitsibakou – Vasalos, E., 2007. *Ancient poetic etymology: the Pelopids, fathers and sons.* Stuttgart.
Untermann, J., 1987. *Einführung in die Sprache Homers: der Tod des Patroklos, Ilias Π 684–867.* Heidelberg.
Usener, K., 1990. *Beobachtungen zum Verhältnis der Odyssee zur Ilias.* Tübingen. (= ScriptOralia 21).
Ussher, R.G. (ed.), 1990. *Sophocles: Philoctetes.* Warminster.
van Groningen, B.A., 1977. *Euphorion.* Amsterdam.
Van Nortwick, T., 2009. *The unknown Odysseus: alternate worlds in Homer's Odyssey.* Michigan.
van Wees, H., 1994. 'The Homeric way of war: the *Iliad* and the hoplite phalanx (I).' *G&R* (2nd series) 41: 1–18.
—, 'The Homeric way of war: the *Iliad* and the hoplite phalanx (II).' *G&R* (2nd series) 41: 131–55.
—, 2004. *Greek warfare: myths and realities.* London.

Van Windekens, A.J., 1949/50. 'Quelques survivances du mot pélasgique *akh- 'eau, rivière, mer' dans l'onomastique Grecque.' *BN* 1: 194–201.
Varias, C., 1998/9. 'The personal names from the Knossos B-tablets and from the Mycenae tablets.' In: J. Bennet – J. Driessen (eds.), *A-NA-QO-TA: studies presented to J.T. Killen.* (= *Minos* 33–34): 349–70. Salamanca.
Ventris, M. – Chadwick, J., 1953. 'Evidence for Greek dialect in the Mycenaean archives.' *JHS* 73: 84–103.
—, 1973 (2nd ed. by J. Chadwick). *Documents in Mycenaean Greek.* Cambridge.
Vergados, A., 2011. 'The *Homeric hymn to Hermes*: humour and epiphany.' In: A. Faulkner (ed.), *The Homeric hymns: interpretative essays*: 83–104. Oxford / New York.
Vermeule, E.D.T., 1986. '‹Priam's castle blazing›: a thousand years of Trojan memories.' In: M.J. Mellnik (ed.), *Troy and the Trojan War*: 77–92. Bryn Mawr.
Vetta, M., 2003. 'L'*epos di Pilo* e Omero. Breve storia di una saga regionale.' In: R. Nicolai (ed.), *ΡΥΣΜΟΣ. Studi di poesia, metrica e musica greca offerti dagli allievi a Luigi Enrico Rossi per i suoi settant'anni.* Rome: 13–33.
Voigt, E.-M. (ed.), 1971. *Sappho et Alcaeus: fragmenta.* Amsterdam.
Wachter, R., 2000. 'Wort-Index Homerisch – Mykenisch.' In: Latacz (ed.) 2000a: 209–34.
—— 2001. *Non-Attic Greek vase inscriptions.* Oxford.
Wackernagel, J., 1877. 'Zum homerischen Dual.' *ZvS* 23: 302–10 (=*Kleine Schriften*: 538–46. Göttingen 1953).
—, 1919. 'Über einige lateinische und griechische Ableitungen aus den Verwandtschaftswörtern.' In: *Festgabe Adolf Kaegi*: 40–65. Frauenfeld.
Wathelet, P., 1988. *Dictionnaire des Troyens de l'Iliade* (2 Vols.). Paris.
—, 1989. *Les Troyens de l'Iliade: mythe et histoire.* Paris.
Watkins, C., 1970. 'Language of gods and language of men: remarks on some Indo-European metalinguistic traditions.' In: J. Puhvel (ed.), *Myth and law among the Indo-Europeans*: 1–17. Berkeley / Los Angeles / London.
—, 1977. 'On μῆνις.' *Indo-European Studies* 3: 686–722.
—, 1986a. 'The language of the Trojans.' In: M.J. Mellnik (ed.), *Troy and the Trojan War*: 45–62. Bryn Mawr.
—, 1986b. 'The name of Meleager.' In: A. Etter (ed.), *O-O-PE-RO-SI: Festschrift für E. Risch zum 75. Geburtstag.* Berlin: 320–8.
—, 1995. *How to kill a dragon: aspects of Indo-European poetics.* New York / Oxford.
Webster, T.B.L., 1958. *From Mycenae to Homer.* London.
West, M.L., 1966. *Hesiod: Theogony.* Oxford.
—, 1974. *Studies in Greek elegy and iambus.* Berlin / New York.
—, 1975. *Immortal Helen.* Inaugural Lecture, Bedford College, London. (=2011b: 80–96).
—, 1978. *Hesiod: Works & Days.* Oxford.
—, 1988. 'The rise of the Greek epic.' *JHS* 108: 151–72. (=2011b: 35–73).
—, 1995. 'The date of the *Iliad*.' *MH* 52: 203–19. (=2011b: 188–208).
—, 1997. *The east face of Helicon.* Oxford.
—, 2001. 'Atreus and Attarissiyas.' *Glotta* 77: 262–6.
—, 2003a. *Greek epic fragments, from the seventh to the fifth centuries BC* (ed. with transl.). Cambridge Mass. (Loeb).
—, 2003b. '*Iliad* and *Aethiopis*.' *CQ* NS 53: 1–14. (=2011b: 242–64).
—, 2007a. *Indo-European poetry and myth.* Oxford.
—, 2007b. 'Phasis and Aia.' *MH* 64: 193–98. (=2011b: 113–9).

—, 2011a. *The making of the Iliad: disquisition and analytical commentary.* Oxford / New York.
—, 2011b. *Hellenica: selected papers in Greek literature and thought. Vol. 1: epic.* Oxford / New York.
—, 2012. 'Towards a chronology of early Greek epic.' In: Ø. Andersen – D.T.T. Haug (eds.): 224–41.
—, 2014. *The making of the Odyssey.* Oxford.
West, S.R., 1988. 'Laertes revisited.' *PCPhS* 35: 113–43.
—, 1998. '‹Meglio la fine di una cosa che il suo principio›. Come comporre una *Odissea*.' In: F. Montanari (ed.), *Omero: gli aedi, i poemi, gli interpreti*: 63–77. Florence.
—, 2001. 'Phoenix's antecedents: a note on *Iliad* 9.' *SCI* 20: 1–15.
—, 2012. 'Some reflections on *Alpamysh*.' In: F. Montanari et al. (eds.): 531–41.
Wiesner, J., 1968. *Fahren und Reiten.* Göttingen.
Wilamowitz-Moellendorff, U. von, 1884. *Homerische Untersuchungen.* Berlin.
—, 1916. *Die Ilias und Homer.* Berlin.
Willcock, M.M., 1964. 'Mythological paradeigma in the *Iliad*.' *CQ* NS 14: 141–54.
—, 1997. 'Neoanalysis.' In: Morris – Powell (eds.): 174–89.
—, 2002. 'Menelaos in the *Iliad*.' In: M. Reichel and A. Rengakos (eds.), *Epea Pteroenta: Beiträge zur Homerforschung (Festschrift für Wolfgang Kullmann zum 75. Geburtstag)*: 221–9. Stuttgart.
Willer, S., 2003. *Poetik der Etymologie: Texturen sprachlichen Wissens in der Romantik.* Berlin.
Willink, C.W., 1986. *Euripides' Orestes.* Oxford.
Yamagata, N., 1994. *Homeric morality.* Leiden.
Yarnall, J., 1994. *Transformations of Circe: the history of an enchantress.* Urbana.
Zanker, G., 1994. *The heart of Achilles: characterization and personal ethics in the Iliad.* Michigan.
Zeitlin, F., 1995. 'Figuring fidelity in Homer's *Odyssey*.' In: Cohen (ed.): 117–52.
Zgusta, L., 1964. *Kleinasiatische Personennamen.* Prague.
Ziegler, K., 1962. 'Odysseus – Utase – Outis.' *Gymnasium* 69: 396–8.

Name Index

Ἀγαμέμνων 3, 7, 31 n. 16, 44–7, 52, 145, 152–3, 163–4, 167
Ἀγαμήδη 59, 147, 152
Ἀγκαῖος 140
Ἀγχίαλος 121 n. 176, 121
Ἀγχίσης 88
Αἴας 3, 9, 10 n. 56, 17, 36–44, 97 n. 40, 144, 153 n. 6, 159, 162–4, 167 nn. 31, 32
Αἰήτης 116
Αἴθων 102
Αἱμονίδης 147
Αἰνείας 21, 87–8, 159, 165
Αἴπυτος (Αἰπύτιος τύμβος) 137
Ἄϊρος 155
Ἀκρόνεως 121
Ἀλέξανδρος 5, 13 n. 78, 83–6, 159, 165 n. 17
Ἀλθαίη 62 n. 198
Ἅλιος 121, 126
Ἀλκιμέδων 12, 123, 142
Ἄλκιμος 12, 123 n. 189, 142, 146
Ἀλκίνοος 63 n. 202, 123, 126 n. 210, 132, 146 n. 91, 152, 161, 166
Ἀλκίππη 123 n. 189, 142
Ἀλκυόνη 14 n. 84, 61, 113
Ἀλύβας 104
Ἀμύντωρ 70, 135
Ἀμφίαλος 121
Ἀμφιάρηος 149
Ἀναβησίνεως 121
Ἀνδρομάχη 71 n. 249, 76, 82–3, 133, 158–9, 165
Ἀντήνωρ 143
Ἀντίκλεια 107, 131, 143 n. 72, 160, 165
Ἀντίνοος 132–3, 143 n. 72, 152, 161, 166
Ἀντιφάτης 149
Ἄντιφος 128
Ἀρήτη 24 n. 133, 27 n. 151, 105, 124–5, 161, 166
Ἁρμονίδης 148
Ἀρσίνοος 147, 148 n. 100
Ἀρχεπτόλεμος 138
Ἀστυάναξ 81–2, 91 n. 10, 164–5, 167

Ἀστύνοος 135, 144
Ἀτρεύς 5, 47–8
Αὐτόλυκος 4, 92
Αὐτομέδων 142
Αὐτόφονος 147
Ἀφείδας 103–4
Ἀχιλλεύς 29–36, 152–4, 156, 157, 163, 167

Βαθυκλέης 56 n. 160, 139
Βριάρεως 139
Βρισηΐς 71 n. 249
Βῶρος 136

Δάρης 149–50
Δευκαλίων 51
Δημόδοκος 126, 143 n. 68
Διομήδη 49
Διομήδης 48–50, 158, 164, 167
Δμήτωρ 134
Δολίος 131
Δόλων 49 n. 117
Δύσπαρις 86

Εἰδοθέη 144
Ἑκάβη 78–9, 158, 165
Ἑκαμήδη 49, 59, 147–8, 152
Ἕκτωρ 19 n. 110, 63, 76, 80–81, 158, 164, 167
Ἐλατρεύς 121
Ἑλένη 71–76, 151, 157, 165
Ἕλενος 75–6
Ἐλπήνωρ 127–8
Ἐπήριτος 104
Ἐρετμεύς 121
Εὔμαιος 129–30, 154, 161, 166, 167
Εὐμήδης 49 n. 117
Εὔνηος 145
Εὐπείθης 133
Εὐρύαλος 121, 128 n. 218
Εὐρυβάτης 141–2
Εὐρύκλεια 130–1, 142, 154, 161, 165
Εὐρύλοχος 127–8
Εὐρύμαχος 128 n. 218, 132–3, 162, 166
Εὐρυμέδουσα 130–1, 142

Εὐρυμέδων 126, 130 n. 237
Εὐρυνόμη 130, 142
Εὐρυσάκης 38, 144
Ἐχένηος 126
Ἐχέφρων 145

Ἠνιοπεύς 138
Ἠπυτίδης 149

Θεανώ 141
Θεοκλύμενος 141, 149
Θερσίτης 22 n. 125, 154 – 5
Θόων 122, 137
Θοώτης 137, 142
Θρασυμήδης 49, 145

Ἰδομενεύς 50 – 3, 157, 164
Ἱπποδάμεια 142
Ἶρος 155
Ἰφιάνασσα 145
Ἰφιδάμας 143
Ἰφιτίδης 138

Καλυψώ 105 n. 94, 114 – 6, 160, 166
Κάστωρ 102
Κεβριόνης 138
Κίρκη 112 n. 128, 116 – 7, 160, 166
Κλεοπάτρη 58 – 61
Κλυτόνηος 121, 126
Κοίρανος 134
Κοπρεύς 149
Κρείων 134

Λαέρτης 4, 11, 106 – 7, 160
Λαμπετίη 144
Λαοδάμας 126, 143, 145
Λαοδίκη 145, 164 n. 9
Λαόδοκος 143 – 4
Λαομέδων 143

Μαίων 129 n. 225, 147
Μάντιος 149
Μεγαπένθης 91, 145
Μέδων 135, 142
Μελάμπους 148 – 9
Μελάνθιος 131
Μελανθώ 131

Μελέαγρος 4 n. 17, 61 – 2
Μέμνων 45
Μενέλαος 46 – 7, 52, 146, 153 n. 6, 158, 164, 167
Μενοίτιος 58, 131 n. 241
Μέντης 90 n. 4, 146
Μέντωρ 63, 90 n. 4, 146
Μέροψ 140 – 1
Μηριόνης 53 – 4, 157, 164
Μίνως 51, 53

Ναυβολίδης 121
Ναυσίθοος 115 n. 142, 125 – 6, 137
Ναυσικάα 4, 121, 122 – 3, 160, 166
Ναυσίνοος 115 n. 142, 125
Ναυτεύς 121
Νέστωρ 3, 9, 63 – 7, 126 n. 210, 157, 164, 167 n. 35
Νοήμων 145 – 6

Ξάνθος 81 – 2, 86 n. 331

Ὀδίος 135, 141
Ὀδυσσεύς 17, 90 – 100, 152 – 3, 156, 160, 163, 167 nn. 31, 32
Ὀϊλεύς 41 n. 71
Οἰνεύς 62 n. 198, 69
Ὀνητορίδης 146
Ὄρμενος 70 – 1, 77
Ὀρσίλοχος 11 n. 66
Ὀρτίλοχος 11 n. 66
Οὐκαλέγων 77
Οὖτις 23 n. 132, 100 – 1, 154

Πάλμυς 135
Πάρις 83, 85 – 6, 159, 165
Πάτροκλος 55 – 61, 157, 163 – 4
Πεισίστρατος 145
Περίβοια 126
Περιμήδης 128
Περίφας 38 n. 55, 149
Περιφήτης 38 n. 55, 149
Πήδαιος 135
Πηλεύς 35 – 6
Πηνέλεως 112
Πηνελόπη 26 n. 148, 110 – 3, 151, 160, 165
Πολίτης 127

Πόλυβος 126
Πολυδεύκης 51
Πολύιδος 149
Πολύκτωρ 137–8
Πολύνηος 122
Πολυπημονίδης 103–4
Πολύφημος 118–20, 160, 166
Πολυφόντης 147
Ποντεύς 121
Ποντόνοος 121, 123, 132, 152, 156 n. 1
Πρίαμος 77–8, 85, 158
Πρόθοος 23 n. 132, 38 n. 58, 136
Πρυμνεύς 121
Πρύτανις 135
Πρῳρεύς 121
Πρωτεσίλαος 19 n. 110, 139

Ῥηξήνωρ 125–6

Σκαμάνδριος 81–2, 135–6, 138 n. 35, 158, 165
Σκάμανδρος 81–2, 86 n. 331, 165
Στέντωρ 140
Στροφίος 135

Ταλθύβιος 141
Τέκτων 122, 148
Τελαμών 38, 42–3
Τερπιάδης 143
Τηλέμαχος 107–10, 133, 144, 160, 164, 167
Τήλεφος 108
Τληπόλεμος 144

Ὑλακίδης 101

Φαέθουσα 144
Φαέθων 144
Φαῖστος 52 n. 136, 136
Φηγεύς 149–50
Φήμιος 90 n. 4, 119, 120 n. 173, 143
Φιλοίτιος 131, 167
Φοῖνιξ 67–71
Φρόνιος 145–6
Φρόντις 146
Φύλακος 135

Χρυσηΐς 71 n. 249
Χρυσόθεμις 145

Ὠκύαλος 121

www.ingramcontent.com/pod-product-compliance
Lightning Source LLC
Chambersburg PA
CBHW050109170426
43198CB00014B/2513